Praise for *Burning Our Money*

'This book is a great guide to how the public sector often spends too much and delivers too little. It lifts the lid on huge budget overruns, grandiose failed projects and very expensive day-to-day services that simply do not deliver the high-quality help you would expect for all the cash expended. Politicians are often criticised for saying in general terms the public sector could do more for less. This work shows us how.'
– Rt Hon John Redwood MP

'Public sector spending was nearly £700bn, some 45 per cent of GDP, in 2011/12. But, as Mike Denham persuasively argues, state spending is not just too big – it is also horrendously wasteful. Moreover, he provides an abundance of evidence to show that the public finances, on current policies, are quite simply unsustainable. Spending has to be cut and radical reform of public sector services is required. His recommendations for making government affordable are constructive and workable. They should be studied and heeded by every policy-maker in the country.'
– Ruth Lea, Economic Adviser, Arbuthnot Banking Group; former Head of the Policy Unit, Institute of Directors

'If you want to understand just how much of your money is being wasted, and how politicians can leave a lot more of it in your pocket, this book is a brilliant place to start. Burning Our Money *is an invaluable account of the incompetence and hubris that have left our economy stagnant and so many families struggling to make ends meet, from an economist with the experience to get to the bottom of it all.'
– Matthew Elliott, Founder of the TaxPayers' Alliance and author of *The Bumper Book of Government Waste*

'The state simply must come to live within the tax base if we are to avoid disaster. Anyone who is serious about the prosperity and wellbeing of their fellow citizens should read this book.'
– Steve

BURNING OUR MONEY

BURNING OUR MONEY

HOW GOVERNMENT WASTES OUR CASH
AND WHAT WE CAN DO ABOUT IT

MIKE DENHAM

Biteback Publishing

First published in Great Britain in 2013 by
Biteback Publishing Ltd
Westminster Tower
3 Albert Embankment
London SE1 7SP
Copyright © Mike Denham 2013

ISBN 978-1-84954-186-2

10 9 8 7 6 5 4 3 2 1

A CIP catalogue record for this book is available from the
British Library.

Set in Sabon and Steelfish

Printed and bound in Great Britain by
CPI Group (UK) Ltd, Croydon CR0 4YY

This book is dedicated to my wife, without whose encouragement it wouldn't have been written.

I'd also like to thank Matthew Sinclair and John O'Connell, both of the TaxPayers' Alliance, for their comments and support.

HOW THE GOVERNMENT BURNS OUR MONEY:

- It spends nearly half of everything we earn (Chapter 1).
- It overpays for supplies and labour, with its staff getting substantially more than private sector equivalents (Chapter 2).
- Its health service is inefficient, underperforms overseas counterparts, and causes thousands of avoidable deaths (Chapter 4).
- It pays welfare benefits to three-quarters of British households, despite our high level of general prosperity (Chapter 6).
- Its state schools are among the world's most expensive, yet performance has slipped down the international league tables and we suffer the worst social mobility (Chapter 8).
- Its criminal justice system costs more than any overseas counterpart, yet our crime rate is one of the highest in the developed world (Chapter 9).
- Compared to the most efficient governments elsewhere, the money it wastes is enough to abolish income tax for everyone earning less than £50,000 (Chapter 10).
- It hides its true costs under a cloak of stealth taxation and disguised borrowing (Chapters 11 and 12).

CONTENTS

ONE

BURNING OUR MONEY

Dear Chief Secretary, I'm afraid there is no money. Kind regards – and good luck!
– Labour Treasury Chief Secretary Liam Byrne – private letter left for his successor, May 2010

It was a foolish letter to write ... I broke the golden rule which is to not write down anything that you are not happy seeing in public and I am sorry that it's made our job arguing against Tory plans harder.
– Liam Byrne, public apology for his letter, May 2010

A WEEK IN THE LIFE

It's the second week of July 2012, and we're in trouble. With the Games of the XXX Olympiad about to start in London, it suddenly emerges we haven't laid on nearly enough security staff. Despite seven years of preparation and nearly £10 billion of taxpayers' cash, the entire event is cast into doubt, and what should have been a glorious celebration of national pride threatens to become a national humiliation.

Fortunately we've still got the army, and, as so often before in our long island history, they're summoned to rescue us from disaster. Already overstretched servicemen and women – some still with the dust of Afghanistan on their boots – find leave cancelled and immediate redeployment to crowd control.

The recriminations are storm force, and all eyes turn to G4S, the huge security company originally contracted to provide the staff. It has failed us catastrophically. The company's share price plummets, and, when its Chief Executive is hauled before MPs for a televised session in the stocks, we all crowd round to hurl stones. But soon the recriminations spread much wider.

For the left, this is a perfect example of how we can never trust the profit-grubbing private sector to deliver public services. Just like all commercial contractors, G4S has obviously put private profit before public duty. In stark contrast, our loyal servicemen have once again put duty first and their own personal interests second. Enough said.

It's a powerful line, but others point out it's not quite as simple as that. For one thing, it's the private sector that's already supplied virtually everything the Games will depend on: stadia, athletes' accommodation, ticketing systems, catering, equipment, drug testing, and a host of other essentials have all being supplied by private contractors. Without the private sector, the Games wouldn't be happening at all.

On top of that, overall responsibility for security rests with the Home Office. Why did it fail to monitor this vital subcontractor? How come it didn't spot the problem before drama turned to crisis? Were its bumbling officials asleep at the wheel yet again?

Because the Home Office has got form – a lot of form. In fact, it's presided over so many bungles that a recent Home Secretary publicly condemned it as 'not fit for purpose'. And right across government, officials routinely mismanage expensive private contractors, with taxpayers suffering the consequences. From defence equipment to IT projects to hospital cleaning, government has a chronic ability to overpay for second-rate delivery.

Neither is it just a problem with managing subcontractors. This very same week in July 2012 brings a stream of reports showing how poorly the public sector performs when it keeps the work in-house.[1]

In education, there's news that our state schools are trailing way behind their overseas counterparts. Research by education charity the Sutton Trust places us twenty-sixth out of thirty-four leading economies in the proportion of pupils achieving top maths scores. And, despite educating nearly 90 per cent of our children, our state comprehensive schools produce virtually none of our top-scoring pupils. It is failure on an epic scale.

In healthcare, a report from the National Audit Office (NAO) – the official spending watchdog – finds that NHS treatment for stroke victims is fatally sub-standard. A thousand victims a year suffer avoidable death or serious disability because of what's known as 'the weekend effect', which is NHS hospitals failing to provide adequate staff cover at weekends, even though strokes – along with many other emergencies – can strike at any time.

A London coroner lambasts the management and staff of a flagship teaching hospital for wholesale incompetence and lack of leadership. The inquest into the death of a 22-year-old cancer patient has found that he literally died of thirst after hospital staff repeatedly ignored his pleas for a drink. Yet those same incompetent staff and managers remain in post.

And despite an annual NHS budget well in excess of

£100 billion, another NAO report concludes that scores of hospital trusts are teetering on the brink of bankruptcy. The system is riddled with financial mismanagement, the cash is running out, and many local hospitals face closure.

Neither is mismanagement confined to the NHS. The latest annual accounts from the Department for Work and Pensions are published, and for the twenty-fourth year in succession the auditors have refused to sign them off. There's so much fraud and error in the welfare system that the Department is unable to account for all the money, and this year it seems nearly £5 billion has gone walkabout. No private sector business could carry on like this, but in the public sector it's just one of those things.

Over at the Ministry of Justice, new figures show that violent criminals released early from its jails go on to commit hundreds of further serious offences. In the previous year alone, they included seventy-eight rapes, fifteen manslaughters, and forty-four actual murders.

In the background, routine public sector waste continues unabated. The Department for Transport has wildly over-estimated the number of passengers likely to use the Channel Tunnel high-speed rail link, saddling taxpayers with an additional debt of £5 billion. The Home Office reveals that it spent half a million pounds on rubber bullets that can't be used. And a high-profile programme to save money by pooling back-office services across Whitehall turns out to have actually cost hundreds of millions more than it saved.

All this, and it's still only Thursday.

A WEEK IN THE LIFE TO COME

It's now the second week of July 2022, and our defeated World Cup squad skulks back home from Beijing. Playing against the hosts in the cauldron of the Mao Stadium, they were overawed and overwhelmed. Except the sports pages reckon the real culprit is the British government. Following the Qatar debacle, it should have accepted Fifa's emergency request for us to stage the tournament. Then we'd have been the hosts, and we'd now be in the quarter-finals.

Talk about wishful thinking. Mr Zhou has made it abundantly clear that China's loans and guarantees to Britain are conditional on robust and visible belt-tightening. The cost of staging the World Cup would have needed specific clearance from the Chinese Directorate of Fiscal Oversight in Whitehall, and they wouldn't have given it. Our government had no choice but to support China's own bid.

Anyway, going without a few circuses is nothing compared to everything else we're now going without. This week the Department of Health admitted there are only twenty-nine NHS GPs left in the whole of London, the rest having gone private or emigrated. The National Audit Office reports that in most areas you can't now get an NHS hip operation in less than three years, and cancer treatment is virtually unobtainable. New statistics show that one-fifth of our state schools have closed since 2019, with the average class size now exceeding forty-five. And yesterday the Prime Minister confirmed the state pension age will rise to seventy-five next September.

That's the problem when there's no money: we have to do what our creditors demand, when they demand it, however painful. Interest on the national debt is now costing more than health and education combined, and, even though we've slashed welfare spending, our taxes have gone through the roof. VAT and the basic income tax rate are both at 30 per cent, but that's just the tip of the iceberg. No wonder the economy has shrunk so much, and people are leaving in droves.

But it's pointless blaming the Chinese for our troubles: we are paying the price for years of wishful thinking.

We were the ones who chose to believe Gordon Brown's fantasy island economics, saddling ourselves with huge debts and an unaffordable government.[2] In 2010, we were the ones who chose to believe a Con–Lib coalition could somehow put things right without causing us distress or inconvenience. Later, when they did try a few distressing things – like reforming the NHS and cutting middle-class welfare – we were the ones who squawked until their nerve failed. Then in 2015, we were the ones who elected a minority Labour government to spend us back to happiness, and reverse the coalition's very few public sector reforms. Even when the Pound nearly died in 2017, we still failed to understand that government was costing far more than we could afford, and required radical surgery.

Well, it's out of our hands now. The Chinese are conducting the required surgery with a large axe and no anaesthetic.

Oh, if only. If only we'd started earlier. If only we'd recognised the pressing need to downsize the state and find more efficient ways of delivering public services. If only we'd had the grit and determination to see the reforms through.

STEP ONE

Thankfully, the Chinese Director of Fiscal Oversight has not yet arrived. We do still have some precious time to sort ourselves out. But to get anywhere, we have to take Step One, the step we have avoided for so long. We have to admit we have a serious problem. And it's not someone else's problem: it's our problem.

The problem is that we've come to expect far more from government than it's capable of delivering, and certainly far more than it can deliver at a price we can afford. Because when we entrust things to the government, waste, inefficiency and failure are guaranteed.

Our week of waste from 2012 was chosen solely because it happened to coincide with the writing of this chapter, but a comparable tally of bungling could have been found in pretty well any week from the last half-century. Here are three humdingers from the last few years:

- The NHS supercomputer – known officially as the National Programme for IT (NPfIT), it was supposed to deliver a standardised patient record-keeping system at an announced cost of £2.3 billion: it's now reckoned to have cost five times that, but not delivered the record system.[3] In fact, it's difficult to find any big government IT project that has *ever* delivered on budget and on time.

- The Nimrod MRA4 spy plane – originally planned to enter service in 2003 at a cost of £95 million each, it fell years behind schedule, ended up costing £400 million per plane, and finally had to be scrapped without ever entering service. The cost to taxpayers was £3.4 billion, and the cost to our servicemen even higher: fourteen of them died when their decrepit previous generation Nimrod crashed in 2006, three years beyond its planned scrappage date. And this was just one of many bungled defence procurements: rifles that jam in use, helicopters that can't fly in rain, aircraft carriers with no aircraft, and all delivered way over budget and way behind schedule.

- The Rural Payments Agency – the government quango responsible for dishing out farm subsidies designed such

a complex new system that it proved impossible to operate. Payments stopped, we got fined by the EU for late
payment, and it cost us over £600 million to put right.[4]
Gordon Brown's Financial Services Authority was a similar disaster – an overblown quangocracy so intent on the
minutiae of its own tick boxes that it entirely overlooked
the rampaging elephant smashing up the financial room.

And beyond these News at Ten headline bungles lies a huge
morass of day-to-day failure that doesn't get nearly as much
publicity as it deserves.

To start with, government routinely overpays for its
supplies. Despite being the biggest customer in the land,
it is forever paying more than you or I would pay in the
High Street. From office accommodation, to Post-it notes,
to drugs, to telecoms, to light bulbs, it wastes money. When
one of Britain's most successful retailers investigated he
reckoned he could save an annual £20 billion 'without even
breaking sweat'.[5]

It also overpays for its labour. Public sector employees
get paid more than their private sector counterparts, and
on top of that they get those famous index-linked pensions.
Depending on how you do the sums, the total overpayment
is between 10 and 40 per cent, which in money terms is £15
to £60 billion a year.[6]

And on top of the overpayment, there's also the issue of
what our public employees actually do. Politicians like to
boast about how many extra doctors, nurses, teachers and
police officers they've employed, but they never mention the
thousands of non-jobs they've also created. Such as:[7]

• Policy and Research Officer with the Nuclear Free Local

Authorities Secretariat at Manchester City Council, on a salary of £38,000.

- Walking Coordinator with Islington Council on £32,000.
- Climate Change Officer with Braintree Council, which was so concerned about its carbon footprint that it offered a salary of £39,000 for someone to keep tabs on it.
- Cheerleading Development Officer with Falkirk Council, salary unknown.

And the over-staffing problem extends much further than non-jobs. Even with its real jobs, the public sector has a chronic tendency to organise itself inefficiently. We've all visited NHS hospitals where the nurses seem to spend more time filling in forms than caring for patients. Contact with social services, or the council planning department, or the tax office, often leaves us trapped in a bureaucratic maze, with hordes of different officials getting themselves involved. And it's no wonder the police are so hard to find when they've somehow managed to organise themselves so that only one in eight officers is 'visible and available' at any one time.[8]

In the private sector such practices couldn't be long sustained, because the business would fail. Costs would escalate above revenues and the operation would have to change or die. But there's no such pressure in the public sector, where organisations can't go out of business through inefficiency. Change is glacial.

According to the government's own estimates, public sector productivity growth is virtually non-existent: indeed, on the latest figures, productivity actually *fell* between 1997 and 2008.[9] In other words, for every additional pound we put in, we got less and less additional output. During a period when private sector productivity was growing strongly, the public sector became even less efficient than it was before – a truly dire performance.

But worse still is the public sector's failure to deliver, especially to those who are critically dependent on it. The death of that cancer patient may be an extreme example, but it's by no means isolated. However much we'd like to believe otherwise, compared to healthcare systems elsewhere the NHS is a killer. Every year, tens of thousands of us die from illnesses that we'd probably have survived if only we'd been treated across the Channel.[10]

In education, around one-fifth of our children leave state schools unable to read and write properly, condemning them to a life bumping along the bottom. And further up the ability range, our brightest children are left unfulfilled and falling well short of the attainment levels achieved by their private school counterparts, let alone their counterparts overseas. A school system that has churned out ever higher exam grades has failed both its ablest and least able pupils, seriously undermining our future prosperity.[11]

As for our welfare system, it now costs an insupportable 15 per cent of our national income, and has consigned millions to dependency. Even at the height of the boom – during which an astonishing 4.7 million additional jobs had been created – we still had over 5 million working-age welfare dependents. Many of them have become, in the words of the legendary William Beveridge, 'habituated to idleness', are often seriously depressed, and are quite possibly now unemployable. The welfare system is a personal, social and financial disaster.[12]

Cost overruns, inefficient organisation and failure to deliver add up to a lot of waste. And, while nobody knows quite how much, research published by the European Central

Bank suggests it's well over £100 billion annually.[13] That's getting on for £5,000 per household every single year.

WE'RE THE ONES PICKING UP THE TAB

It is the proud boast of our public services that they're free. Irrespective of our own personal means, they give us free healthcare, free education for our children, free housing and free cash hand-outs.

That's a very seductive proposition, and if only it was true we wouldn't need to worry about poor standards and waste. We could just look upon our public services as a disappointing gift – a gigantic version of those knitted socks Aunt Agatha sent for your tenth birthday.

Unfortunately, it isn't true. The state is not some rich benefactor paying for services out of her own pocket. Everything the state provides has to be paid for by us.

Of course, the bill is not spread evenly, and that allows many of us to believe that someone else is paying – someone else like the idle rich, or perhaps those evil multinational companies we hear so much about.

But that comforting belief is also largely a delusion. Companies may apparently pay nearly 15 per cent of total taxes, but, as lifeless legal constructs, they can't actually pay those taxes any more than they can drink beer. Their taxes always end up being passed on to us, either through higher prices, or lower wages, or lower dividends on our investments. As we'll see later, we pay their taxes without even realising it.

And, while the rich certainly pay much more per capita than the rest of us, half of all tax ends up being paid by what's become known as the squeezed middle – the 40 per cent of households on annual gross incomes between around

£25,000 and £60,000. They have to pay because as a group
they're the ones with most of the income. Not that the poor
escape scot-free: around one-eighth of all tax is paid by
households on incomes below £10,000.[14]

The uncomfortable reality is that, in one way or another,
we all pay. Indeed, millions of us are in the absurd situation
of receiving state benefits with one hand and simultaneously
paying tax with the other. In the trade that's known as fiscal
churn, and it means the state is robbing Peter to pay Peter.
Worse, Peter doesn't get back as much as he's paid in because
a chunk is lost paying for the tax collectors and other
government officials needed to administer the circularity.

MAKING US ALL POORER

Public sector waste and failure makes us poorer because we
have to pay for it through higher taxes – *much* higher taxes.
In fact, if the public sector stopped wasting that £100 billion
a year, we could abolish income tax for everyone earning less
than £50,000.

But the waste and inefficiency also make us poorer in
another way. There is now considerable evidence that
beyond a certain point – generally put at about one-third
of GDP – increasing government spending as a share of
national income undermines long-term economic growth.
Productivity growth is much lower in the government sector,
and the taxes to pay for public spending act as a drag on
the wealth-creating private sector, eroding incentives to
enterprise and effort.[15]

For example, the European Central Bank analysed the
twenty-eight leading industrialised economies over the period
1970 to 2004, a period which saw their average government
spending increase from 35 per cent of GDP to 44 per cent.

It found that each 1 percentage point increase in that share cut the average annual growth rate of GDP per capita by an estimated 0.12 per cent. Another study, carried out by the OECD, put the effect at 0.15 per cent, and there are a large number of other studies pointing to an effect in the range 0.1 to 0.2 per cent.[16]

Over the last few years public spending here has absorbed nearly half of our national income. Back in 1997 it was only about 40 per cent. On the basis of the OECD's estimate, that increase may have cost us something like 1.5 per cent off our long-term growth rate. Even if we make some adjustments for the current recession, the surge in public spending under the last Labour government is likely to have knocked between 0.5 and 1 per cent off the rate.

Given the current state of the global economy, that kind of handicap is not one we can afford. If we're serious about growing our way back to prosperity and high employment, we have to cut the burden of public spending substantially.

Of course, that doesn't mean cutting it all the way back to zero. As we'll discuss later, there are some things – like defence, law and order, and basic infrastructure – that are essential for long-term prosperity, and only government can provide them. And in a modern economy, one necessary component of basic infrastructure is a population which has mastered the 3Rs, some basic science and a few other things besides. So some level of public spending is necessary, however inefficiently the money is spent. It's just that the current level is way beyond that minimum.

It's also way beyond what was envisaged when Beveridge wrote his famous welfare report back in the 1940s. Benefit levels have soared far above any basic safety net, and they've become an entitlement rather than something to be earned.

State education has expanded hugely beyond the elimina-
tion of basic ignorance – although it has shamefully failed
to eliminate illiteracy. And the NHS now provides a vast
range of costly treatments not even dreamed of when it
was founded.

Moreover, there's no relief in sight. In fact, looking
forward, the problem will only intensify. Our population
is aging dramatically, driving up spending on pensions, the
NHS and care services. Even after the planned increases in
pension age, the increasing elderly population is expected to
force spending up by a further 4 or 5 per cent of GDP over
the next half-century. Which would further increase taxes,
and cut our growth rate by perhaps another 0.5 per cent. We
are staring at a spiral of decline.

If only we had that rich benefactor, none of this would be
a problem. But we don't, and it is. Our bloated, inefficient
public sector is a major drag on future prosperity, and we
have to find ways of making it fitter and much leaner. Unless,
that is, we fancy a future of economic stagnation, declining
living standards and public services run into the ground.

WE CAN'T VOTE FOR LESS WASTE

When G4S bungled its Olympic security contract, the left
were delighted. This was the clearest possible demonstration
that the private sector cannot be trusted with public service,
and if the army hadn't galloped to the rescue the Games
would have descended into chaos.

And it cannot be denied that private sector companies are
just as capable of bungling as the public sector: mistakes
happen, circumstances change, and even the most successful
organisations get complacent. But the vast majority of private
sector companies face competitors, and those that make too

many mistakes risk going out of business. Customers can simply choose to spend their money elsewhere.

That doesn't happen in our monopolistic public sector. As customers, we're forced to pay for the state's services whether we like them or not. We're not free to choose whether to pay our taxes, and so unless we're very rich we're locked into using public services – however bad they are.

True, when there's a particularly egregious public sector failure, the organisation concerned will promise to 'learn lessons'. It may rearrange a few deckchairs, and in extreme cases may even transfer its head elsewhere. But once the dust has settled, experience shows that these organisations carry on pretty much as before. The hospital that killed that 22-year-old remains managed and staffed by the same people. And despite a quarter-century of failure, the DWP won't be able to account for next year's spending any better than this year's.

Now in theory it's not meant to be like this. In theory, we're supposed to exercise control via the ballot box: if our public services fail to deliver we can throw out the rascals in charge and replace them with a new lot. We have the power to elect a new board of directors.

The reality is miles away from that. To start with, there's often little to choose between the alternative boards on offer – most now comprise career politicians who've spent their entire working lives inside the Westminster bubble, and whose perspectives on public services and spending are remarkably similar. Their main priority is to get elected, which means sticking to 'the centre ground'. Consensus politics has undermined electoral choice.

Second, even if we do somehow elect a board that is minded to make radical change, it then has to confront a leviathan that doesn't want to budge. The public sector is heavily unionised, and has powerful supporters in the left-leaning media, most notably the tax-funded BBC. Politicians who threaten the status quo can expect to face huge resistance and the roughest of media maulings. In the words of one Prime Minister:

> You try getting change in the public sector and the public services. I bear the scars on my back after two years in government and heaven knows what it will be like after a bit longer. People in the public sector [are] more rooted in the concept that 'if it has always been done this way, it must always be done this way' than any group of people I have come across.[17]

Tony Blair says he now regrets not pushing harder, but given Labour's dependence on union funding he was never going to make much progress. Even our most radical post-war Prime Minister, Margaret Thatcher – most definitely not a consensus politician and not in the unions' pocket – failed to reform public sector working practices.

In reality, our ability to control the quality and cost of public services via the ballot box is virtually non-existent. With our own shopping we can effect change simply by switching our purchases to a competing supplier: we can vote directly with our wallets. But with our public services we're reduced to shopping via a political class bunched on the centre ground, and a unionised workforce clinging tenaciously to the status quo.

To get better and cheaper public services we have to go beyond merely electing a new set of directors and managers. We have to be much more radical. We have to restructure the entire relationship between government and its customers: that is, all of us.

FACING UP TO A NASTY TRUTH

To understand how and why the public sector wastes so much, we're going to take a close look at four of the biggest spending programmes, together comprising nearly three-quarters of all spending. They are health, welfare, education, and law and order.

We'll see how the public sector is weighed down by amateurism and lack of accountability at the top, combined with inflexibility and union militancy at the bottom. We'll see how politicians promote failure by twisting priorities and decision making to suit their own agendas. And we'll see how we ourselves generate waste by making demands government simply cannot deliver.

Alongside the problems, we'll look at some solutions. Perhaps surprisingly we'll find plenty of them, mostly based on successful systems operating elsewhere in the world. We'll also find a surprising measure of political agreement on what needs to be done. But against that we'll see how political action is stymied by an unwillingness to confront our collective wishful thinking.

The NHS is a prime example. In our national mythology it's the very best of British, the envy of the world – why, we even gave it a starring role in our Olympics opening ceremony. Yet, as we've already noted, its performance is fatally second-rate compared to its counterparts across the Channel. And the fundamental reason for that is that, unlike our nationalised monolith, the major European healthcare systems operate on the basis of choice and competition, keeping suppliers on their toes.

So for the last twenty-five years successive British governments have been trying to introduce similar market competition into the NHS. And not just Conservative governments: one of the most enthusiastic market reformers was Labour Health Secretary Alan Milburn. However, such has been the opposition from within the NHS, and the power of the myth, they've all backed off. Milburn eventually got so frustrated he walked away from government altogether 'to spend more time with his family'. And the most recent reform attempt by Conservative Andrew Lansley was stopped by his own Prime Minister, who after prolonged exposure to adverse headlines contracted a terminal case of cold feet.

Yet – tempting though it is – we can't simply blame our politicians for lack of bottle. True, many of them believe one thing in private and say another in public – as perfectly highlighted by Liam Byrne's 'no money' letter from May 2010. But they're politicians, and they've seen what happens if they get branded as nasty. We can't really expect them to confront our myths head-on, when so many of us are still believers.

No, the real fault lies not in our politicians but in ourselves. We're the ones who've failed to grasp the extent of the problems. We're the ones who've failed to insist on change. And we're the ones who've failed to accept the tough decisions needed to get us back on track.

The time has come for us to face up to this nasty truth. Because with all the money gone, muddling through is no longer an option.

TWO

EXPERTS IN WASTE

While the Royal James *was bringing towards the dock, we went out and saw the manner and trouble of docking such a ship, which yet they could not do, but only brought her head into the Dock, and so shored her up till next tide. But, good God! what a deal of company was there from both yards to help to do it, when half the company would have done it as well. I see it is impossible for the King to have things done as cheap as other men.*
– Samuel Pepys, Clerk of the Acts to the Navy Board, 1662

James Hacker: It's very popular with the voters, Humphrey. Gives them a chance to help us find ways to stop wasting government money.

   Sir Humphrey Appleby: The public doesn't know anything about wasting government money. We're the experts.
– Yes Minister, 1980

Government has always wasted our money. Whether repairing the Navy's warships, staffing the Circumlocution Office, or buying paperclips for the Department of Administrative Affairs, you can be sure it will spend way more than it ought to. As Pepys discovered 350 years ago, when the government has things done, bungling, duplication and overpayment are inevitable.

Waste permeates every level of government activity, and as we examine each of the main areas of government spending we'll find many examples. And we'll see how the same underlying failures crop up over and over again. Let's run through them, starting with the public sector's chronic tendency to overpay.

THE SIMPLE SHOPPER: PAYING TOO MUCH FOR ITS SUPPLIES

The government is by far the biggest shopper in Britain. Every year it spends around £240 billion with its thousands of suppliers. Unfortunately, it's hopeless at it.

Throughout history governments have routinely over-paid, over-ordered and bought the wrong things. Even during the Second World War, with minds concentrated by the fear of national extinction, vast amounts of useless kit were purchased, much of it later hidden from public view in disused coalmines (it's said there are 500 tons of left-footed Wellington boots down a mineshaft somewhere in Nottinghamshire).

In 2010, the government asked billionaire retailer Sir Philip Green to examine government shopping and suggest ways of saving cash.[18] He discovered a shambles, with government failing miserably to exploit its scale and status. Different bits of government were buying basic supplies like paper and printer cartridges individually and at wildly vary-ing prices: the most expensive were *nine times* the price of the cheapest. Prices paid for basic services like telephony and office accommodation were far above what big commercial businesses would pay. Laptops available to anyone over the internet for £800 were being bought for £2,000.

The really alarming thing is that this was happening in 2010 – ten years after the Blair government established the Office for Government Commerce (OGC) specifically to make government procurement work efficiently. Green was appalled: 'We couldn't work like this, we'd be out of business ... The only reason the government can ... is that they've got a printing press that prints money and we don't.'[19]

He estimated that if government adopted the hard-nosed professional buying practices employed by big private sector businesses, it could save taxpayers £20 billion annually 'without even breaking sweat'.

But there's a problem: the public sector doesn't have the hard-nosed professionals required to manage the process. Here's how a senior executive at one of the big defence contractors describes their negotiations with the MoD:

> Sometimes you feel you're in a process of asymmetric warfare. From industry you have professional contract negotiators whose job is to extract the best deal on the best day. From the MoD side, generally you don't have professional procurement executives. You do have a situation where on one side you have accountability, deliverability, decision-taking, and on the other a less so process.
> – Robin Southwell, Chief Operating Officer of EADS[20]

This lack of professionalism pervades negotiations throughout the public sector, as we'll see later.

Moreover, it isn't just a matter of paying the wrong price. Unlike paper and printer cartridges, much of what the government buys is not something you can simply pick up from Tesco. The big ticket items – military equipment, software systems, new hospitals – are usually bespoke.

And as everyone who's ever employed a builder knows, with bespoke projects you have to specify precisely what you want upfront. Changing your mind halfway through a project is fearsomely expensive and prone to disaster. Yet that is precisely what public sector buyers do all the time.

A good example is the NHS supercomputer. The Department for Health originally specified a highly standardised and centralised system, and a fixed price for delivery. But as the project got underway it met with huge opposition from within the NHS itself, and, under mounting pressure from media and politicians, the Department began to flip-flop away from the original specification.

In theory, they'd locked their suppliers into fixed price contracts, and they tried to make those prices stick. They'd even appointed their own hard-nosed professional from outside to drive the contractors, whom he treated like dogs pulling a sledge:

> When one of the dogs goes lame, and begins to slow the others down, they are shot. They are then chopped up and fed to the other dogs. The survivors work harder, not only because they've had a meal, but also because they have seen what will happen should they themselves go lame.[21]

But in practice the hard talk didn't work. As the Department flip-flopped on the specification, the contractors started to lose big money, and they weren't prepared to absorb it. In 2006, the international consultancy firm Accenture pulled out, writing off several hundred million in the process. They were later followed by a second huge supplier, Fujitsu. In 2007, the husky-driver himself jumped overboard. The project disintegrated into a catastrophic and expensive muddle.

We've seen this many times. Governments agree a price for a bespoke project, only to be forced to pay more later. Either the complexity of the project has been grossly underestimated (as was the case with the Nimrod spy plane), or there are big specification changes (as with the supercomputer and Britain's new aircraft carriers).

A recent analysis of 240 public sector projects showed that they had overrun initial budgets by an average 38 per cent. By far the worst was that NHS supercomputer, but plenty of others incurred overruns well in excess of 100 per cent.[22]

And governments elsewhere aren't much better. A study by Danish economists looked at public transportation projects around the world and found nine out of ten overrunning, with an average overrun of 28 per cent. Moreover, their analysis suggested that overruns are not always the result of naive optimism:

> Project promoters routinely ignore, hide, or otherwise leave out important project costs and risks in order to make total costs appear low. Politicians use 'salami tactics' whereby costs are only revealed to taxpayers one slice at a time in the hope that the project is too far along when true costs are revealed to turn back.[23]

The London Olympics was a classic example of salami tactics in action. When the original bid was made in 2005, the government reckoned it would cost taxpayers £2.3 billion. It later emerged that that figure was pretty well plucked out of the air, presumably not to alarm anyone too much.[24] And as soon as we were locked in, it rocketed to £9.6 billion – a fourfold increase. Moreover, there were a few hidden extras

– such as using the army for security – so the true overall cost was probably even higher.

But whether we blame optimism or salami slicing, the problem of underestimated costs is all too real. In fact, it's so real that it's been given an official name by the Treasury: they call it 'optimism bias'. Based on past experience, the Treasury now insists that capital project proposals incorporate an additional optimism-loading on the initial cost estimate, ranging from 2 per cent for standard building projects, right up to 200 per cent for some equipment and development projects.[25] In other words, the Treasury reckons that the true costs of projects like new defence equipment and computer systems will run out at *three times* the initial estimate. Which is quite a lot of optimism, let alone salami.

So to summarise, our simple shopper is an optimistic salami slicer, who overpays, is incapable of specifying exactly what he wants, is highly likely to change his mind halfway through and is unable to manage supplier contracts. Apart from that, he's just the man to send to the shops with £240 billion of our hard-earned cash.

THE CULT OF THE AMATEUR

A recurring theme in almost all of these shopping disasters is that of public sector amateurism. It's long been observed that the senior levels of the civil service – what used to be called its administrative class – overwhelmingly comprise gentlemen amateurs who know virtually nothing about what goes on below stairs, where our public services are actually delivered. They may be Sir Humphrey Oxbridge thorough-breds, but their interests are high policy and the governance of Britain, not the more mundane tasks of management and efficiency.

An official report on the civil service summarised the problem this way:

> Administrative class officials ... move too frequently from job to job with no specific professional education or formal training for their work. The Service lacks skilled managers ... most of the work of most Senior Civil Servants is not managerial, but rather relates to matters such as the preparation of explanatory briefs and answers to parliamentary questions ... there is not enough contact between the civil service and the rest of the community ... because Civil Servants are expected to spend their entire working lives in the Service...[26]

The striking thing about that passage is that it was written half a century ago, yet it still rings true today. Certainly, the civil service does now employ large numbers of specialists in various technical functions, but those at the top are still very much generalists. They still flit from post to post, and department to department, never building the kind of nitty-gritty managerial experience required to get a grip on public sector waste. The median time in post for a senior civil servant is under three years, and it's still the case that few have ever worked outside the public sector.

Take the current Permanent Secretaries at the three biggest-spending departments.[27] Robert Devereux, who heads the Department for Work and Pensions, worked his way up through Overseas Development, HM Treasury, the Department of Social Security and the Department of Transport. Along the way he did have a secondment with the Guinness brewing company, but his entire career progression has been in Whitehall. Chris Wormald, head of the Department for Education, progressed through three

government departments and the office of the Deputy
Prime Minister before landing the top job back at his first
department. Una O'Brien, head of the Department for
Health, admittedly does have a somewhat different career
background, having set up a charity before joining the civil
service. But the bulk of her career has been spent in Whitehall
and NHS administration.

Now, nobody says Sir Humphrey is an amateur in terms
of running civil service departments and helping ministers
develop policy – far from it. The charge is that he's an
amateur in terms of getting us value for money.

Time and time again, expensive policies fail because of
shockingly poor implementation. Senior mandarins make
plans without knowing precisely how they will be implemented, or even whether they are practical. And subsequent
monitoring of progress is often woeful or non-existent.
Labour's attempt to reform working practices in the NHS
was a prime example, costing billions but failing even to
collect information on whether it was succeeding.[28]

Accounting can be shambolic. Public sector bodies are
entrusted with billions of our cash, but they can't necessarily
account for how it's spent. The accounts of the European
Union haven't been signed off by auditors for two decades,
because of unresolved errors and irregularities. And, as we
saw earlier, the accounts of the Department for Work and
Pensions – our biggest-spending department – have been
qualified every single year since 1988/9: there's so much
fraud and error that auditors won't sign them off.

The management of costs and finance has never received
as much attention inside government as it does in the
commercial sector – even though government budgets far
exceed those of most commercial organisations. Professional

managers and so-called bean counters rarely make it to the top. In the words of the National Audit Office: 'Staff can still be promoted to senior positions in departments without having demonstrated an ability to deliver cost-effective operations, which sends a message within the organisation that performing well on financial matters is not important for career progression.'[29]

With amateurs in charge, we really shouldn't be surprised that the government spends our money so unprofessionally.

PAYING THEMSELVES TOO MUCH

If the public sector is hopeless at shopping and managing commercial suppliers, it's even more hopeless at managing its own labour costs, now running at £170 billion annually.

Traditionally, our public employees were supposed to be paid modestly. The idea was that high financial rewards were incompatible with a public service ethos and could attract the wrong sort of chap. Far better to stress the intrinsic rewards of service, the security of employment, the pension and the honours for loyalty.

Over recent years this has changed, most markedly under the last Labour government. With an ambitious and expensive spending programme to push through, they soon became deeply frustrated by the lack of professional management skills they found among top officials. They concluded that to make progress they'd need to buy in some top talent from the private sector: they had to stop paying peanuts, and start elbowing the monkeys aside.

One such external recruit was Richard Granger, the IT consultant brought in to deliver the NHS supercomputer. It's said that he took a pay cut to join the Department of Health, but he still got paid considerably more than any other member of staff, with reported annual earnings of £270,000–£285,000.[30] And he was typical of several high-profile appointments from the private sector.

The problem was that these much higher pay levels didn't stop with the relatively small number of senior people recruited in from outside to undertake specific and vital roles. Soon they spread out right across the public sector, lifting rewards for incumbent staff, both deserving and undeserving. Packages ballooned well into fat-cat territory.

In 2010, a study found that 38,000 public employees were being paid over £100,000 p.a. Nine thousand – including 362 local council bosses – were getting more than the Prime Minister's £142,500. And over a thousand were pulling in more than £200,000, among them ten GPs on over £300,000.[31] The very highest-paid public employee was Mark Thompson, the Director-General of our 'public service' broadcaster, who was pulling in £838,000. Altogether the BBC had seven of the ten highest-paid public employees, and 331 managers on more than £100,000. And that's without taking account of the eye-watering packages paid to their newsreaders and other performers.

And to put these figures into perspective, remember that a salary of £100,000 puts an individual in the top 2 per cent of earners across the entire country. Pay of £200,000 puts him in the top half of 1 per cent.[32]

But it isn't just public sector bosses: taking account of all grades and levels, *average* public sector pay is higher than in the private sector.

This striking fact has been known for years, and nobody disputes the basic figures. However, until recently, public sector unions and their supporters were able to contend that the difference reflected a skills and qualifications gap, with the public sector on average employing higher-quality work-ers doing more responsible jobs. That contention has now been blown away by a detailed pay analysis from the Office for National Statistics (ONS).[33]

The ONS analysis looks at relative pay *after* adjusting for differences in the mix of employees in terms of gender, age, occupation, region and qualifications. And it estimates that even after taking account of all those factors, average public sector pay is still 8 per cent higher than in the private sector.

What's more, over the ten years for which the ONS has published figures, the gap has been growing. It grew sharply as the Blair government dished out a series of inflationary public sector pay awards in the early noughties, and rose further as the recession crushed private sector earnings but left the public sector relatively unscathed.

The message is that the public sector is paying too much for its labour. And an 8 per cent gap on its £170 billion labour bill comes to a chunky £14 billion per year.

But the true overpayment is even more than that, because public sector pensions cost a lot more than those in the private sector. We'll be looking further at pensions in a later chapter, but to get a fairer comparison of employment costs we need to add the higher employers' pension contributions on to the pay gap figures already quoted. ONS analysis shows that adding on employers' pension contributions increases the gap between public and private sector employment costs by getting on for 10 per cent (average for full-time employ-ees).[34] That takes the labour cost gap from around 8 per cent up closer to 20 per cent.

But that still isn't the end of the story. Because, despite recent reforms, the public sector's year-to-year pension contributions are insufficient to fund the pension liabilities it's accruing. There's a shortfall that will ultimately have to be made good by taxpayers. According to the Public Sector Pensions Commission, the true cost of the average public sector pension is around 45 per cent of annual pay.[35] But since the combined contributions of both employees and employers is only about half that, there's a 20 per cent shortfall facing future taxpayers. That needs to be added to public sector labour costs.

The bottom line is that on a like-for-like basis, the public sector could be overpaying for its labour by up to 40 per cent. Even a gap of 30 per cent translates into waste of £50 billion annually.

The problem is exacerbated by the public sector's use of national pay scales. In the private sector, labour costs are considerably lower in regions away from London, but in the public sector that isn't the case. Despite some limited use of regional pay weightings, national pay scales mean the public sector tends to underpay those working in the London area, but overpay the bulk of its employees who work elsewhere. The result is the worst of both worlds: an excessive total wage bill, combined with recruitment difficulties in London and the south east.

And the damage inflicted by national pay scales goes well beyond the financial costs. For example, state schools in London and the south east have to pay their teachers more or less the same rates as those in the north east, even though local wage rates outside the profession are as much as 50 per cent higher. As a result, the average quality of their teachers is likely to be lower than in the north east, and the education given to pupils correspondingly worse. According to one recent study, the effect is to reduce exam scores by around one grade for every 10 per cent shortfall in wage rates.[36]

In the NHS, the consequences are even worse. Because NHS hospitals in high-wage areas can't attract enough permanent staff, they have to hire temporary agency staff, and their success in treating patients falls well short of the standards achieved elsewhere. An LSE study found that survival rates among heart attack victims are directly related to local wage rates: in high-wage areas more victims die than in low-wage areas. Or to put it another way, the NHS adherence to national pay scales is literally killing people in London and the south east.[37]

HELD TO RANSOM BY THE UNIONS

A key reason the public sector pays too much for its labour and has inflexible national pay scales is that it's heavily unionised. And the unions have done a great job extracting and defending above-market rewards for their members.

Back in the 1970s, trade union power stretched right across the economy. However, membership in the private sector subsequently nosedived, partly because of Thatcher's union reforms, but more fundamentally because increasing global competition wrought a radical change in our industrial structure and workforce attitudes. In the market sector, employees came to recognise the risks to their own jobs of excessive wage demands and union intransigence. But in the public sector, things just carried on as before.

Today, over 60 per cent of the remaining union members are in the public sector, despite the fact that it employs only a fifth of the workforce.[38] Fifty-six per cent of public employees are union members, four times higher than the private sector's 14 per cent. And that heavy public sector unionisation makes us an outlier against international competitors. Average union membership across the OECD is 18 per cent, whereas ours is 27 per cent.[39] We're significantly more unionised than the US, Japan, Germany and even France.

As a result, our public sector is virtually impossible to run efficiently. Not only are labour costs stuck at their excessive level, but the unions constitute a fearsome obstacle to organisational reform. They block change, frequently forcing politicians into expensive and unsuccessful workarounds. In the NHS, with its seventeen separate unions, billions were spent under Tony Blair in a doomed attempt to buy more flexible working practices.[40]

The ultimate union weapon of course is the strike, and public sector unions have never been shy about using it. Over the last fifteen years, the number of days lost to industrial disputes in the public sector has averaged half a million annually.[41] That's nearly five times the number lost in the private sector, even though the private sector is four times bigger. Or to put it another way, the average public sector worker is nearly *twenty times* more likely to strike than her private sector counterpart. She went out even while Blair's government was pumping huge amounts of extra cash into her pay packet.

It is deeply ironic that trade unions originally established to fight for workers against the barons of unbridled capitalism now direct most of their efforts to fighting their fellow working man in the private sector for a bigger share of his wallet.

And there's something even more extraordinary: taxpayers are actually subsidising these public sector unions. For one thing, union officials are given paid time off to conduct union business – including organising all those strikes. In 2011/12, over 3,000 full-time equivalent public sector staff were paid by us while working on union business, at an estimated cost of at least £92 million. On top of that, the unions receive direct payments from us to fund member education programmes. In 2011/12, that amounted to a further £21 million, giving them a total subsidy of £113 million.[42]

Clearly it's outrageous that taxpayers should be made to pay for activities that are directly contrary to their own interests. But in the public sector, that's exactly what happens.

We'll come back to this in a later chapter, where we'll also look at the unhealthy financial relationship between public sector unions and the Labour Party.

LACK OF ACCOUNTABILITY

During the latter months of 2011, after years of uninterrupted growth, Tesco suffered a marginal decline in its UK business. Within weeks its Chief Executive was heading for the exit. Despite his undoubted abilities and unblemished previous career record, something had gone wrong in the business, and, as the top man, he had to carry the can.[43]

Contrast that with what happened at the Home Office in 2005–6. A long series of management blunders had culminated in more than a thousand foreign prisoners being erroneously released from our jails. On top of that, the department's financial accounts had broken down and it was unable to account for all of the £13 billion it had received. Which, if it had been a private sector company, could have put its directors at risk of a jail sentence, never mind dismissal.

Yet despite that, and despite the Home Secretary being sacked and his successor famously describing the department as 'not fit for purpose', the Permanent Secretary who'd presided over the chaos was *not* sacked. In fact, just before the financial blunders became public knowledge, Sir John

Gieve was lifted out of the Home Office and installed as Deputy Governor of the Bank of England. And there – of all things – he was put in charge of financial stability. Two years later, of course, our financial stability itself went up in smoke.

The contrast is stark and undeniable. And such a contrast cannot help but influence and shape personal behaviour.

Indeed, public sector employees are usually safe even when they're known to be incompetent by their bosses and colleagues. Teaching is a shocking example. We all know that incompetent teachers can destroy life chances, yet it's estimated there are as many as 17,000 of them employed in British state schools today. Rather than sacking hopeless staff, head teachers find it much easier to write glowing references and help them move on to another school. The roll-call of those who've actually been 'struck off' the teachers' register due to incompetence numbers only eighteen in the last four decades.[44]

The public sector has always operated on the basis of collective responsibility – committees and rule books rather than individual executive authority. And as long as individuals act in accordance with the rules – as long as all the right boxes have been ticked – they are usually pretty safe from the consequences of poor results. It's much more difficult to get sacked for poor performance in the public sector than in the private.

But by downplaying personal accountability, the public sector makes it much less likely that mistakes will be corrected quickly, and much more likely that failure will be repeated – even by the very same people who failed in the first place.

POLITICIANS

We can't blame it all on our civil servants: many of Britain's biggest waste disasters can be traced directly to decisions made by their political masters.

Of course, in the broadest sense we might blame the entirety of government waste on politicians, because they're the ones who've presided over the huge growth in public spending. And they're the ones who came up with half-baked policies like 'free' healthcare and one-size-fits-all education. But let's focus here on their chronic tendency to meddle in policy implementation.

According to the traditional view, ministers are at the wheel of a finely tuned Rolls-Royce. All they need do is point it in the right direction and they'll be conveyed effortlessly to their chosen destination. In other words, once they've set the strategy they can happily leave their civil servants to take care of its implementation.

In practice, it's never been like that. Ministers find their departments are more Austin Allegro than Rolls-Royce, and, as government has grown, they've been increasingly drawn into implementation. After all, they're the ones who have to answer on *Newsnight* for public sector failure, and with their necks on the block they want some control. Unfortunately, while politicians may have their uses, achieving value for taxpayers' money is not one of them.

Again, the NHS supercomputer provides a classic example. It was ordered right at the top, at a Downing Street seminar chaired personally by Tony Blair. It seems he'd recently chatted with Microsoft's Bill Gates about the potential power of IT in delivering healthcare, and had been deeply impressed.[45] He reckoned the NHS must have fallen way behind the curve, missing out on massive efficiency gains, and it was time to apply the Prime Ministerial boot.

But shooting the breeze with Bill Gates proved no substitute for a true understanding of NHS IT requirements. And it provided no insight into the real-world difficulties of development and implementation, about which Blair was ignorant.

Of course, Health Department officials should have immediately flagged up the problems. But it takes a particularly courageous Sir Humphrey to speak up when the Prime Ministerial boot is flying around. They therefore agreed to a preposterously tight timetable and a preposterously low budget. The project went ahead even though many people must have realised right from the start that it was likely to end in failure. And once begun, a project personally ordered by the Prime Minister cannot be revisited: the mission must be accomplished whatever the cost. Or rather, the doomed project must grind on until there's a change of government.

A similar thing happened when the Rural Payments Agency (RPA) was instructed by ministers to implement the new EU policy on farm subsidies using a system far more complex than that used anywhere else. Defra's Secretary of State Margaret Beckett made a terrible, ill-informed decision in favour of the 'dynamic hybrid' system, and that was that – there was nobody to say no. Another fiasco duly unfolded, costing taxpayers hundreds of millions, producing huge delays, and reportedly causing suicides among farmers unable to access their subsidies.

Defra's ministers blamed their civil servants for not having warned them of the likely problems ahead. Farming minister Lord Bach said: 'I don't think that was satisfactory from senior civil servants whose job is to tell ministers the truth. I don't think they were deliberately trying to mislead me but there was a slight conspiracy of optimism.'[46]

A conspiracy of optimism is a nice way of putting it, but his civil servants were damned either way. Today's ministers arrive steeped in the DVD box set of *Yes Minister*, ready to jump on Sir Humphrey's attempts to stymie them. Civil servants know that behaving like Sir Humphrey will have them spending the rest of their careers in some distant outstation counting sheep. Advancement depends on pleasing ministers with a 'can-do' attitude, even when officials privately think the ideas hare-brained.

Failing to question the judgement of a powerful boss has spelled doom for many organisations. It's said that Hitler's top generals believed his invasion of the Soviet Union would end in catastrophe, but none spoke up. At the Royal Bank of Scotland, senior executives later claimed to have seen disaster coming, but none had the nerve to tackle CEO Fred the Shred.

Politics trumps taxpayer value in all kinds of other ways as well. For example, the age-old policy of buying British means that we often end up paying a higher price for an inferior product, especially in defence procurement. When the Nimrod spy plane contract was awarded to British Aerospace back in the 1990s, it's widely believed that the RAF would have preferred to buy the tried-and-tested Lockheed Orion.[47] But even though the US company offered to source 70 per cent of the proposed new plane from UK suppliers, and even though there were good prospects for future export orders, our politicians ruled that BAe should get the deal.[48] The apparent clincher was a super-keen price squeezed in below Lockheed's – except that, in the end, that price proved to be undeliverable.

When it comes to value for money, political intervention is rarely a plus.

IT'S NOT THEIR MONEY

Towards the end of his long and distinguished life, the economist Milton Friedman shone his light on the different ways of spending money:

> There are four ways in which you can spend money.
>
> You can spend your own money on yourself. When you do that, why then you really watch out what you're doing, and you try to get the most for your money.
>
> Then you can spend your own money on somebody else. For example, I buy a birthday present for someone. Well, then I'm not so careful about the content of the present, but I'm very careful about the cost.
>
> Then, I can spend somebody else's money on myself. And if I spend somebody else's money on myself, then I'm sure going to have a good lunch!
>
> Finally, I can spend somebody else's money on somebody else. And if I spend somebody else's money on somebody else, I'm not concerned about how much it is, and I'm not concerned about what I get. And that's government.[49]

Friedman has homed in on the vital issue of incentives. And what he highlights is that government has very few incentives to spend our money wisely. It's not their money, and they're using it to buy stuff for someone else.

Moreover, the situation is even worse than he suggests. Because not only is it someone else's money, and not only are the purchases made for someone else altogether, but the public officials doing the spending have absolutely no contact with those paying for it. As we'll see in the next chapter, our taxes disappear into the government's big black pot, and are ladled out in ways so convoluted and obscure that even the government's own accountants can't always fathom them.

Of course, the public sector's spenders must keep their bureaucratic paymasters sweet, and their bureaucratic paymasters must keep their political overseers sweet, and their political overseers must from time to time keep their electorates sweet. But by then, the incentive to deliver value is so attenuated it's virtually disappeared. And that's quite apart from the fact that those who vote for high-spending politicians may well not be the same people who have to pay the additional taxes.

Unlike Tesco, or any other private business, those who provide our public services can pretty well ignore those who have to foot the bill. The value imperative that drives efficiency in the private sector barely exists in the public.

PRODUCER CAPTURE

So government overpays for its supplies and labour, organises itself inefficiently, and is managed by people who aren't too bothered about delivering value. But there's something even more troubling.

All too often our public services seem to have been organised for the convenience of staff rather than customers. Despite the fact that we now live 24/7 lives, major services close at five or earlier and most don't operate at all over the weekend. Queuing is standard, and if we complain, we're directed to prominent notices warning us not to hassle staff members. We sit and wait, left with the distinct impression that the staff are doing us a favour by even speaking to us. As customers, we're made to feel like an unwelcome distraction.

What we're experiencing is the effect of producer capture. Instead of the customer being king, public sector management and staff have grabbed the throne for themselves, organising things to suit them rather than us. They make us wait, they pay themselves too much, and they evade responsibility for poor performance. It's costly, irritating and, at 2 a.m. in A&E, frightening.

The underlying cause is straightforward: most of us are unable to take our business elsewhere. The public sector operates a virtual monopoly across its key services, and monopolies always give priority to the interests of producers rather than consumers. Worse, in the case of these tax-funded monopolies, we have to pay for them whether or not we use their services.[50]

And we've only got ourselves to blame. We're the ones who've created these giant state monopolies by expecting so much from government. On top of its traditional functions of defence and the rule of law, we've piled education, healthcare, pensions, sickness pay, unemployment pay, child support, housing, social care, transport, international charity and even entertainment.

We've chosen to believe that government can provide all of these things for us dependably, efficiently and preferably with someone else paying. It's time to recognise that isn't possible.

THREE

THAT'S THE WAY THE MONEY GOES

A billion here, a billion there, and pretty soon you're talking real money.
– Attributed to US Senator Everett Dirkson

The government spends a colossal amount of our cash. In fact, it's so colossal it's become meaningless. Politicians and Whitehall mandarins may toss around billions here there and everywhere, but the scale is so far removed from our own experience that we can't relate to it. Somehow it doesn't seem like real money.

In numbers, public spending is well over £700 billion a year. That's a seven with eleven noughts after it: £700,000,000,000. If each of those pounds was one second, they'd last 22,000 years. If we stacked them up as one-pound coins, they'd stretch to the moon and back three times. Laid edge to edge, they'd orbit our planet 400 times. We are talking cosmic numbers.

In spending terms, £700 billion is twenty times what we stuff into the tills of Britain's mega-retailer Tesco every year, and eight times what we spend on all our food and drink put together. It's equivalent to *all* our own spending on everything, apart from housing. So that's food, drink, clothing, heating, household goods, transport, holidays, entertainment – the lot.

Government now spends £27,000 per household per year, or well over £500 per week. It is a big Big Spender.

OUR GOVERNMENT SPENDS MORE THAWN THE INTERNATIONAL AVERAGE

It's always useful to benchmark ourselves against major competitors, and on government spending, we're now towards the top of the table.

Over the period 2007 to 2011, covering both pre- and post-crash years, UK government spending averaged 49 per cent of national income. Across the OECD as a whole, the average was only 43 per cent.[51] And as the following chart shows, we are now the third highest spender among the G7 group of leading industrial countries.

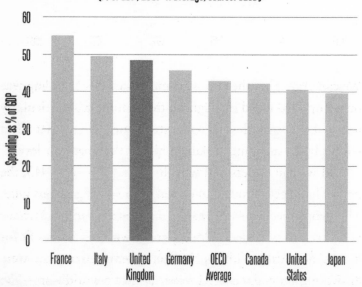

Our High Spending Government
UK public spending vs G7 members and OECD average
(% of GDP; 2007–11 average; source: OECD)

IT ALSO SPENDS MORE THAN ITS PREDECESSORS

At the start of the twentieth century, government spending accounted for less than 15 per cent of our national income. By 2011, it was close to 50 per cent, the highest in our peacetime history and higher even than during the First World War. The following chart tells the story.[52]

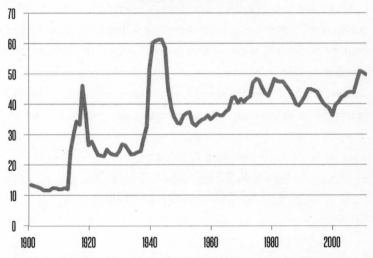

Government Spending Just Keeps Growing
General government expenditure as % of GDP
(1901–2011; source: ONS and OECD)

We can clearly see the two wartime spikes, but spending was on an upward trend throughout the century. It's particularly noticeable how both wars had a strong upward ratchet effect – after both, spending remained higher than pre-war levels.

And we can understand why. In both 1918 and 1945, the nation had been through an ordeal of the most grievous kind. The people needed some respite and reward, and politicians were keen to provide it. Lloyd George with his 'homes fit for heroes' and Attlee with his New Jerusalem welfare state were answering a popular call. Moreover, the two world wars – like all big wars – necessitated a widening of the tax net, and, once widened, politicians have always been reluctant to shrink it again. It gives them the chance to beat swords into plough-shares, which in twentieth-century terms meant diverting wartime taxes from defence to welfare spending. And it was the expansion of welfare that drove spending growth.

Before the First World War, by far the biggest spending item was defence, accounting for around 40 per cent of the government's budget. Spending on what we now call the welfare state – health, education and benefits – was well under 20 per cent, equivalent to just 2 per cent of national income.[53] Today, welfare comprises two-thirds of government spending and consumes 30 per cent of national income.

The welfare state was officially born during the Second World War, although its origins go back much further. It provided more generous cash benefits, more spending on education and, for the first time, a 'free' (that is, free at the point of access) nationalised health service. And for the next twenty years it meant public spending at around 35 per cent of national income, compared to 25 per cent in the mid-1930s.

It wasn't until the 1960s that it reached the next level. Harold Wilson's government ramped up welfare right across the board and, in just six years, spending leapt to 42 per cent of national income.

It was reckless and unsustainable, and the 1970s were a disastrous decade both for the public finances and the economy. As two successive oil price shocks and militant trade unionism sent the economy into a tailspin, government spending peaked at a scary 48 per cent of national income, far exceeding tax revenues. 1976 brought the ultimate humiliation of an IMF bailout, even if we did somehow manage to retain our AAA credit rating.

Margaret Thatcher's government was elected in 1979 with a mandate to curb union power and get the economy moving again. But first they had to grip the government's finances, which collapsed further as the economy sank into another recession. They imposed severe restraint on public spending, becoming hate figures for the left in the process. Yet, contrary to the myth, they never did cut spending overall. Instead, it was a resurgence of economic growth that eventually brought the spending ratio back down to 40 per cent by the late 1980s.

The next recession in the early 1990s pushed unemployment up to 3 million and drove the spending ratio back up to 45 per cent. And once again, it was renewed economic growth rather than spending cuts that brought it back down. By the time the Conservatives were voted out of office in 1997, the ratio had fallen to 41 per cent.

New Labour came to power having pledged to stick with the previous government's spending plans for the first three years – to demonstrate they could be trusted with the economy. And they were as good as their word, so that by the year 2000, public spending was down to 37 per cent of national income – right back where it had been when Wilson came to power in 1964. To widespread amazement, it seemed a Labour government had voluntarily put fiscal prudence ahead of welfare spending.

You will need no reminder of what happened next. In the new millennium the Blair government reverted to type. In just five years, a reckless frenzy of spending propelled it from 37 per cent of national income up to 44 per cent – a faster rate of increase than even Wilson had managed. The public finances rested on an increasingly preposterous fantasy that boom-and-bust had been abolished. So, when the inevitable bust hit, the spending ratio shot through the peacetime roof, exceeding 50 per cent in both 2009 and 2010.

Cramming a century of spending history into a few paragraphs can never do justice to all the twists and turns along the way, but let's pick out the six key messages:

1. Since 1900, the growth of public spending has outpaced the growth of national income by an average 1.2 per cent per year. If we carry on at that rate, some time around 2070, spending will absorb our entire income.

2. Big wars increase spending permanently.

3. Labour governments have increased spending more than Conservative governments. Each period of Labour government since 1951 has increased spending by an average 4 per cent of national income. Each period of Conservative government has increased it by an average 1 per cent, and that was entirely attributable to the disastrous 1970–74 Heath government.

4. It's a lot easier to raise spending than to cut it. It took just eleven years from 1964 to increase spending from 37 per cent to 48 per cent of national income; it then took twenty-five years to get it back down to 37 per cent again.

5. Outside of the years immediately following the two world wars, modern governments have rarely cut spending. The only significant exception was the Callaghan government, forced to cut by 4 per cent in real terms as a condition of the IMF bailout in 1976. Even under Thatcher, spending grew by 12 per cent in real terms.

6. Given that outright cuts have been so difficult, after every period of overspending, economic growth has been essential to bring the public finances back into balance.

Clearly, several of these messages resonate especially loudly in our present difficulties. We will return to them.

WHO GETS THE CASH?

The conventional way of analysing government spending focuses on how it's allocated across the main functional programmes – health, education and so on. And we'll adopt that approach in the chapters that follow.

But just as interesting is to analyse spending in terms of who actually gets the cash. And the answer may surprise you.

We can identify four main groups of recipients:

1. Public sector employees – both active and those drawing pensions.
2. Welfare recipients, including state pensioners.
3. Private sector suppliers – both those who supply goods such as fighter aircraft and pharmaceuticals, and those who supply services such as IT consultancy and hip operations.
4. Holders of government debt.

And when you add up all the numbers, it turns out that the biggest slice of government cash goes not to welfare recipients or public sector employees, but to private suppliers. They get around £240 billion a year, one-third of all spending.[54]

Of course, governments have always bought things from commercial businesses, especially weapons and capital infrastructure. But since the Thatcher government began outsourcing services like hospital cleaning in the 1980s, purchases have grown enormously.

Today, suppliers include not only arms manufacturers like BAE Systems, and construction companies like Skanska, but also big service companies like Serco and ISS. And let's not forget the global IT contractors such as Hewlett Packard, the international drugs giants like GlaxoSmithKline and the Olympics security blunderer G4S. They are all big suppliers to HMG. And behind them there's a long tail of smaller companies who might only be supplying the local council with maintenance services.

Then there are various suppliers who sound like they're in the public sector but aren't. NHS GPs are a good example, with most being private contractors rather than direct employees. Universities are another example: they sound like they're in the public sector, but in reality they are private sector bodies, albeit heavily dependent on public funding.

Overall, it adds up to very big business, making the government and its various agencies by far the juiciest customer in the land. And in theory that ought to mean great terms from the government's suppliers, even better than the ones Tesco extracts from its suppliers. Unfortunately, as we saw in the previous chapter, government has never been much good at shopping, so a substantial chunk of that £240 billion is made up of overpayment.

The next biggest group of recipients are those on welfare benefits, who together get £200 billion. Identifying them is easy: it's pretty well all of us. As we'll explain later, three-quarters of British households are now in receipt of at least one cash benefit. From child benefit to state pensions, more often than not there's something you can claim. Unless, that is, you're in work with no dependent children – in which case, you're out of luck.

£170 billion goes to public sector employees, comprising 5.8 million on the current payroll and 3.3 million receiving public pensions.[55] The number on public payrolls multiplied under the Blair government, rising by 600,000, including

100,000 additional public administrators. It's since fallen back a bit, but the net increase since 1997 still stands at 400,000.[56] Public sector pay rates also boomed under Blair.

Finally, £44 billion goes to government debt holders, split roughly 70/30 between British and foreign investors. Traditionally, British recipients largely comprised insurance companies and pension funds. However, since the Bank of England began buying up government debt in 2009 as part of its programme of quantitative easing (QE), a growing share of the debt interest has been going there. In effect, on around one-quarter of its debt, the government is now paying itself. We'll come back to the implications of that later.

SOME REGIONS DO A LOT BETTER THAN OTHERS

Once we start tracking who gets the cash, something else becomes obvious: certain regions of Britain get a whole lot more than others.

In particular, the devolved areas of Scotland, Wales and Northern Ireland all get much more than England. According to the Treasury's regional analysis – which tracks over 80 per cent of all spending – spending per head in the devolved areas is between 14 and 25 per cent higher than in England. In Scotland's case it means they get £7 billion more than if spending was held at the English level. That's £1,700 extra for every single Scot compared to her English counterpart.[57]

This preferential treatment goes back many years, and in Scotland's case was formalised in the now notorious Barnett formula during the 1970s. But since the establishment of devolved governments in the 1990s, the inequality has attracted much more attention. English taxpayers have increasingly questioned why they are being forced to pay for higher levels of public spending north of the border

– especially when the Scots are given free public services not available to the English, such as free university tuition.[58]

But even within England itself there are big differences between regions. For example, the north east gets 25 per cent more spending per head than the south east, a gap of £2,000. And if we exclude London, the north in general gets much more than the south. Different people have different views on whether this is fair, but there's no avoiding the fact that it's taking place. Indeed, in some regions public spending now constitutes the major part of the local economy. In the north east, it's up to around two-thirds of regional output – the kind of ratio last seen in Eastern Europe prior to the fall of Communism.

WHAT IT'S SPENT ON

Two-thirds of public spending goes on just three programmes. Welfare is by far the biggest, weighing in at £230 billion, or 35 per cent of all government spending. Health comes second, on £120 billion; and education third, on £90 billion. Those three programmes together constitute what we refer to as the welfare state, costing us £440 billion a year.

By comparison, the historic core functions of the state – defence and the maintenance of law and order – are cheap. With defence on £39 billion and law and order on £34 billion, they come to a combined 11 per cent of total spending.

Worryingly, debt interest is now the fourth biggest spending item, reflecting the explosive growth of government borrowing over recent years. Already consuming 7 per cent of spending in 2011/12, interest is set to increase much further. We'll be taking a close look at the implications of this later.

Outside of these main areas, spending goes on a huge

assortment of other activities including transport, housing, environmental protection, sport and culture, and international aid.

WHO SPENDS IT?

Logically enough, the bulk of the spending is channelled through Whitehall's spending departments, or their devolved counterparts in Scotland, Wales and Northern Ireland. Budgets are set by department, spending is done by department, and each department's top civil servant, known as the Departmental Accounting Officer, is directly answerable to Parliament for stewardship of the cash.

By far the largest-spending department is the Department for Work and Pensions. It spends £160 billion annually, and employs 116,000 civil servants to sign the cheques. Following them is the Department of Health, with an annual budget of well over £100 billion.[59]

Surprisingly, the third biggest spender is the Chancellor of the Exchequer, the person who's supposed to stop his colleagues spending our money, not to spend it himself. And for eight centuries, that had been the function of all our Chancellors – from Eustace of Fauconberg to Gladstone to Healey to Clarke.[60] Until Gordon Brown took over, that is. Brown didn't much like being Her Majesty's Master of Prudence, so he grabbed a few of the benefits previously administered by the Department of Social Security, notably child benefit. The gamekeeper turned poacher, leaving the system without a full-time gamekeeper.

In fairness, half of the Chancellor's £80 billion spending comprises debt interest. But the fact that the Chancellor now hands out tens of billions in benefits means that accountability for welfare spending is blurred.

And that accountability problem extends much further than just welfare. Throughout the public sector, responsibility for key functional programmes is split across a confusion of spending departments and other organisations. Labour minister Jeff Rooker once described it as 'a bowl of spaghetti'.[61] He was referring to the complex and confusing morass of government funding streams aimed at regional development, but he might just as well have been talking about government spending as a whole.

The reality is that the huge growth of spending over the years has never followed a coherent plan. It's happened in fits and starts, with departments gaining or losing responsibilities and budgets according to the political clout of their ministers rather than organisational logic.

There have of course been reorganisations – lots of them. And some have been considered attempts to rationalise things. But just as often, change has been driven by the need to be seen to do something. A good example is what the government describes as public order and safety (law and order to you and me). Spending on that is currently spread across *ten* separate departmental groupings, including the Home Office and the Ministry of Justice. Until 2007, the two were joined, but, after a series of operational disasters and Home Secretary John Reid's famous diagnosis that the Home Office was 'not fit for purpose', they were split. It's not clear the split improved efficiency, but it answered the immediate political imperative to be seen to do something.

The chopping and changing has been accompanied by a whirl of new names and initials. The Department for Education is a classic, with five name changes in twenty years. In fact, it's been through so many it's now run out, and it's recycling one it first thought of in 1992.[62]

Sometimes the changes have been so half-baked they've been abandoned immediately. Back in 2005, the ragbag Department of Trade and Industry was relaunched as the more dynamic-sounding Department for Productivity, Energy and Industry. It was only when the new nameplates were screwed up did they realise there'd been an altogether more serious screw-up. Ordering an immediate return to the old name, embarrassed Trade Secretary Alan Johnson explained that DPEI sounded like 'penis and dippy'.[63]

QUANGO STATE

Although the big central departments have overall responsibility for their high-level budgets, much of the actual spending is channelled down through a labyrinth of arms' length organisations. The most important are local councils, police authorities and a vast array of so-called quasi-autonomous non-governmental organisations – quangos for short.

Over recent decades, quangos have become notorious for waste and lack of accountability, with successive governments promising to make bonfires of them. But that's proved virtually impossible – no sooner has one quango been torched than another springs up from the ashes.

One problem is that nobody can quite agree on what they are, with the official list looking a lot shorter than the ones compiled by outside analysts.

In their comprehensive analysis published just before the last election, the TaxPayers' Alliance (TPA) focus on public bodies that are dependent on central government for funding and where central government has a big say in goals, strategies and senior appointments.[64] They liken them to subsidiaries in the private sector, and estimate that there were 1,148 of them in 2008, employing three-quarters of a million staff and spending over £90 billion of our money. But even that excludes a slew of quasi-autonomous NHS trusts, employing a further 1.4 million people and spending another £90 billion. It also excludes academy schools, which now number nearly 2,000 and get £6 billion direct funding from central government.[65]

The irony is that many of the big-spending quangos were established with the specific aim of boosting public sector efficiency. The theory is that, distanced from the Whitehall bureaucracy and political interference, they are free to focus all their energies on the specialist task assigned. But as the TPA analysis highlights, in practice quangos have some serious drawbacks.

For one thing, the issue of accountability is blurred. Quangos may be technically accountable to Parliament, but there are now so many that scrutiny is limited. On the other hand, the existence of a quango creates a kind of firewall behind which ministers can hide from their own responsibilities. This happened in 2006, when education ministers blamed a school test fiasco on their exam quango, even though a subsequent inquiry showed their own 'fingerprints were all over it'.[66]

Duplication is another problem: with so many quangos in existence, duplication and unnecessary costs are unavoidable. And the quasi-independence of quangos means they inevitably lobby for more powers and larger budgets. Indeed, the TPA estimates that tax-funded lobbying costs us around £40 million annually.[67] That's government lobbying itself, at our expense. And although the appointments process is now more open and transparent than in the early 1990s, ministers still have huge influence over who gets the well-paid senior jobs. There is a widespread perception of political cronyism, a perception that has been fuelled by appointments such as that of long-time Labour insider Trevor Phillips to the £110,000-a-year chairmanship of the Commission for Racial Equality.

Local councils are not quangos, because taxpayers get to elect those in charge. But in reality, today's councillors have limited authority. Their councils may once have been proudly independent, but that was when they raised most of their cash from local ratepayers. Today, they answer to paymasters in Whitehall. Grants from central government are running at over £100 billion annually, which is 85 per cent of council revenue funding. And that dependence makes them much more like quangos than independent entities. Elected councillors may squawk about it, but he who pays the piper generally ends up calling the tune.

This dependence on central funding undermines account-ability to local taxpayers, and there is growing evidence that it undermines efficiency. Instead of shaping their services and costs to meet the needs and preferences of their local commu-nities, councils have been obliged to follow one-size-fits-all boilerplates laid down by Whitehall. Local taxpayers have little control over this because their council tax payments constitute only a small part of their council's revenue. Overall, they still have to pay broadly the same amount of tax, but by routing it via central government they have much less control over local service delivery.

Most of our major competitors have far less fiscal centrali-sation than us. In fact, we have the fourth most centralised system out of all twenty-three developed economies analysed by the OECD, and we seem to be paying a big price in terms of efficiency. International comparative studies suggest we could save tens of billions annually by decentralising more, in line with our competitors.[68]

Drawing this together, of the £700 billion the government spends each year, £160 billion is spent by local authorities. And depending on how you count them, a further £190 billion is spent by quangos of one kind or another. Which means that around half of all spending is actually carried out by arms' length bodies, rather than directly by the big-spending departments.

All of which makes the link between what you spend in tax and what you get back in services pretty opaque.

THE LENGTHY JOURNEY FROM PAYMENT TO SERVICE

Let's follow £100 of your tax as it leaves your wallet and travels through the system to where it gets spent on services. Because, as one of our Prime Ministers reminded us: 'It is your tax which pays for public spending. The Government have no money of their own. There is only taxpayers' money.'[69]

First stop is HMRC's bank account. And since tax collectors don't do it for love, they keep £1 for themselves.[70]

What remains then gets divvied up among the spending departments we looked at earlier, and paid into their bank accounts. We'll follow the £17 that goes to the Department of Health.

The Department keeps £1 to cover central costs including administration. The rest it dishes out to its vast array of quangos, including – in England alone – ten Strategic Health Authorities, 191 Primary Care Trusts (PCTs) and fifty assorted others.

About £15 goes to the PCTs, who are responsible for delivering NHS services in your local area. Except they don't actually deliver anything – they pay other people to do it. After deducting around 50 pence for administration, they pay £7.50 to hospitals, £2 to GPs and dentists, and the rest to a slew of other suppliers like pharmacists and mental healthcare providers.

So when you visit your GP, you are sitting four layers away from where your payment was originally made. Unlike when you visit Tesco, the payment and the service are completely detached. The layers of complexity leave you with little idea of how the cost of your tax payments relates to the services you receive.

That detachment is even more pronounced when taxpayers are funding services they will never use. For example, few taxpayers will ever go to the Royal Opera House, yet it gets an annual government subsidy equivalent to a £1 surcharge on *everyone's* income tax. Setting aside the immorality of forcing poor taxpayers to subsidise a gilded playground for the rich, when the cash largely comes from people who never use the service it's impossible for anyone to connect up payment and service delivery.

This is a structure tailor-made for waste and inefficiency. Quite apart from the administrative costs of having so many layers, insulating suppliers from those who ultimately pay breaks the vital link that drives efficiency in the market economy. Public sector suppliers don't need to keep the customer satisfied, because the customer has to pay whether she's satisfied or not. Indeed, she has to pay even if she doesn't want the service at all.

LUNCH IS NEVER FREE

Throughout the entire country, there are millions of us who depend on government for our incomes. Whether we're working directly for the public sector, or working for a private sector contractor, or drawing welfare benefits, it's the government's cash that puts food on our table. Which goes

a long way to explaining why public employees such as BBC
staff are so keen on public spending.

The government also supplies all of us with a huge range
of services. They may be a bit rickety, and we may be able
to buy much better for ourselves from private suppliers, but
they're free. It's a very seductive proposition.

Except – as we must keep reminding ourselves – in the real
world none of this is free. Whenever the government raises
pensions, or hires another 20,000 nurses, or buys a new
Olympic Park, sooner or later we have to pay an equivalent
amount in taxes. And with a billion here, a billion there,
pretty soon you're talking real taxes.

Looked at like that, the question is: why do we let the
government arrange our education, healthcare and telly
programmes, rather than doing it ourselves? After all, we
manage to buy our own food and car insurance, and for
most of our public services there are already plenty of
alternative private suppliers available.

We'll ponder that question as we examine the problems
in what many hold to be our very finest public service –
the NHS.

FOUR

SICKNESS IN THE NHS

I am well into my recovery and I felt that you should know what excellent care I have received, Mr Mohammed is a perfect gentleman and his team are total professionals, well done to all concerned and good luck to you in the future, you have changed my life and restored my faith in the health service.
– Feedback comment by anonymous patient at South Tyneside NHS Foundation Trust

[My partner] had a terrible evening. He had a very distressful twenty-four hours. They are understaffed. They have got terrible facilities. The toilets are appalling ... He suffered terribly. What are you going to do? All you do is walk around and make yourself known but you don't do anything to help anybody.
– Sharon Storer, waylaying Tony Blair on his pre-election walkabout at the Queen Elizabeth Hospital Birmingham, 2001

No area of the public sector stirs our emotions more than the NHS. We all need healthcare at some point during our lives, and when we need it we really need it. For six decades, the NHS has been there for us – protection from a world of pain, free at the point of use, and available to all irrespective of means. It literally saves our lives. You bet we feel emotional.

In this chapter, we'll look at what the NHS costs and how it performs. We'll examine how well it's used all the extra funding it's had over the last decade or so. And we'll see how it does in the crunch business of keeping us alive. We'll find plenty of waste, and some very serious questions.

In the next chapter, we'll look for answers to those questions and see how applying market principles to healthcare could deliver better value for money.

But first we're going to look at something that often surprises people.

MORE MONEY DOESN'T BUY LONG LIVES

We all know that medicine has conquered many dread diseases over the years. And we all know that new drugs and fantastically clever technology are able to extend our lives as never before. So, given that most of us want to live long and prosper, spending more money on the NHS has to make sense. Right?

Well, not necessarily. When we look at experience across the developed world, we discover that there is virtually no correlation between the amount countries spend on healthcare and their average life expectancy.

Sure, in poor countries with little existing healthcare, additional spending on things like immunisation programmes can have a huge pay-off in terms of lives saved. But in Britain today we're not in that position, and we need to compare ourselves against other rich countries.

The following chart shows the picture for the twenty richest members of the OECD in 2009.[71] Life expectancy at birth is plotted on the vertical axis, and healthcare spending on the horizontal axis. And, as we can see, spending more money is not reflected in higher average life expectancy. Indeed, some of the biggest spenders have the lowest life expectancy.

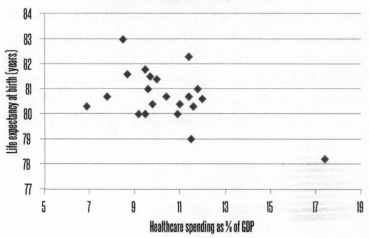

Thus, among the richest countries, the biggest spender – which is the US – has the lowest average life expectancy. And the country where people live longest – Japan – is the third lowest spender. We're around the middle of the pack. We spend a bit less than the average, and we die a bit sooner.

Precisely what accounts for variations in average life expectancy is the subject of much current research, but differences in diet and lifestyle obviously play a big role. A population stuffing itself with supersized junk food while slumped in front of the telly is going to be less long-lived than one eating steamed vegetables and taking regular exercise. And we seem to have a particular problem here in Britain, with a quarter of our population now classed as obese, compared to, say, less than 5 per cent in Japan.

The point we need to register here is that, for a developed country, more healthcare spending does not automatically translate into long life expectancy or healthy lives. Those things depend crucially on how people manage their own health and that of their families. And as we'll discuss later, there are countries that manage to spend less than us on healthcare while achieving better health outcomes like life expectancy.

WHAT THE NHS COSTS US

Government spending on health – largely comprising the NHS – costs us more than any other area of government activity except for welfare payments. In 2010/11, it totalled £121 billion, 18 per cent of all government spending, and nearly £5,000 per household.

That's a lot of money, and a large chunk of it reflects the huge growth of spending under the last Labour government. Between 1997 and 2010, spending in real inflation adjusted terms literally doubled, climbing to over 8 per cent of national income.

Growth on that scale was unprecedented. In its first fifty years up until 1999/2000, the cost of the NHS gradually increased from around 3 per cent of national income to just over 5 per cent. Or to put it another way, NHS costs grew by 60 per cent more than the growth in national income.[72] But in just ten years, between 1999/2000 and 2009/10, costs relative to GDP surged by a *further* 60 per cent. Growth that had previously taken fifty years was piled into just ten. And the cost to taxpayers jumped from 5 per cent of GDP to 8.

We'll look at what we got for all that extra money later, but we need to recognise that this spending surge did not arrive out of a clear blue sky. There was an important historical context.

The previous two decades had been difficult ones for NHS budgets, as a Conservative government struggled to restrain the growth of public spending after the excesses of the 1970s. Taking one year with another, they succeeded, with NHS spending being held down to roughly the same share of national income it had reached in the 1970s. But in the meantime, people were living longer, and treatments were getting more sophisticated and expensive by the year. Services were under pressure, and waiting lists were lengthening for a whole range of potentially life-saving treatments. By the late 1990s, there was a widespread view that we simply weren't spending enough on health.

It was a view reinforced by comparisons with other developed countries. As a percentage of national income, all our major competitors were by then spending considerably more than us: France and Germany were both spending 3 to 4 per cent more, and the US an extraordinary 7 per cent more. Something had surely gone wrong.

Now, in making international spending comparisons we always need to make sure we're comparing apples and apples, and that's especially important with healthcare. Because different countries fund their healthcare systems in very different ways, and government spending is by no means the only source of funds.

For example, it's well known that US healthcare relies heavily on private insurance arrangements rather than public funds. And even countries with universal public health systems often levy user charges, whereby patients have to pay if, for example, they visit a GP. Indeed, the NHS itself charges for certain services, such as prescriptions and dentistry, not to mention the millions of us who pay for private medical services. Overall, around 15 per cent of UK health spending is paid for out of our private funds, and about 10 per cent of the population have private health insurance.[73]

So, to get a true international comparison of spending on healthcare, we need to take account of all forms of spending, both public and private. And that's the basis of the following chart, showing the latest available comparison against other rich countries (again defined as the twenty richest members of the OECD).

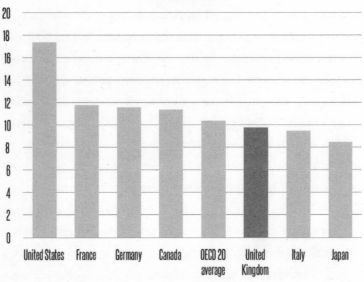

So despite Labour's unprecedented spending surge – health spending doubled in real terms during their tenure – we're still spending less than most of our major competitors. We spend 9.8 per cent of GDP compared to a rich-country average of 10.4 – a relative shortfall of just over 5 per cent. Even if we exclude the high-spending US – which is a real outlier – there's still a relative shortfall of 2 per cent.

Perhaps more striking is the comparison against our

near neighbours France and Germany. Although we've now caught up with where they were in the mid-1990s, their spending has since grown by *another* 1 to 2 per cent of GDP. It seems we've been running just to stand still.

The fact is that healthcare spending has been increasing all around the world, and we'll come back to the implications of that in the next chapter.

WHAT THE NHS DOES FOR US

The NHS provides medical care for pretty well the entire nation – a huge undertaking. Around 10 per cent of us have private medical insurance, but that's generally just a top-up to our basic NHS package, confined to non-emergency hospital treatments. For most routine services, from GP visits to childbirth, virtually all of us depend on the NHS.

And the NHS delivers on a heroic scale.[74] In England alone:

- It deals with 1 million patients every thirty-six hours, with each of its 39,000 GPs seeing an average 140 patients a week.
- Its doctors write out nearly 1 billion – yes, *1 billion* – prescriptions a year, equivalent to seventeen prescriptions for each and every one of us. Overall, it spends an annual £11 billion on drugs to treat us.
- Its hospital consultants complete 17 million 'consultation episodes' a year. In 2010/11, they performed 10 million operations, almost one for every five of us. (Well, strictly speaking, they performed 10 million of what the NHS snappily labels 'finished consultant episodes with a procedure', so they didn't all involve the knife.)[75]
- Its hospitals deliver 650,000 of our babies every year.
- Its A&E departments deal with around 16 million attendances annually, of which a quarter require an X-ray.

What's more, we generally seem very happy with what the NHS delivers. The official annual survey of patient satisfaction with their GPs regularly reports that nine in ten patients are at least 'satisfied', with over half saying they are 'very satisfied'.[76] Similarly, the annual survey of inpatients at NHS hospitals finds that nine in ten rate their overall care as 'good' or higher. Nearly half rate their care as 'excellent'.[77]

There's more good news when it comes to equity. In broad terms, the NHS does seem to deliver on its mandate to treat everyone the same irrespective of means. Yes, there are complaints that the sharp-elbowed middle class get more than their fair share, but that's not what the official statistics say. According to the stats, those in the lower half of the income distribution benefit from a quarter *more* NHS spending than those in the top half.[78]

As we'd expect, to do all this takes a lot of staff, and in England alone the NHS employs a staggering 1.4 million people (2010).[79] That makes it by far the largest employer not just in Britain, but also in Europe. Even worldwide, it's only exceeded by the Chinese People's Liberation Army, the US armed forces, a couple of Chinese state industries, and US retailer Wal-Mart.[80] Closer to home, we can compare it against Britain's largest private sector employer, Tesco. Tesco also maintains a presence in virtually every town and city, and also carries an awesome responsibility – that of feeding one in three British families. But at 300,000 staff, Tesco's UK employment is well under a quarter of NHS employment. The NHS really is a monster.

But by no means all NHS staff are those famous 'doctors 'n' nurses' who feature so heavily in political point scoring. In 2010, out of 1,431,557 staff employed by the NHS in

England, just 141,326 were doctors and 410,615 qualified nursing staff – less than 40 per cent of total staff numbers.[81] There's a long tail of other staff, not least the 41,962 labelled as managers and senior managers.

We can put this into an international perspective by comparing the staffing of our health system against the average in other rich countries. And we can do the same for various other headline medical resources. The following chart shows comparisons for the number of doctors, nurses, acute-care hospital beds and MRI scanners, all expressed relative to population.[82] Again, the international benchmark comprises the twenty richest OECD member countries.

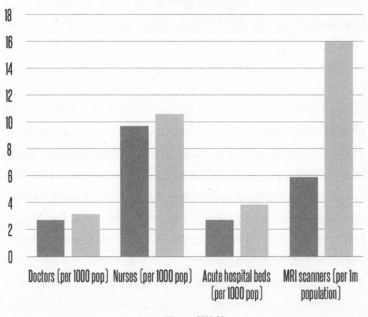

Comparison of Medical Resources
UK vs rich country average – numbers relative to population
(2009; source: OECD)

The chart casts a very revealing light on the NHS. It may be one of the world's biggest organisations, but relative to population it provides us with fewer doctors, fewer nurses, fewer acute-care hospital beds and *much* less high-tech equipment than its counterparts abroad.

On the face of it, such a comprehensive shortfall in medical resources is worrying. We may be spending 5 per cent less than the international average, but surely that can't explain a 15 per cent shortfall in doctors, or a 30 per cent shortfall in hospital beds, or a staggering 60 per cent shortfall in scanners. What on earth is the NHS doing with the rest of the money?

Opponents of NHS reform have long suggested that these apparent shortfalls actually reflect the efficiency of the NHS. Because it is an integrated system it can deliver healthcare more cheaply, and it can reap economies of scale denied to the fragmented systems elsewhere. It doesn't waste resources on duplication, which is what happens where there are competing providers operating in a market system. Big is beautiful because integration is more efficient. Far from being a problem, Britain is getting a bargain.

Let's see if that view is supported by the evidence.

DO WE GET VALUE FOR MONEY?

We've looked at the costs of the NHS, and we've looked at what it delivers to us. To assess value for money, we need to weigh the costs against the delivery.

There are two key issues. First, whether the NHS is efficient in the way it uses its people and other resources in delivering healthcare – otherwise known as productivity. And second, whether the NHS manages to keep costs down by negotiating keen terms with its suppliers – especially its suppliers of labour.

We'll start with productivity. That's about comparing NHS inputs against its outputs, and assessing how efficiently it converts the former into the latter. We'll look at how NHS productivity has changed over time, and how it compares against health services overseas.

For many years, NHS productivity was a complete mystery. The official line was that, since its services are provided 'free', it wasn't possible to measure the value of its outputs, so we'd just assume they were always equal to the inputs. In other words, NHS productivity was assumed to remain unchanged, world without end, forever.

That was always pretty thin, and the Office for National Statistics has now finally produced some more helpful figures. It's done so by measuring the key NHS outputs independently.[83]

Essentially, the statisticians take all those stats we've just listed – on the number of GP appointments, operations, prescriptions and so on – add them all up, and derive an estimate of how NHS output is changing year by year. They've done it for every year since 1995 and, over the thirteen years to 2008, they calculate that NHS output increased by 61 per cent.

But that's just the *quantity* of output (the number of consultations, prescriptions etc.). To get a more complete picture they also attempt to take account of changes in the *quality* of that output. For example, survival rates from various treatments increased through the period and the overall output measure ought somehow to take account of that. The statisticians have therefore added on an estimated quality adjustment, which lifts the total increase in output from 61 per cent to 69 per cent.

Now, a 69 per cent increase in NHS output over just thirteen years sounds pretty impressive. At an average annual growth rate of 4.4 per cent, it compares very well with almost any other sector of the British economy.

But when we bring in the costs, and compare the increase in estimated output against the huge increase in health service spending over that period, a rather different picture emerges. The statisticians estimate that over the thirteen years, cash spending increased by a whopping 167 per cent. Obviously a large chunk of that was health service inflation, but even adjusting for that, real spending still increased by 75 per cent – significantly more than the growth of output.

So although estimated NHS output increased by 69 per cent, productivity declined by over 3 per cent through the period.

Moreover, the size of that quality adjustment is open to debate. Early versions of the calculation didn't include it, and it was only after pressure from NHS bosses that it was brought in. Without it, output growth would fall back to 61 per cent, and the decline in productivity would come in at 8 per cent.

The conclusion is clear: for as long as we've got figures, whichever way we measure it, NHS productivity has been getting progressively worse. As the NHS has got bigger, it's become less efficient.

The NHS also comes out poorly in productivity comparisons with its counterparts overseas. Again, international productivity comparisons in healthcare are a new field of statistical analysis, but work by the OECD is starting to give us the key numbers.

In one recent study, researchers examined the performance of different healthcare systems in delivering what are known as health outcomes.[84] In particular, they looked at the potential gain to life expectancy if each country's healthcare system operated at the same efficiency level as the world's best. That is, without spending any more money, how much longer would each healthcare system keep the average person alive if its efficiency matched the world's best?

They found the NHS to be among the developed world's least efficient systems. It underperforms all of its G7 counterparts except for the US. And if it operated as efficiently as the world's best, then, *without spending any more money*, we'd all live an average three and a half years longer. Gargantuan scale has certainly not made the NHS efficient.

These productivity findings are important not just because they tell us today's NHS is inefficient, but also because they fly in the face of that long-held view that big is beautiful. Even if there are economies of scale in healthcare, it's clear the NHS doesn't benefit from them.

Let's now turn to our second question – whether the NHS keeps costs down by getting keen prices from its suppliers. Because even if the NHS is very efficient at turning inputs into outputs, it still won't deliver value for money if it persistently overpays for those inputs, be they doctors, drugs or facilities.

This has always been a vexed issue for the NHS, which has steadfastly maintained it faces an inflation rate unavoidably higher than for the rest of the economy. For as long as anyone can remember, NHS bosses have argued that unless they are given above-average budget increases, spending in real terms must get squeezed. It's an unavoidable result of expensive advances in medical technology.

And it's perfectly true that the price of NHS inputs has risen faster than prices in the economy generally. The analysis from the Office for National Statistics shows that from 1995 to 2008, NHS inflation was running 0.7 per cent per annum faster than the rest of the economy (as measured by the GDP deflator).[85] But the key question is: why?

It turns out that the excess was *not* down to the escalating cost of new-fangled medical kit or drugs. It was entirely down to increases in NHS pay rates, which accounted for the *whole* 0.7 per cent excess.

That's a very important conclusion. What it tells us is that if the NHS had kept proper control over its pay rates, NHS inflation could have been kept in line with average inflation elsewhere. Instead of which, the NHS awarded its doctors, nurses, managers and other employees a series of eye-watering pay rises during Labour's years of plenty.

OVERPAYING FOR WHAT IT BUYS

Well over half the increase in NHS spending under Labour was lost to NHS inflation, especially its inflationary pay deals.

Most notorious was the new contract for GPs, which resulted in their average earnings shooting up by nearly 60 per cent in just two years. Under the deal, many GPs were suddenly able to earn well over £200,000 per annum, and a couple of GPs were later discovered pulling in an astonishing £475,000 per annum.[86] What's more, GPs were simultaneously able to reduce their hours, close their surgeries on Saturdays and abandon their traditional but tiresome out-of-hours service for home visits. The NHS had somehow agreed to pay considerably more cash in exchange for considerably less work.

The GPs' contract epitomised the spectacularly inept negotiating practices of NHS managers. Viewed from the other side of the negotiating table, one of the doctors' negotiators from the BMA union later recalled: 'It was just stunning. Nobody in my position had ever believed we could pull it off, but to get it … was a bit of a laugh.'[87]

Unfortunately, it wasn't so much of a laugh for taxpayers.

According to the OECD, the deal made our GPs the best-paid of *any* in the developed world – including the US.[88]

The real irony here is that these huge pay deals were supposed to boost NHS productivity. The original idea had been to get staff to accept new and more productive working practices in exchange for extra pay. But when the National Audit Office later analysed the results from the largest component of the programme it concluded:

> The Department of Health ... has not carried out a specific exercise to demonstrate the productivity savings resulting ... nor have trusts attempted to measure the resulting efficiency or productivity gains. Without the means to measure the specific impact ... it is not possible to determine whether the productivity savings have been achieved...[89]

So, despite all the cash that had been lavished on it, and despite all the promises that it would boost productivity, NHS bosses had not even bothered to monitor and assess its results. The entire programme had been an exercise in wasting money.

The reality is that NHS staff are highly unionised, and their unions have been more than a match for the weak NHS management.

In fact, like those doomed British car manufacturers in the 1970s, the entire organisation is riddled with unions – as many as seventeen by one count. Some – like Unison, Unite, and the GMB – will be well known to you from their regularly televised strike threats. But others may not be so familiar – or at least, you may not realise they're trade unions.

The Royal College of Nursing (RCN) is one example. It may sound like an official body for maintaining the highest professional nursing standards, but it is in fact the country's fourth largest trade union with around 400,000 members, most of whom are employed by the NHS.

The British Medical Association (BMA) is another example. It too sounds like a professional body charged with upholding the Hippocratic oath, and its chairman is often heard opining on that very basis. Yet, in reality, the BMA is a trade union representing around 140,000 doctors and medical students. In the decade to 2009, the BMA was Britain's second fastest-growing union, with membership expanding by 29 per cent.[90]

The primary focus of both the BMA and the RCN is on improving the terms and conditions of their members. And like all NHS unions they are heavily resistant to any reform that could threaten their members' interests – which pretty well means any reform at all. It's something worth remembering when one of their representatives pops up on TV to comment on government reform proposals.

Another factor that increases NHS labour costs is the high staff absence rate due to sickness. According to an independent report commissioned by the Department of Health, the average NHS employee takes 10.7 days a year off sick, 50 per cent higher than the average in the private sector.[91] 45,000 staff call in sick per day, and the direct cost is put at £1.7 billion annually. The cost of hiring additional staff to cover for the absentees pushes the figure even higher.

But if NHS managers have failed to keep wage costs under control, they've done no better purchasing goods and services from outside suppliers. For example, the National Audit Office investigated purchases of so-called consumables, and found that NHS hospitals were routinely overpaying by about 10 per cent.[92] There was a lack of coordination leading to a failure to achieve proper bulk discounts. Among other things, the NAO discovered that hospitals were buying no fewer than 652 different types of medical gloves.

The £11 billion annual drugs bill is another area where the NHS can easily overpay. At present, the prices of branded drugs are mainly controlled under the Pharmaceutical Price Regulation Scheme, a voluntary five-year agreement between the Department of Health and the pharmaceutical industry that places a fixed cap on the profits drugs companies are allowed to make from the NHS. But while that may sound comforting, the financial and marketing sophistication of these giant global corporations means the comfort may be more apparent than real. Ominously, the last five-year agreement had to be scrapped halfway through when an Office for Fair Trading probe revealed that the NHS was paying hundreds of millions more than it needed to.[93]

Then there's the whole issue of PFI hospital projects, the costs of which have often been allowed to escalate beyond anything the sponsoring trusts could sensibly afford to finance over the medium term. Indeed, several are now in serious financial difficulties, with the South London Healthcare Trust losing so much money on its £69 million annual PFI charge, it's had to be put into administration.[94] One of its three big hospitals may yet have to close, depriving hundreds of thousands of Londoners of local care.

In the case of the Norwich & Norfolk Hospital PFI contract, NHS negotiators were so far out of their depth that the private sector investors were able to walk away with a bonus of £82 million, boosting their rate of return to an astonishing 60 per cent. The Chairman of Parliament's Public Accounts Committee commented: 'This was a poor deal ... It is hard to escape the conclusion that the [NHS] staff managing the project were not up to the rough and tumble of negotiating refinancing proposals with the private sector.'[95]

But perhaps the single best example of cost overruns during Labour's spending surge is the now infamous National Programme for IT (NPfIT), otherwise known as the NHS supercomputer. This was an attempt to provide the entire NHS with a single unified patient record-keeping system, covering tens of millions of people and accessible by any properly authorised member of the NHS staff from anywhere in the country. In theory it was supposed to improve efficiency right across the NHS, and to make things safer for patients.

When the project was launched in 2002, at a summit personally chaired by Tony Blair at No. 10, its cost was budgeted at a chunky £2.3 billion. But the Department of Health – not an organisation previously known for its IT management skills – soon discovered that the technical challenges in delivering the thing were somewhat greater than it had assumed. In fact, it turned out the Department had bitten off the biggest civilian IT project in the entire history of the world.

The result was a Grade A fiasco. From the initial £2.3 billion budget, the official estimate of costs soon spiralled fivefold to £12.7 billion. The real prospective cost was almost certainly even more, with Labour Health Minister Lord Warner at one point blurting out a figure of £20 billion.[96] Eventually the succeeding coalition government pulled the plug on the whole thing, leaving taxpayers billions out of pocket with virtually nothing to show for it.

So, to summarise, the overall picture is of an organisation that has achieved a lot in boosting output over the last fifteen years. But in doing so it has become progressively less efficient. And in the area of cost control it has performed badly, especially during the period when its budget was being ramped up by the last Labour government.

In terms of value for money, the NHS has been heading in the wrong direction. We're certainly getting more healthcare than we had fifteen years ago, but we're spending a lot more on it. Pound for pound, we're worse off.

But of course, when it comes to healthcare, money isn't everything. And there are aspects of the NHS that are far more troubling than its record in wasting money.

THE DARK SIDE OF THE NHS

We've all had our own experiences of the NHS. Some have been excellent, such as when it literally saves a loved one's life. Some have been irritating but bearable, such as waiting hours for treatment in an A&E department. And some have been little short of horrific.

Let's start with those waiting lists. The NHS has always had a problem with waiting lists for hospital treatment, and successive governments have struggled to contain it.

For the last Labour government it was a major priority, with hospitals being set a series of targets for maximum waiting times. And they certainly achieved some success: according to the official figures, the total waiting list for in-patient treatment at English hospitals halved between 1997 and 2010.

But from the perspective of a sick patient, NHS waiting lists can still feel pretty long. As of August 2011, the average wait was just over six weeks, with 2.6 million patients in the queue. Ten per cent of those patients had been waiting for more than eighteen weeks.[97] That is, they'd been

waiting more than eighteen weeks to see a hospital specialist for a problem sufficiently serious that their own GP had
been unable to deal with it. Either that, or they were queuing
for admission as an in-patient for surgery.

After six decades of the NHS, we've all got so used to these
waiting lists that we tend to assume they're the natural order
of things. But they aren't. In many countries, such as France
and Germany, hospital waiting lists are largely unknown.
In fact, it's very difficult to compare our waiting lists with
those abroad because many countries simply don't collect
the stats – they don't need to.

True, for many people, waiting is little more than an
inconvenience. But it's certainly not the mark of a world-
class health system, and for some unfortunates, it could be
a killer.

Another area where the NHS falls well short of the world's
best is in the standard of general nursing care.

For example, very many of us will have been appalled at
the treatment meted out to an elderly relative in hospital.
We'll have seen with our own eyes the lack of attention, the
failure even to ensure patients are eating and drinking properly, and the shambolic, unhygienic condition of the wards.

And it's hardly a hidden horror. The problem constantly
features in the media, and there's been a steady stream of
damning official reports. A report from the Care Quality
Commission in 2011 said it had carried out unannounced
inspections at 100 hospitals with wards caring for the elderly:

> Around half of the hospitals we visited gave our inspec-
> tion teams cause for concern. Twenty hospitals were not
> delivering care that met the standards the law says people
> should expect.

This means that one in five of our inspections ... picked up care that posed risks to people's health and wellbeing.

... Time and time again, we found cases where patients were treated by staff in a way that stripped them of their dignity and respect. People were spoken over, and not spoken to; people were left without call bells, ignored for hours on end, or not given assistance to do the basics of life – to eat, drink, or go to the toilet.[98]

A fifth of NHS hospitals failing to deliver even minimum legal standards is third world healthcare. And to that we can add a host of other horror stories from recent NHS history.

There was the surge in deaths from the hospital-acquired infections MRSA and Clostridium difficile. At its peak, up to 10,000 patients a year were dying from these two nasty infections, largely attributed to inadequate standards of hygiene in NHS hospitals: infection rates in private hospitals were close to zero. It took an emergency programme of deep cleaning and new work practices for NHS hospitals to get on top of it, and even now deaths still run in the thousands every year.[99]

Then there are the various scandals at individual NHS hospitals. One such hospital was the Kent & Sussex Hospital in Tunbridge Wells: its death rate from Clostridium difficile went so high that locals nicknamed it the Kent & Snuffit. But the real shock was the catalogue of failure uncovered by the subsequent inquiry. Not only were nursing and hygiene standards judged wholly unacceptable, but management took no serious action even once they realised there was a problem. For a finish, not only was the senior management cleared out, but the entire hospital later had to be closed and the work transferred elsewhere.

Even worse was the Mid-Staffordshire Hospitals Trust,

where the official inquiry estimated that between 400 and 1,200 patients had died 'needlessly' because of shockingly poor care:

> Patients … described one ward as a 'war zone' and people were often left waiting in A&E for hours covered in their own blood and without pain relief even though they had serious injuries. Others were left without food or drink, some received the wrong medication – or none at all – and blood and faeces was left on lavatories and floors.[100]

These and many other such incidents speak very badly of NHS staff, both ward staff and management. And quite rightly, we're appalled. But we need to understand that working conditions for the staff themselves can also be pretty bad.

For example, it's well known that the NHS has a serious problem with staff bullying. According to the annual NHS Staff Survey, around 15 per cent have experienced bullying from patients and their families, and, more shockingly, 15 per cent have experienced it from their managers or work colleagues.[101] Indeed, 14,000 staff say they have been the victim of an actual physical assault by their managers or colleagues.

Now, nobody's saying we should judge the NHS solely on the basis of its catastrophes. But what these failures highlight is that the real NHS is quite a long way from the shining beacon of our imaginations. The organisation has a dark side, and it can be very dark indeed.

WASTING OUR LIVES

We'll end this chapter by assessing the NHS's record on the most vital duty it has – keeping us alive.

As we've already seen, in the six decades since the NHS was founded, life expectancy has increased by thirteen years for men and fourteen years for women. Which proves that the NHS is doing a great job, right?

Well, no. In the five decades before we had the NHS, life expectancy increased even more: by twenty years for men, and twenty-one years for women.[102] In particular, there was a dramatic fall in infant mortality, all achieved without the NHS.

The truth is that life expectancy has been increasing for well over a century right across the developed world. The key drivers have been improvements in diet and huge advances in medical knowledge and technology, all of which has been taking place irrespective of the NHS. We may give the credit to the NHS, but it should really go to the scientists and pharmaceutical companies who've given us so much life-saving technology.

When we look at the performance of the NHS against that of other healthcare systems, we start to get a very different picture. We start to see that, in terms of helping us live longer, the NHS has actually been doing a rather poor job.

One widely used yardstick is the cancer survival rate. Cancer is a common life-threatening disease and, once you've been diagnosed, your survival depends critically on the effectiveness of the clinical care you receive. So looking at the percentage of patients who survive at least five years after initial diagnosis can tell us something about the performance of the healthcare system.

The following chart shows the UK's performance for three common cancers compared to the OECD average. The NHS underperforms right across the board.

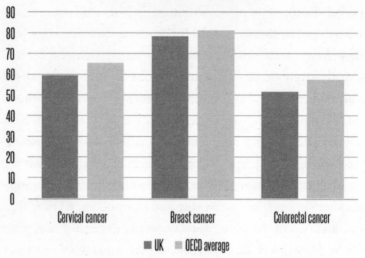

NHS Underperforms on Treating Cancer
5-year survival rates (%) 2002–2007
(Source: OECD Health Care Quality Indicators)

And note that these OECD averages include countries that are considerably poorer than us. The richer ones like the US and Japan do much better than the averages. For example, the chance of surviving breast cancer in Japan and a number of other countries is now close to 90 per cent, compared to our 78 per cent.

It's a similar picture on other cancers: for all the common cancers, your chances of survival with the NHS are lower than they are with most of its counterparts elsewhere. And it's the same with the other great modern killers. For example, if you're unlucky enough to have a stroke, your chance of survival in an NHS hospital is only about half the average elsewhere in the OECD.

A broader yardstick brings all these various treatable diseases together in a single measure known as 'mortality amenable to healthcare'.

The idea is that with today's advanced drugs and medical technology, many previously fatal diseases are perfectly treatable. With effective and timely healthcare, victims should have a good chance of surviving, so, if they die, that may signal a failure by the healthcare system. By counting up everyone who's died from one of these diseases – up to a certain cut-off age (usually seventy-five) – we can work out the number of people who've died prematurely when they might have been saved.

Of course, there's room for debate over precisely which serious diseases *are* amenable to healthcare, but there's a broad measure of agreement over the main ones. The list includes the three cancers in the chart above, a wide range of other cancers, infectious diseases like pneumonia and TB, and diseases of the circulatory system (e.g. heart disease).

The OECD has crunched the numbers for 2007, and the results for members of the G7 group of leading industrial nations are summarised in the following chart.[103]

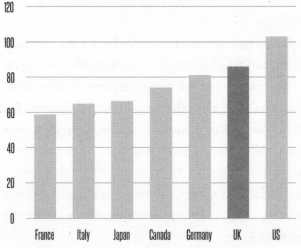

Too Many Premature Deaths
Mortality amenable to healthcare – deaths per 100,000 population
(2007; source: OECD)

The chart shows that the UK has a premature mortality rate of 86 per 100,000 people. That means that every year, over 50,000 people under the age of seventy-five die from diseases that should have been treatable. It's equivalent to the population of Salisbury.

Of course, in the real world, no healthcare system could ever save all of these sick people, which is why we need to compare across countries. We need to benchmark the NHS against a standard that is actually achievable.

The French healthcare system is the world leader. France has the best results in the G7, and it's also the best among all thirty-one OECD members in the study. If the NHS could somehow match the performance of the French healthcare system, it would save 16,000 lives a year. Even if it just matched the European average across France, Italy and Germany together, it would still save well over 10,000. That's how far behind it is.

To drive the point home with a sledge hammer, what these numbers are saying is that thousands of us die needlessly because of shortcomings in the NHS. If we lived just across the Channel our chances of surviving many serious diseases would be significantly higher.

And this isn't a shortcoming that has suddenly appeared out of nowhere. The NHS has been failing to save lives for years.

A chilling analysis by the TaxPayers' Alliance looked at its performance every year from 1981 to 2008.[104] It found that, compared to an average of European healthcare systems, the NHS currently loses just over 10,000 lives a year to these treatable diseases (roughly in line with the OECD's research results). But back in the early 1980s it was losing many more – in excess of 40,000 a year. Even as recently as the mid-1990s it was losing 30,000 a year.

Adding up the figures over the entire twenty-eight years, the TPA analysis points to an overall death toll of 780,000 people. That's 780,000 people who would probably have lived had they been lucky enough to be treated by a European healthcare system rather than the NHS.

For all of us depending on the NHS for our healthcare, these figures are deeply disturbing. For years it seems the NHS has been consigning hundreds of thousands of us to a premature death. And although it's improved somewhat recently, it still lags woefully behind the leading healthcare systems right next door to us in Europe. It's not too much to describe it as a national scandal.

In the next chapter we'll look at what could be done about it.

FIVE

TIME FOR MODERN MEDICINE

A free health service is pure Socialism and as such it is opposed to the hedonism of capitalist society.
– Aneurin Bevan, Labour founder of the NHS, 1952

Tony Blair explained his priorities in three words: education, education, education. I can do it in three letters: NHS.
– David Cameron, Conservative leader, 2006

And always keep a-hold of Nurse
For fear of finding something worse.
– Hilaire Belloc, *Cautionary Tales for Children*

WHERE'S THE ANGER?

Given the costs, and the inefficiencies, and the catastrophes, and, most of all, the avoidable deaths, you'd think we'd be pretty angry about the NHS. You'd think we'd be demanding radical action. Yet somehow, we're not.

Compare this with our attitude to road traffic deaths. There's huge public anger about death on the roads. Pressure groups like Brake – whose slogan is 'Stop the carnage' – campaign vigorously to have speed limits cut and police enforcement increased. Their stated long-term goal is zero deaths, and they command considerable airtime to promote their message via the almost universally supportive media.

Yet we suffer far fewer road deaths than the estimates of avoidable NHS deaths we examined in the last chapter. In 2009,[105] there were 2,337 deaths on UK roads. What's more, as a percentage of population, the UK had the lowest number of road deaths of *any* OECD member. Indeed, deaths have since fallen even further, to below 2,000 in 2010. In this aspect of life preservation at least, we are literally the world leader, and we should rightly be patting ourselves on the back.

But you'd never realise that from the public debate. In road safety, it seems being the best in the world is not good enough.

So why aren't similar campaigning groups going after the NHS, which is clearly not the best in the world, and seems to be responsible for far more needless deaths than Britain's drivers?

A large part of the explanation is that most of us simply don't know the facts. We don't know about the deaths in the NHS, whereas we do know about deaths on the road. Sure, we all know lots of people who've died while under the care of the NHS, but that was only to be expected – they were sick. The fact that many would have survived had they been treated across the Channel is not widely known.

But our ignorance reflects something deeper. We don't know the ugly facts because, deep down, we'd prefer not to know them. They're inconvenient and rather worrying. We'd prefer to believe our NHS is the envy of the world. We prefer the myth.

TRAPPED BY MYTH

According to legend, the NHS is the very best of Britain, a shining beacon of hope that makes us proud. From cradle to grave, from generation to generation, it's been there for us:

universal healthcare, irrespective of personal means and free at the point of use. We are blessed with a healthcare system that is the world's gold standard, and the envy of less happy lands.

It seems the vast majority of us subscribe to this belief. We may have our grumbles about some NHS services, and we may be shocked when individual hospitals fall short of the high standards we've been given to expect. But, given sufficient money, men and women of goodwill can surely fix these things. The NHS is a vital and much-loved British institution. It keeps us safe in a big scary world. We must cling on tight.

The problem is that, with the NHS held as an article of faith, there's very little room for rational debate. Heretics who challenge the faith are branded heartless, probably in the pocket of private healthcare providers and almost certainly payrolled by the evil Big Pharma.

Recalling his time as Chancellor, Nigel Lawson put it this way:

> The National Health Service is the closest thing the English have to a religion, with those who practise in it regarding themselves as a priesthood. This made it quite extraordinarily difficult to reform. For a bunch of laymen, who called themselves the Government, to presume to tell the priesthood that they must change their ways in any respect whatever, was clearly intolerable. And faced with a dispute between their priests and ministers, the public would have no hesitation in taking the part of the priesthood.[106]

On the left, of course, there's no need to challenge. The NHS has always been the embodiment of socialist ideals: from each according to his ability, to each according to his health needs. Aneurin Bevan himself described it as 'pure Socialism', and although today's Labour politicians tend to avoid the 'S' word, they still proclaim *their* NHS as 'social justice in action'.

On the right, many like Lawson are more sceptical, recognising that the NHS is highly inefficient and that it underperforms its counterparts overseas. But such is the esteem in which it's held by the electorate, today's Conservative politicians have learned to keep such thoughts to themselves. Questioning the NHS is seen as political suicide. Conservatives must show that the NHS is 'safe in their hands', and prove it by outbidding their Labour opponents on NHS funding.

Thus, the power of the myth smothers public debate and makes radical reform 'quite extraordinarily difficult'. Which is unfortunate, because without reform the myth only works if supported by an ever-increasing flow of money.

We can see that from our changing attitude towards the NHS. According to the annual British Social Attitudes Survey, back in 1997 – the year Labour came to power – only one-third of us were satisfied with the NHS. But by 2009, that proportion had doubled, with nearly two in three declaring ourselves satisfied.[107] What had changed in between, of course, was that Labour had doubled health spending in real terms. That's a good trick if you can do it, but no government in the foreseeable future will be able to. The myth is coming up against harsh fiscal reality.

TO INFINITY AND BEYOND

What do you reckon is the world's biggest industry?

Sex?

No, the global sex industry is thought to have an annual

turnover of well under 1 trillion dollars per year (a trillion
being one million million).

Guns, then.

Well, no again. The arms industry is worth a mere $1.5
trillion.

No, the world's biggest industry is healthcare. Its annual
turnover is already 5 trillion dollars, or 8 per cent of global
GDP, and it's growing at a phenomenal rate.

There are two main drivers. First, there's the escalating
cost of treatment. Whereas leeches were always relatively
inexpensive, treatments involving $1.5 million MRI scan-
ners and $50,000-per-course cancer drugs are not. And with
every passing year, the ingenuity of medical researchers and
pharmaceutical companies delivers yet more in the way of
high-tech and high-price treatments – treatments that we
quite naturally demand.

Second, largely as a result of those expensive new treatments, we're all living much longer. When the NHS was
founded in 1948, life expectancy at birth was about sixty-five
for men and seventy for women. The corresponding figures
today are seventy-eight and eighty-two. Even more striking,
the rate of increase seems to be speeding up: in recent years,
average life expectancy has been increasing by four to five
months *every single year*.[108]

Of course, the fact that modern medicine is allowing
us to live longer is good news. But unfortunately, it's also
hugely expensive. Not only are there more old people to
look after, but their healthcare costs are much higher than
those of the young. According to the official estimate, the
annual healthcare cost for those aged eighty-five or over is
six times higher than for those aged between sixteen and
forty-four.[109]

Treatments aimed at staving off imminent death are especially expensive, with more than a quarter of all acute healthcare costs incurred trying to save those in the final year of life. Indeed, it's sometimes said that the NHS keeps us alive through a series of cheap illnesses only so we can die from a really expensive one later on.

Now, these trends are certainly encouraging for the healthcare industry. But they're much less encouraging for British taxpayers.

Projections of future health spending show a continuing rise, stretching away as far as anyone can see, quite possibly all the way to infinity.

The government's own Office for Budget Responsibility expects public spending on health to rise from its current 8 per cent of GDP up to around 10 per cent by 2060.[110] Add in private spending and that would take us to perhaps 12 per cent. But that seems much too optimistic: a 2 percentage point rise over the next fifty years looks pretty tame against the near 5 per cent rise we've had over the last fifty. Moreover, it would only take us up to where Germany is *today*, and leave us well short of the current US level.

This mounting cost of healthcare is a major challenge for all developed nations. But with a nationalised health service we face a particularly difficult challenge: all the money has to be found from within a government budget subject to a hard and prolonged squeeze.

Faced with such a challenge, business as usual is not a serious option. And whatever they may have said in public, all our recent Health Secretaries have known that.

MINISTER, WE CAN'T GO ON LIKE THIS

When Dr John Reid heard he'd been made Secretary of State

for Health in a Cabinet reshuffle in 2003, he reportedly said, 'Oh fuck, it's health.'[111]

Because, although founding the NHS may have ensured Nye Bevan's place in political history, ever since then the health portfolio has been a bed of increasingly sharp nails. It's destroyed promising Cabinet careers from John Moore's to Patricia Hewitt's. And it's a striking fact that, from the moment the NHS opened its doors in 1948, no Health Secretary[112] has *ever* gone on to become leader of their party, let alone Prime Minister. The job is literally a hospital pass.

The fundamental problem is that our Health Secretaries have the impossible job of squaring myth and reality. However starry-eyed they may have been previously, once they open that red box they're confronted head-on with the inefficiencies and the needless deaths. They're thrust onto *Newsnight* to apologise for the latest hospital horror and explain why it could never happen again. And, most of all, they're shown the secret Treasury books proving that taxpayers cannot go on funding a healthcare system still organised as a nationalised industry from the age of Stalin.

Bevan's original vision of the NHS was one in which the men from the ministry were responsible for managing everything. Or, as he put it, 'the sound of a bedpan dropped in a distant hospital should reverberate through Whitehall.' And that was pretty much how the NHS stayed right up until the 1980s: huge, top-down and highly inefficient.

For years, health ministers tried to improve things by pulling levers and issuing directives, just as Bevan intended. But efficiency didn't improve. There was more money – as we saw earlier – but much of it disappeared in yet more inefficiency.

It was unsustainable, and, starting under Thatcher, the

politicians began experimenting with much more radical solutions. Solutions that moved a long way from Bevan's vision.

Importantly, it wasn't just Conservative ministers who realised the state monolith needed such drastic surgery. Although some old-time socialists – such as Blair's disastrous first Health Secretary Frank Dobson – still believed that more money was the answer, other Labour ministers realised that wasn't enough. Foremost among them was Blair's second Health Secretary, Alan Milburn, and it's worth quoting at length what he told a hostile audience of NHS bosses in 2003. Because Milburn laid out very clearly the route map to reform:

> ... The era of one-size-fits-all public services is over. At the heart of concerns about the NHS is the sense that its services are simply too indifferent to the needs of its patients. Staff and patients alike are up against a system that feels too much like the ration-book days of the 1940s...
>
> I believe we can open up more choices to NHS patients ... And by linking the choices patients make to the resources hospitals receive ... we can provide real incentives to address under-performance ... Giving people the power to choose between services will drive standards up...
>
> These reforms are about embedding choice across the NHS – from primary care to hospital services...
>
> They will require changes in the way the NHS works. Choice requires diversity in capacity ... Some will be run by NHS providers. Others by private-sector providers. In making their commissioning decisions, PCTs will need to consider how best to use both existing and new private-sector provision for the benefit of NHS patients ... They will also need to consider how best to use voluntary-sector providers.

And choice will only work if there are the right incentives in the system. From this April, we will begin to move to a new system of payment-by-results for NHS hospitals. Resources will follow the choices patients make so the hospitals which do more, get more; those which do not, will not ... An increasing proportion of each hospital's income will come as a result of the choices patients make.

Choice in other words is not just about making patients feel good about the NHS. It is about giving the patient more power within the NHS.[113]

Choice, competition and money following the patient. This is a very different vision to Bevan's. What Milburn had understood was that you can't make an aged elephant dance simply by giving it instructions from Whitehall. The only realistic way forward is a more disaggregated and responsive system based on choice and competition. In this vision of the NHS:

- The centralised command-and-control bureaucracy is scrapped.
- GPs and hospitals are given a much greater degree of autonomy.
- New healthcare providers are encouraged, including private sector providers.
- Patients are given choice over both their GP and their hospital.
- Money follows the patient.

In other words, the NHS is reorganised as a market, with individual suppliers competing for customers and driving up efficiency in the process.

And although the precise details vary, this is the vision of the NHS that has driven all serious attempts at NHS reform over the last twenty years.

We'll examine the merits of this approach later, but first let's reflect on the huge obstacles facing would-be reformers.

OVER MY DEAD BODY

To start with, any reformer is up against that myth. And in particular, the myth that competition and the market spells the end of 'free' healthcare for all. As we'll see in the next section, that isn't true, but it's proved all too easy for opponents of NHS reform to suggest that it is. And the idea that we and our families might be left with no proper healthcare at all is a very powerful reason to oppose change.

Also, in the minds of many of us, markets are associated with greed and profiteering, and we fear what that would mean if applied to healthcare. Surely we're not commodities to be traded like so many pork bellies? Can it be right to leave something as important as our health up to the markets? We somehow forget that it's markets that put food on our plates and clothes on our backs.

Reforming politicians recognise this problem and try to sidestep it by downplaying the vital market aspect of their plans. Instead, they stress the bit about better customer choice – just as Milburn did in his speech. But even if that helps reassure some of the customers, it does nothing to overcome the second major obstacle to reform – entrenched opposition within the NHS itself.

In 2006, Health Secretary Patricia Hewitt felt the full force of that opposition when she addressed the annual conference of the Royal College of Nursing. Or rather, when she attempted to address it. Such was the outrage at her reform programme that the nurses booed and heckled her into silence, all carried live on the rolling news channels. It was a classic Ceauşescu moment, and her political career effectively ended there and then.

Alan Milburn himself is another good example. Within a few months of making that courageous speech we quoted, he'd resigned his post, citing a desire to 'spend more time with [his] family'. After four bruising years slugging it out with the NHS establishment and the unions, he'd simply had enough, walking away not just from the Health job, but from his entire Cabinet career (although he did later make one brief reappearance).

And, in fairness, Milburn had lasted longer than most. The average tenure of a here-today-gone-tomorrow Secretary of State for Health is just two years – sixteen years less than the average tenure of a Tesco Chief Executive.

Driving through radical reform in any mature organisation is difficult. But when that organisation comprises nearly 1.5 million heavily unionised public sector employees long insulated from the chill blast of competition, it verges on the impossible. As Tony Blair famously complained, public employees are rooted in the concept that 'if it has always been done this way, it must always be done this way'.[114]

So we've reached a virtual stand-off. In private, most senior politicos understand that the NHS needs radical surgery. They understand that it needs to be dismembered into smaller pieces, and that those pieces need to compete for customers. They understand that if we're to have a healthcare system that is both efficient and affordable, we need to inject the power of the market.

But performing the actual operation is a whole different matter. The patient doesn't want to be treated, and the rest of us are scared by the patient's screams.

Any would-be surgeon needs a will of iron to proceed. And more than that, he needs the strong and unflinching support of his colleagues, especially the Prime Minister. Which – as we saw so vividly illustrated when David Cameron pulled the rug from under his own reforming Health Secretary Andrew Lansley in 2011 – is not something any surgeon attempting to operate on the NHS can ever rely on.

True, there have been reforms, but often they've been abandoned or even reversed within a few years. And yes, there have been some steps in the right direction, such as paying hospitals and clinics by results rather than via the opaque funding formulae used previously. But overall, progress has been painfully slow.

So what can be done? How can we shift the obstacles to reform, or at least weaken them enough to make faster progress?

It would help if we all knew a bit more about the alternatives to the NHS that are already successfully operating elsewhere. Then at least we could see that using the market to drive efficiency does not mean losing the most treasured features of the NHS, such as universal healthcare. And we could see that, deployed in the right way, the market could actually help realise the original ideals of the NHS.

MODERN ALTERNATIVES TO THE NHS

Defenders of the NHS like to tell us that it's superior to all the alternative ways of organising healthcare. In particular, they like to scare us with lurid tales of the US healthcare system, which costs a fortune but fails to provide anything like universal coverage. Worse, many US doctors and hospitals work quite openly for profit – repellent behaviour in those caring for the sick and surely not something we would ever tolerate here.

And it is true that the US system has serious problems. It *is* expensive – at 17 per cent of GDP, it's the most expensive in the world. It *doesn't* provide universal coverage – according to the OECD, the main private insurance arrangements cover just 58 per cent of the population, with another 27 per cent covered by government programmes for the elderly and very poor, leaving 15 per cent without any cover at all.[115] And it *does* perform pretty badly on some key measures, such as infant mortality and mortality amenable to healthcare (see previous chapter). If you're rich, you get the finest healthcare available anywhere, but if you're middling poor and uninsured, you're in trouble.

But, scary as these things are, they're a red herring. Because nobody is seriously suggesting we adopt the US system as an alternative to the NHS. The model we really need to explore is the social insurance system used by most of our European neighbours.

The details of these European systems vary from country to country, but most share the following key features:

- Universal coverage – according to the OECD, the healthcare systems of all Western European countries have 100 per cent coverage, or very close to it (e.g. the Netherlands only manages 98.6 per cent coverage, but that's because orthodox Calvinists and certain other religious minorities have been allowed to opt out on conscientious grounds).[116]
- Insurance based – European systems feature standalone health insurance organisations which are separate from the providers of healthcare itself; in different countries the insurers may be state-owned or private, but either way it

contrasts with the NHS, which has long been a monolithic provider of medical services funded from general taxation.

- Customer choice – in most European systems, patients have always had a choice of medical providers, both with GPs and hospitals; although, like here, GPs in many countries act as gatekeepers with respect to hospital services – you can't just pitch up for a colonoscopy whenever you feel like it.

- Competing providers – as well as competing GPs, most European systems have a good mix of competing hospital groups, some owned and operated by the state, some by non-profit bodies and some by commercial companies.

So the typical European healthcare system incorporates the advantages of choice and competition, without sacrificing universal coverage. Nobody is denied medical care because they're poor.

A very important point about this European social insurance model, and one that distinguishes it from the US private insurance system, is that insurance is compulsory, just like car insurance is compulsory for British drivers. Everyone with a job has to have a policy with an authorised provider. Premiums are generally paid by a combination of the employee and the employer, but children and those without jobs may have their premiums paid by the state (although the cost may be deducted from pensions and benefits).

Another key difference from the US is that insurance companies offering the product are not allowed to decline customers on health or any other grounds, and not allowed to load premiums for higher-risk groups. What's known in the trade as 'cream skimming' – where only low-risk customers are accepted – is thereby eliminated.

Let's see how this works in the context of a specific country. The Dutch system was overhauled in 2006 and now incorporates many of the best elements of the European social insurance model. According to the OECD statistics, it outperforms the NHS both in preventing deaths from treatable diseases and in terms of overall efficiency.

In the Netherlands it is compulsory for everyone (except those Calvinists) to take out basic medical insurance covering regular GP and hospital services. But, just like with car insurance, they have a choice of insurance companies, which are privately run and compete on price. Insurance premiums average around £1,000 per year, with the insured's employer paying about the same again. Children are covered free, and those on limited incomes are subsidised by the government.

On the supplier side of the market, the insurance companies must provide a basic minimum package of cover as laid down by the government regulator, although they can also offer optional upgraded packages for higher premiums. They must accept all comers and are not allowed to refuse cover or load premiums. But, to ensure that individual companies are not disadvantaged by somehow attracting a disproportionate number of high-risk clients, there is a risk-pooling arrangement to smooth things out between companies.

Individuals choose their own GP, and GPs levy a charge which is later reimbursed by the insurer. The GPs also act as gatekeepers for hospital services, and there is a good choice of hospitals, many of them privately run on a non-profit basis.

Thus, the Dutch system combines universal healthcare provision with competition among providers. There's competition among the insurers, and competition among doctors and hospitals. Moreover, the competitive pressure on insurers means they should have a strong incentive to negotiate keen terms for their clients from those doctors and hospitals. Just like Tesco does with its suppliers.

Now it is true that this system does not cover the entirety of Dutch healthcare spending. Long-term treatments, especially those requiring hospitalisation, are excluded and financed through a separate government insurance levy. General taxation is also used to fund part of the overall costs. And it's also true that competition seems not to have delivered quite the pressure on costs originally hoped for. Which is why the government is increasing the scope for price competition between hospitals, and increasing the incentive for insurers to negotiate low prices from providers.

But what the Dutch system has that we haven't traditionally had is that element of choice and competition driving overall efficiency. They've harnessed the power of the market to drive value for money, but within a system that provides healthcare for all, irrespective of means.

The European systems are living proof that bringing the market into healthcare doesn't mean the end of universal provision. And neither does the participation of privately owned insurers and hospitals. In fact, the OECD's analysis finds that the European systems based on competing private insurers – such as the Netherlands and Germany – do *better* than the NHS in delivering equality of healthcare across the different income levels.[117]

The conclusion is clear. Opponents of NHS reform who tell us that the market means the end of universal healthcare are plain wrong.

For the NHS to have any chance of providing acceptable levels of healthcare in future, modern market-based reforms along European lines are essential. There simply isn't the money to repeat Labour's spending surge, and the system has to be made more efficient.

But choice and competition will only take us so far. There is a far more difficult issue we will have to confront before too long – one that raises fundamental questions about personal responsibility and the role of the welfare state.

GRASPING THE NETTLE OF FREE HEALTHCARE

A couple of years ago, Tesco mispriced its chocolate oranges, erroneously marking them down to 10 per cent of their normal price. Almost immediately, there was a stampede into Tesco's stores and the shelves were stripped bare. One chocoholic snapped up 246 of these exquisitely moreish confections before the error was discovered; or to put it another way, she snapped up 227,000 calories along with 7.3 kilos of fat.[118]

It was a timely reminder of the perils of free healthcare.

The principle of healthcare free at the point of use was the very core of Bevan's original vision. And for sixty years now, champions of the NHS have been repeating and reinforcing his message. All our political parties publicly support it and, it's fair to say, most of us see it as essential and non-negotiable.

Unfortunately, it's a principle that ultimately threatens the very existence of the NHS. Because when expensive but desirable things are provided at little or no direct cost to ourselves we tend to consume far too much of them.

Back in 1948, the NHS was launched as a completely free service, and as soon as it opened its doors it was overwhelmed by a stampede for every kind of medical treatment, spectacles, dentistry and even wigs.[119] Following the inevitable funding crisis, charges were imposed for some of these items, including prescriptions (triggering the resignations of Bevan and Harold Wilson). But the vast bulk of NHS treatment remains free to this day, just as Bevan intended. Hospital treatment is free, as are visits to your GP. Even prescriptions are largely supplied free because so many patients are exempt from the charges.[120]

Our natural response is to consume a lot of healthcare. We have absolutely no incentive to economise on its use because it's free. We can call on it 24/7 at no direct cost to ourselves, and we can make and break appointments without financial penalty. We can abuse our bodies as we like, safe in the knowledge that the NHS will pick up the pieces at no cost to us. Or at least, no direct and obvious cost to us.

Of course, in the real world, we can't actually consume as much of this free healthcare as we'd like, because it isn't available. As Alan Milburn acknowledged in his speech, we're rationed. We may not always register that fact until the moment we ourselves try to access treatment, but waiting lists and non-availability of treatments have been features of the NHS ever since it began. It's a version of the Soviet bread queue, with no prospect at all of chocolate oranges.

But rationing is no way to run healthcare in the twenty-first century. It means that the amount of healthcare we get is determined not by what we want and are prepared to pay for, but by what our politicians decide we should have. It means the system answers to the politicians and not to us, with all that flows from that in terms of poor customer service. It means the chronic inefficiency of state enterprise. And it means boom-and-bust healthcare – bouts of wasteful, unsustainable spending growth under Labour, followed by long and painful periods of retrenchment under the Conservatives. All of which we documented in the previous chapter.

And free-at-the-point-of-use has another highly damaging consequence. It gives us no incentive to take responsibility for our own health. Whereas car insurance rewards us with no-claims discounts if we drive safely and accident-free, we get no tax discounts for living a healthy life and not claiming healthcare from the NHS.

Obesity is a very good example. We know that Britain has a ballooning obesity problem, with getting on for a quarter of us now clinically obese – more than twice the average rate in France, Germany and the Netherlands.[121] And the health consequences are feeding through into massive additional costs for the NHS: the Department of Health expects them to exceed £6 billion annually by 2015. Which, given the fixed NHS budget, means less money for treating all our other health problems.

One option might be to use NHS funds to grip the problem directly. For example, we could make gastric bands widely available on the NHS, which would presumably cut the obesity rate in fairly short order. Except that an operation to fit a gastric band costs up to £8,000 and fitting them into a quarter of the population would cost £120 billion – the entire annual NHS budget.

And anyway, just why should taxpayers fund the health-care costs of obesity? Given that it arises from overeating and lack of exercise, why shouldn't individuals take responsibility for their own behaviour rather than expecting someone else to pick up the bill for the consequences? And the same goes for people who make those other famously harmful lifestyle choices, such as smoking, or drinking to excess (although smokers and drinkers do at least contribute to their costs via heavy excise duties).

An obvious way of addressing these problems is to make

patients pay a charge whenever they access healthcare. That would make it clear to everyone that healthcare has a cost, and provide some incentive for individuals not to overuse the system.

And a number of European countries do precisely that. For example, in France a consultation with a GP costs around £20. Part of that is later reimbursed by the patient's insurer, but patients are at least made aware that the service is not free. The idea is to dissuade people from making frivolous visits to the doctor, and many British GPs privately agree that we should institute a similar arrangement here.

The country that has gone furthest along this road is Singapore. Like us, but unlike the US, Singapore has a universal healthcare system. But in contrast to the NHS, the bulk of its funding (around two-thirds) comes from its customers rather than the government. Apart from the very poor, individual healthcare expenses have to be met by the individual or her family *at the point of use*.

To manage those expenses, all workers and their employers have to contribute to a compulsory individual savings account called Medisave, which can be drawn on to defray hospital bills when the need arises. And to cover against the risk of catastrophic illness, they also have to take out a separate insurance policy, either with the government Medishield scheme or a private insurer. But the key point is that when Singaporeans want to access healthcare they generally have to pay.

And the approach seems to have been spectacularly successful at delivering high-quality healthcare combined with tightly controlled costs. Singapore spends less than 4 per cent of its national income on healthcare, well under half what we spend. Yet their life expectancy is more or less the same as ours – if anything, a bit higher. And infant mortality is *half* our rate. In fact, Singapore has the second lowest infant mortality rate in the world.

We will have to learn from places like Singapore. However much we'd like to keep our healthcare free at the point of use, it simply isn't going to be affordable over the long term. The continuing upward pressure on costs and our reckless habit of living unhealthily are landing taxpayers with a bill they will not be prepared to carry indefinitely.

In the immediate future, there is clearly scope for getting more from the current budget by bringing in the market, as Alan Milburn recommended a decade ago. But it will only take us so far. Sooner or later we will have to abandon that cherished principle of 'free' healthcare.

The reality is that healthcare is not free, and never has been. We cannot go on behaving as if it is.

SIX

WE CAN MAKE YOU RICH

Ask me my three main priorities for Government, and I tell
you: education, education and education ... We are thirty-
fifth in the world league of education standards. Thirty-fifth.
They say give me the boy at seven and I'll give you the man
at seventy. Well, give me the education system that's thirty-
fifth in the world today and I'll give you the economy that's
thirty-fifth tomorrow.
– Tony Blair, 1996

What we are really describing is a failure of the education
system. A system where half of all kids fail to get five decent
GCSEs simply means that five years later we spend billions
offering them remedial training to make them work-ready.
– David Frost, Director General of the British Chambers of
Commerce, 2011

Politicians have a tendency to describe all public spending
as investment, and Tony Blair's New Labour were notorious for doing so. But investment involves a sacrifice today
in return for an economic pay-off tomorrow, whereas most
public spending is consumed today with no such longer-term
pay-off. Put bluntly, it's no more investment than eating a

meal – there's a value to it, but we can't expect a pay-off tomorrow. Except for education. Education can yield a pay-off tomorrow. Education can make us rich.

Governments have been investing our money in state education since Victorian times. The driving force then was the need to keep up with foreign competitors – especially the newly united Germany – and that's pretty well remained the pitch ever since. Over that time, politicians of all parties have pledged to improve our education system, and they've backed their pledges with huge amounts of our cash.

Yet the results have often been disappointing. The economic pay-off has never quite measured up to the promises, with employers constantly bemoaning our lack of skills compared to foreign workers. In attainment – despite Blair's commitments – we've slipped even further down the international league. And in social mobility – the other great promise of state education – we've gone backwards over the last forty years.

In this chapter we'll look at what we spend, what we get back and how our system falls short. We'll see what we can learn from our competitors, and identify some more tough choices.

WE'RE PAYING A PREMIUM PRICE...

Blair came to power in 1997 promising to prioritise education, and over the next thirteen years, spending soared by over 70 per cent in real terms. By the time of the 2010 election, it was running at £90 billion, or 6.3 per cent of our national income, up from just 4.6 per cent in 1997.[122]

As a result, our state schools are now among the most expensive in the world. The OECD says that the cost of putting a child through primary and secondary education in Britain exceeds $100,000, which is 10–15 per cent above the norm. Germany, France, Italy and Japan all provide school education at a substantially lower cost.[123]

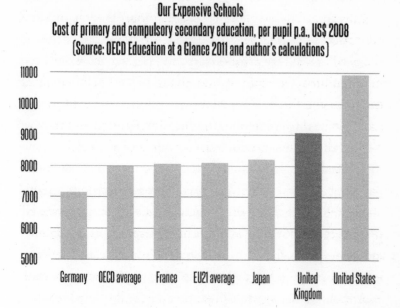

Our Expensive Schools
Cost of primary and compulsory secondary education, per pupil p.a., US$ 2008
(Source: OECD Education at a Glance 2011 and author's calculations)

...BUT WE'RE NOT GETTING A PREMIUM SERVICE

The most respected international league table of educational attainment is produced by the OECD's Programme for International Student Assessment (PISA). Begun in 2000 and run on a three-year cycle, PISA tests thousands of fifteen-year-olds for literacy in reading, maths and science. It uses independent standardised tests, rather than national exams such as GCSEs, so it gives us a good idea how our system is performing relative to our competitors.

The most recent assessment was for 2009 and places us well down the league. Out of the thirty-four OECD member countries, we were ranked twentieth in reading and twenty-second in maths, putting us well in the lower half. Only in science do we rank in the top half, coming in at eleventh.[124]

Compared to the top scorers – Korea and Finland – we're a long way behind, and we're comfortably beaten by key competitors like Germany, Japan, Canada, the Netherlands, Switzerland and Australia. The survey also assessed thirty-one less developed economies and, worryingly for our future prospects, the top performer *in the entire world* is the Chinese city of Shanghai, with Hong Kong close behind.

A particularly troubling finding is that, within the overall averages, we produce far fewer top-scoring students than our competitors. In maths, for example, only 1.8 per cent of our students achieve the top score, compared to an OECD average of 3.1 per cent and an extraordinary 27 per cent in Shanghai. Even in science, where at least we do better than the average, the percentage of our students achieving the very highest attainment levels still trails way behind Shanghai, Singapore, Finland, New Zealand, Japan, Hong Kong, Australia, Germany, the Netherlands and Canada.

And we seem to be getting worse. Since the first PISA study, we've dropped thirteen places in reading, fourteen places in maths and seven places in science. So in just nine years – years in which we ramped spending ever higher – we've slumped an average eleven places in the international league table of attainment.

Now, it must be said that the OECD describes our current position in the PISA study as still broadly in line with the OECD averages for reading and maths, and somewhat ahead for science. But the direction of travel is all too clear.

So, despite spending an extra £20–30 billion annually on education, we've slipped further down the league. Something is going seriously wrong.

PRIZES FOR ALL

Of course, according to the government's own official measure of exam output, everything has been going swimmingly. Even as we sank down the world rankings, output rose every single year for two decades.

The headline measure of output is the percentage of 15–16-year-olds gaining five or more GCSEs at grade C or above. When GCSEs were launched in 1987/88, just 30 per cent managed that, but by 2011, the proportion had soared to nearly 80 per cent. And, to take an even longer perspective, in the old O level and CSE exams that preceded the GCSE, the proportion who got five or more top grades never exceeded one quarter.

Success at A level has also seen a staggering rise. After years of uninterrupted improvement, the failure rate dropped to just 2.2 per cent in 2011, and the proportion of candidates achieving at least a C grade rose to 76 per cent. The proportion getting an A or A* grade reached 27 per cent, compared to just 10 per cent back in the 1960s.[125]

The same apparent success has been delivered by our universities. Since the mid-1990s, despite a big increase in student numbers, the proportion awarded firsts has virtually doubled. It now stands at 14 per cent. Back in the 1960s, with far fewer students, even the very top universities failed to deliver more than about 8 per cent.

It may not quite be prizes for all, but it's got very close.

FOOL'S GOLD FOOLS NOBODY

The problem is that the prizes themselves have become seriously devalued. With each successive summer of yet higher grades and yet more crowing by politicians and the education establishment, public scepticism has grown. Such achievements must mean the exams are getting easier and we're suffering a chronic bout of grade inflation.

Our top universities certainly believe that. Not so long ago, A levels were seen as 'the Gold Standard' of school achievement, and a dependable basis for university entrance. But standards have slipped so much that several universities now set their own entrance tests. The Rector of Imperial College London says:

> In some subjects, like mathematics, what you can do is take the current A level maths paper and compare it to the papers of ten, fifteen, twenty years ago and look at the performance of students. One can probably say with a degree of confidence that the papers currently are somewhat easier.
>
> How can it be that the quality of teaching has improved so dramatically and we have such an extraordinary change in the intellectual ability of our population? Do we really believe it is the quality of teaching or do we believe that the quality of the examination has been declining?[126]

Oxford physics professor Frank Close is blunter: 'Every physics department has been aware that A level students do not have the same knowledge base they did even ten years ago. This is no reflection on intelligence, but an indication that the syllabus has been dumbed down.'[127]

And the problem doesn't just affect our top students. Employers are constantly appalled by the poor educational standard of school leavers, with apparently qualified candidates who are barely literate. Sir Terry Leahy, the long-serving boss of Tesco, summed up their exasperation:

> As the largest private employer in the country, we depend

on high standards in our schools. The government said that secondary school standards had never been higher. Sadly, despite all the money that has been spent, standards are still woefully low in too many schools. Employers like us ... are often left to pick up the pieces.[128]

So just how far have exam standards slipped?

It's difficult to make watertight comparisons between today's exams and those from thirty or forty years ago. We know that grade scores have increased, but that doesn't necessarily mean the exams are easier. Syllabuses have changed, teaching has changed and a larger proportion of the population are now sitting the exams. Comparisons are tricky.

However, we do have information on how pupils of similar academic ability performed in the exams of twenty years ago compared to now. A widely quoted study of A level results for the Office for National Statistics used data from standardised ability tests carried out in 1,400 schools to examine this. And it concluded that, on average, over the last two decades, students of similar academic ability have seen their grades increase by around two whole grade levels.[129]

Indeed, in some subjects the increase in grade scores for pupils with the same ability levels was even higher. In maths it was an extraordinary three and a half grades. The authors conclude:

A level grades achieved in 2006 certainly do correspond to a lower level of general academic ability than the same grades would have done in previous years. Whether or not they are better taught makes no difference to this interpretation; the same grade corresponds to a lower level of general ability.

So, for a given level of general ability, today's A levels give a reading that is, on average, two grades higher than those of twenty years ago. Or to put it the other way, today's average A level grade is worth two grades less than the average twenty years ago.

Whether we call it dumbing down or recalibration, today's exams are a whole lot easier than they used to be.

GOLD AS CLASS-BASED ELITISM

Not everyone thinks grade inflation and the loss of the Gold Standard is a problem. In 2008, Labour Education Minister Lord Adonis told us:

> It is the class-based elitism that instinctively wants to ration success and cap the aspirations of the less advantaged. The underlying premise is that there is a fixed pool of talent in society.
>
> So every August we are told that increased success rates demonstrate declining standards in state schools (increased success in private schools, by contrast, is usually put down to hard work and good teaching).
>
> I reject this ration-book view of talent and opportunity. It was a bad recipe for the twentieth century and is a disastrous one for the twenty-first. Successful societies flourish above all else by mobilising talent and educational potential.[130]

We'll skip over His Lordship's swipe at private schools (one of which educated him), and his failure to acknowledge that exams have got easier. Let's focus on his ration-book point.

Up until the 1980s, our major public exams awarded grades on the basis of *relative* performance, just like Olympic medals. For example, A levels awarded an A grade to the top 10 per cent of candidates in that year, a B grade to the next 15 per cent, and a C grade to the next 10 per cent. That meant just 35 per cent of candidates were awarded A–C grades, against 76 per cent now. The top grades were rationed to the top performers in that year.

Clearly, that was very helpful to universities in selecting entrants and very helpful to employers in selecting recruits. The exam grades constituted an excellent signalling device, ranking each candidate's performance relative to peers. And in relative terms, top talent is always rationed.

But the approach has drawbacks. Candidates can work hard and score high marks, yet still fail to get good grades. Moreover, if marks are closely bunched, small differences can result in hugely different grades. To many people like Lord Adonis, that never seemed fair. It says no matter how hard you work, you can never have a prize because you're not as good as your peers.

So in the 1980s, the grading system was switched from Olympic medals to driving tests. Under the driving-test approach, grades are awarded according to the individual candidate's absolute marks, not relative to other candidates. Thus, in the current A level, A* grades are awarded to all candidates achieving 90 per cent or more, A grades to those between 80 and 90 per cent, B grades between 70 and 80 per cent, and so on. In theory, every single candidate could get an A or A* grade.

The driving test certainly ended the rationing of top grades, and in that sense it was fairer: good teaching and hard work can now deliver success irrespective of the scores of others. However, switching to the driving test exposed the entire system to abuse.

Because everybody – politicians, teachers, parents and

pupils – always wants improving results, and there's always pressure to relax standards. Grade rationing anchored the system to prevent standards drifting down, but now there's no anchor. True, the various exam boards were supposed to withstand the pressure and uphold standards, but, since they've wanted more schools to choose their particular exams, they too have had a strong incentive to dumb down.

In theory, there's no reason why driving-test exams had to go this way. With rigorous supervision it ought to have been possible to maintain standards. But with no fixed anchor, once exam scores became the official target for schools, dumbing down was inevitable.

ANOTHER CENTRAL PLANNING DISASTER

When Tony Blair made exam results the scorecard for his central education plan, their fate was sealed. Scoring was guaranteed to take priority over maintaining educational standards.

Here's how the man put in charge of Blair's central plan described its operation:

> Large-scale reform driven from the top down; designing all the materials at the national level and training everybody in a cascade out; using the accountability system to publish results and school inspection to check that people were adopting better practices.
>
> We also had a very tough agenda for dealing with under-performing schools: closing some, starting some fresh, and turning around others. We began intervening in very troubled local educational authorities … It was very difficult to do but important.
>
> The basic premise of our first phase of education reforms

was that in order to achieve a certain minimum floor you have to first set those standards top down and drive them centrally.[131]

To anyone with a knowledge of Soviet state planning, this is familiar territory: top-down orders, output quotas and inspections, summary execution for backsliders and everything driven from the centre. It certainly commands the attention of managers and workers, but, as the Soviets discovered over half a century ago, there are some serious drawbacks.

The plan set each school minimum output targets for test and exam results. The best-known was that at least 30 per cent of each secondary school's pupils should gain at least five good GCSEs (grade C or higher). Falling short meant the school being publicly branded as a failing school, and repeatedly falling short meant the school being put into 'special measures' – a sinister term borrowed from Stalin's gulags.

The targets were designed to concentrate minds, and they succeeded. For school heads and their teachers, GCSEs became what's known as a 'high-stakes test'. If they failed the test, they faced the chop, so failure was not an option. And, as we've seen, the proportion of pupils getting the magic five good GCSEs soared. The plan worked.

However, just as under Stalin's Five-Year Plans, do-or-die targets have side effects. In particular, they tend to get met only at the expense of some other vital but untargeted area suffering unintended and perhaps catastrophic damage. So, while more pupils were getting five good GCSE grades – as demanded by the plan – it emerged that many were doing so only by avoiding English and Maths. Schools were 'gaming the system' by channelling their less able pupils into easier subjects. The losers were pupils who already had problems with literacy and numeracy, and who were now giving up altogether on those vital skills.

That eventually became a scandal, and in 2004 a damning report from a former Chief Schools Inspector demanded change. Henceforth, schools were required to ensure that at least 30 per cent of pupils achieved five A–C grades *including* English and Maths. But for hundreds of thousands of pupils the damage had already been done.

The targets also disadvantaged less able pupils in another way. And that was by driving teachers to adopt so-called 'triage teaching'.

School league tables meant teachers had long been teaching to the test, with an increasingly narrow focus on the exam curriculum rather than a broader understanding of the subject. But given this tough new targeting regime, that wasn't enough. Under relentless pressure, they adopted a desperate battlefield technique developed by French doctors in the First World War: they surreptitiously categorised casualties (pupils) into those who were going to live anyway, those who were going to die anyway, and those where medical attention might make the difference between life and death.[132]

Triage teaching focuses a huge and disproportionate amount of teaching effort on children at or just below the critical pass mark – in this case, the boundary between the C and D grades. They're the ones who could pass *or* fail, and it's *their* success that's vital to the school's overall score. Which means that brighter children – the ones who are going to pass *anyway* – get left to their own devices rather than being stretched. And for the 20 per cent of pupils who are struggling at the bottom – the ones who are *never* going to pass – they can forget it. They are pretty well written off.

The results have been grim. The bottom 20 per cent of our fifteen-year-olds lack even the most basic skills in reading and maths.[133] After at least ten years of formal education, they have still not acquired the means to participate effectively and productively in life. Their school careers have been a waste of our money and a colossal waste of their own life chances.

Another unintended consequence has been the growth of soft subjects, such as the notorious Media Studies A level, now taken by 25,000 pupils each year. They've certainly bulked up school exam scores, but only because they're easier than traditional subjects like Maths and Physics. A detailed study concluded that subjects like Media Studies, Film Studies and Photography are between one and two grades easier than traditional science subjects, with a wider gap at lower grade levels.[134]

Unfortunately, because everyone knows they're soft, they don't carry much weight. Indeed, top universities now advise anyone thinking of applying not to take them. Cambridge has published a list of twenty they will not count as hard subjects for admission purposes, including Media Studies and the aptly named Leisure Studies. Doing such subjects might be enjoyable, but they have limited career value.

So, while the central plan boosted exam scores across the board, it did so only at terrible cost: standards were dumbed down; pupils were encouraged into easy subjects with little long-term value; and those at the top and bottom suffered from grossly inadequate attention. Hundreds of thousands of our children have had their lives permanently blighted.

It was quantity without quality, the classic hallmark of Soviet production.

THE 50 PER CENT UNIVERSITY TARGET

Blair's other big education target was to get 50 per cent of young people going to university. And again, the headline numbers tell us he very nearly succeeded. When Labour came to power, the so-called higher education initial participation rate was running at under 38 per cent. By 2010, it had reached 47 per cent.[135] There were then 2.5 million students enrolled at British universities.[136]

On one level, it was a fantastic achievement. But, once again, there's that issue of quantity versus quality.

To start with, just as in our schools, there's been rampant grade inflation. Between 1997 and 2010, the proportion of first-class degrees awarded more or less doubled to 14 per cent. And the proportion awarded firsts or upper seconds reached 60 per cent, with some universities pushing it beyond 80 per cent. Forty years ago it was 30 per cent.[137]

On top of that, many of the newer universities – those that used to be polytechnics and colleges of higher education – have expanded their intakes on the back of what are known as 'non-traditional subjects'. As well as 30,000 students doing the inevitable Media Studies, we've also seen Golf Studies at Lincoln University and the infamous football module, nicknamed 'David Beckham Studies', at the University of Staffordshire.[138]

Now, when the 50 per cent target was launched in 1999, the government justified it on economic grounds. It claimed that the average degree was worth £400,000, so expanding participation would bring a huge payback. In reality, the average degree was never worth anything like that, as the government was later forced to admit. According to the OECD, it's actually worth about £130,000, after taking account of the individual's costs of study.[139]

But even that lower figure is based on the earnings of past graduates, and it was always optimistic to assume we could massively expand their numbers without eroding their earnings advantage. Moreover, unless the new students are going to match existing graduates in terms of ability, rigour and subject choice, the economic returns are bound to be lower. Which is precisely what's now happening.

One sign of that is the graduate unemployment rate, which, since the financial crisis, has doubled for recent graduates: it now stands at around 20 per cent. On top of that, many of the graduates who do get work are taking jobs that don't require a degree – jobs that were previously filled perfectly well by school leavers. The ONS says over a third of recent graduates now do such lower-skill work.[140]

Which leads on to another vital point. It was long ago realised that the acquiring of a degree (and other qualifications) may be valuable to the individual not only because it imparts additional productive skills or knowledge, but also because it acts as a signal to prospective employers that the individual himself is highly able. So it can make sense for an individual to get a degree, in order to open the door to a well-paid job. But for society as a whole, there may be little or no increase in overall output to compensate for the costs, including the loss of output while people are studying. Taxpayers could end up spending billions on an investment with no pay-off.

The fundamental concern here is that we're now producing far more graduates than we need. And while those graduating from the top universities and top courses will doubtless continue to command an earnings premium, those with lesser degrees may well find their expensively obtained certificates turn out to be virtually worthless. As with our schools, we've pumped up quantity at the expense of quality.

We need to look more closely at education as an investment. And, in particular, what we as taxpayers get back for all the money we put in to educate other people's children.

DOES IT MAKE US RICHER?

Compulsory state-funded education dates back to Frederick the Great of Prussia. He instituted it because he believed that state schooling would turn out good Prussians – literate, numerate and drilled to serve; as he himself put it, 'an educated people can be easily governed'. Given subsequent unfortunate events in Prussia and elsewhere, that's not how anyone would put it today – although plenty still argue that taxpayers benefit from the social cohesion state education supposedly fosters.

These days, the standard case for tax-funded education is based on the economic argument advanced so powerfully by Tony Blair. In today's globalised knowledge economy, it says, a well-educated workforce is crucial to national economic success. Taxpayers should stump up because by educating other people's children they are investing in their own future prosperity. We all stand to gain.

That basic line has now been pushed by our politicians for well over a century, and it has wide acceptance. Easy to understand, it has the attraction of a financial payback to taxpayers, reinforced by a fear that if we don't make the investment, we'll be swallowed up. Education is the new arms race.

But here's the striking thing: although the argument is

taken as read, there's very little evidence to support it. For fifty years, economists have been searching, and they just can't come up with the killer facts.

What we do know is that for developed economies there is no direct link between education spending and economic growth. For example, Denmark spends more than the OECD average, but has experienced a long period of below-average growth. Whereas Australia spends less than average yet has enjoyed above-average growth.

Here's a chart showing education spending against economic growth for the fifteen largest developed economies over the last two decades.[141]

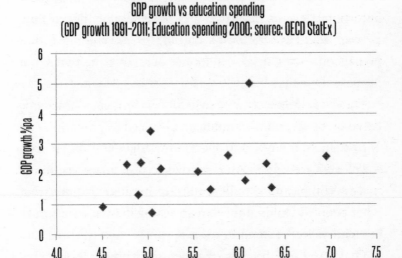

No Link Between Spending and Growth
GDP growth vs education spending
(GDP growth 1991-2011; Education spending 2000; source: OECD StatEx)

So GDP growth bears virtually no relationship to what's spent on education. In general, countries spending under 5 per cent of GDP seem to do just as well as countries spending a quarter or a third more. And that raises a huge question mark over our recent move from 4.6 per cent up to 6.3 per cent.

(In case you're wondering, the outlier with 5 per cent growth is South Korea, which was arguably still a developing economy in the early years; exclude it, and even the vaguest perception of a relationship disappears.)

Of course, academic economists do far more than look at a simple scatter chart, and they've produced reams of learned papers on the subject. But they've still never managed to demonstrate a robust link between more spending and more growth. As a detailed survey of the work published by the OECD drily put it in 2001: 'Answers that are sufficiently accurate and robust to allow confident conclusions are some way off.'[142]

Now, nobody is saying education is irrelevant to growth. Studies of developing economies have shown that general literacy and numeracy are crucial for development. But for already developed economies like Britain, that's not particularly helpful. The issue for us is not whether to scrap education altogether, but whether taxpayers should be forced to fund ever more of it.

And in these straitened times, the same question is being asked right across the developed world. The focus has shifted from spending more to delivering more: higher quality for less cash. And we know that's possible: for example, the German school system comprehensively outperforms ours in the OECD's PISA tests, yet costs considerably less.

Researchers are also focusing on the relationship between high-quality education and a country's ability to generate new ideas and to innovate. The idea here is that we will increasingly depend on a critical mass of highly educated workers who can keep our economy at the forefront of new techniques and new industries. Not many people are capable of that, but for those that are, it's worth pumping them full of expensive education because they will generate big spill-over benefits for the rest of us. The PhDs who've built the world-leading IT businesses around Cambridge are often cited as a model.

Of course, it's easy to sketch out potential linkages; rather trickier to exploit them. But it does underline the point that simply pushing more of our children through more exams and more years of school and college doesn't automatically make us richer. On the other hand, it could make a lot of sense to subsidise the highly able through university, but only if the universities maintain the highest standards of entry and academic rigour.

The bottom line is that despite the rhetoric, we can have no confidence that additional spending on education will have any economic pay-off. Or, to put it another way, over the last decade or so, the politicians have increased our annual tax bill by 30-odd billion on a hunch.

AND WE HAVEN'T GOT SOCIAL MOBILITY EITHER

Now, money don't get everything, it's true, so let's examine the other great promise of tax-funded education – that it gives everyone a fair chance to get on. Irrespective of parental income, free education provides a ladder up which bright, hard-working children can scramble.

Back in the old days, of course, that was precisely what our state grammar schools did. They offered children from poor backgrounds (including your author) a ladder to climb. And for thirty years following the Second World War, social mobility was reckoned to be pretty high.

The extent to which the grammars drove that mobility has always been hotly disputed, but one thing we do know is that the left's imposition of comprehensive schools has definitely not worked. Social mobility in Britain today is poor. In fact, it's shockingly poor: according to the OECD, we are just about the least mobile of any developed country they've studied.[143]

The OECD's key statistical measure of mobility is the correlation between an individual's earnings and that of his parents. The idea is that if people with high incomes are mainly the children of parents who also have high incomes, then that shows social mobility from one generation to the next is very limited – the rich stay rich and the poor stay poor. They call it the intergenerational earnings elasticity, and it measures the proportion of one generation's relative earnings position that gets transmitted down to the next (a reading of zero means no discernible transmission, and a reading of 1 means a perfect link).

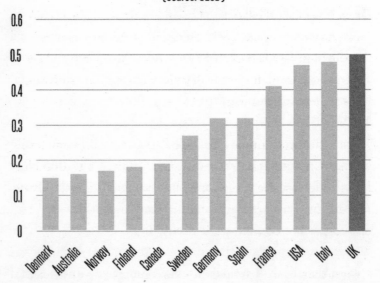

UK Top of Social Immobility League
Intergenerational earnings elasticity
(Source: OECD)

So, according to the OECD, here in the UK 50 per cent of the economic advantage that high-earnings fathers have over low-earnings fathers is transmitted to their sons. That's the highest legacy rate among the countries studied, and much higher than in most of our European neighbours. In terms of social mobility, our education system is a catastrophic failure.

Faced with this, the Blair government tried direct action. It was spearheaded by the multi-billion-pound Sure Start programme. Based on the US Head Start programme, Sure Start was an attempt to support the most disadvantaged children from long before they reach school age. Indeed, it was hoped to identify them while still in the womb, and to provide intensive parenting support all the way from pregnancy to school entry.

It sounded like a good idea, but, once again, the results have been disappointing. For one thing, the programme's subsidised childcare facilities have been gatecrashed by more affluent working parents. David Cameron blames people like himself:

> There is a criticism sometimes with Sure Start that a great new centre is established and the 'sharp-elbowed' middle classes, like my wife and me, get in there and get all the services ... It can't just be a service that everyone can jump into and get advantage out of. It is really there for those who are suffering the greatest disadvantage.[144]

Worse, the programme has failed to lift attainment levels among its target children. A detailed study of 117,000 children found that the programme had produced absolutely no improvement in reading, vocabulary or maths scores.[145] The lead researcher commented:

> Given the resources put into early years initiatives, we expected

to see a rise in literacy and numeracy scores in schools, so it's disappointing that there has been no improvement. Our findings reinforce the concern that the poorest families in our society are not accessing the full range of educational opportunities and resources designed to help them.

Bluntly, direct action at the pre-school level has been an expensive flop.

There's also been late-years intervention, directed at our top universities and pressuring them to discriminate in favour of candidates from state schools. It's argued that state school candidates are generally weaker than private school candidates – not least because they attended state schools – so the playing field needs levelling up.

The problem, of course, is that if our top universities discriminate, they're almost certainly admitting less qualified students for what ought to be highly demanding courses. And although it's suggested that lagging state school pupils can 'catch up', there's no serious evidence that happens. More likely, courses have to be run at a gentler pace, possibly with remedial classes tacked on the side: university resources are stretched thinner and course standards diluted.

And if prosperity in the global knowledge economy depends on having a cluster of super-bright, super-educated people, dumbing down our top universities would be a disaster. Which highlights a key issue we need to confront if we're to get better value from our educational investment: the hugely inconvenient conflict between equality and national prosperity.

HOW TO GET MORE FOR LESS

Over the last two decades, the amount taxpayers spend on education has doubled. Our school places are now among the most expensive in the world. Yet there's no serious evidence that our educational standards have improved, or that we're benefiting in terms of faster economic growth. Moreover, despite the establishment of comprehensive education, and despite several costly attempts at remedial action, 20 per cent of our school leavers still fail to attain basic literacy. And, despite wholesale dumbing down of grade standards, nearly half still fail to get five good GCSEs including Maths and English.

Somehow we seem to have been landed with the worst of both worlds. We've got a state education system that's become much more expensive but which has delivered neither the economic returns nor the social justice originally promised. We urgently need to get more for less.

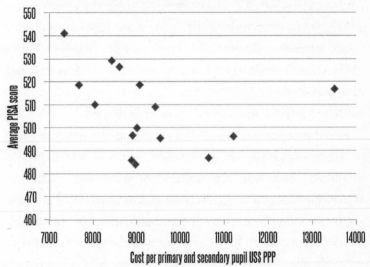

Cheaper Can Be Better
PISA attainment scores vs cost of schooling
(Average 2009 PISA scores vs annual cost per school pupil US$; source: OECD)

Here's another chart based on the OECD's comparative study of pupil performance we looked at earlier (PISA). For each of the fifteen largest economies, it shows average pupil scores across reading, maths and science as compared to the cost of a school place.[146] And, contrary to what you'd expect, what jumps out is that the cheaper systems are delivering the best results.

And this is not some false confession extracted from the data under torture. The OECD itself says:

> Among high-income economies, the amount spent on educa-
> tion is less important than how those resources are used…
>
> After a threshold of about $35,000 per student … expend-
> iture is unrelated to performance. For example, countries
> that spend more than $100,000 per student … show similar
> levels of performance as countries that spend less than half
> that amount.[147]

As we saw earlier, we're now one of those countries spending in excess of $100,000.

So how do cheaper systems deliver better results? There are no magic formulas, but the OECD research has identified two key factors:

- Quality of teachers – having high-ability teachers is far more important than having small class sizes; for example, in top-performing Korea and Finland, teachers are only recruited from the top 10 per cent of graduates.
- Expectations – schools must set high standards and must be intolerant of failure. There can be prizes for all, but only once they've been properly earned.

Of course, the climate of expectation within a school devel-ops over years, and depends heavily on the quality and commitment of senior staff. It's not something that can be ordered from above.

And that echoes another strong theme from the research: the systems that do best tend to be those where schools have more independence to manage their own affairs and develop their own culture and teaching methods. They are not operating a top-down central plan.

All around the world, from Sweden to the US, governments are responding to this research by granting state-funded schools more independence. And to encourage innovation, new private providers – including profit-making firms – are being allowed into the market, supplying education that remains funded by the state but which is no longer supplied by a state school. Enrolment in privately run but publicly funded schools now exceeds 50 per cent in the Netherlands and 35 per cent in Australia and Korea.

But independence is being accompanied by accountability. In particular, parents are being given more choice over which school their child should attend. Three-quarters of pupils across the OECD now attend schools which are competing for pupils with at least one other. Choice and competition – otherwise known as the market – are being used to drive improvement. It's exactly how our private school system has been operating for years.

The results have been encouraging. The OECD finds:

> … a clear relationship between the relative autonomy of schools and schooling outcomes across systems when autonomy is coupled with accountability…
>
> … school systems that provide schools with greater discretion in making decisions regarding student assessment policies, the courses offered, the course content and the

textbooks used tend to be school systems that perform at higher levels...[148]

This is the traditional power of the market applied to tax-funded education. Teachers are trusted to know their business far better than politicians or central government bureaucrats, but they have to deliver results to their customers or lose that business. It's as simple as that.

And the good news for British taxpayers is that it really shouldn't cost anything. In terms of compulsory education, we're already spending more than most competitors, and far more than the OECD's critical cost threshold: in fact, we ought to be able to get better results from *less* money. And while we are spending a bit less than average at university level, given our growing surplus of graduates it's not obvious we'd lose much if we trimmed back further (as we saw earlier).

In fairness, the coalition government is moving in the right general direction. They are promoting school independence, with more academies and new free schools. They are promoting parental choice, and they are trying to ensure that oversubscribed schools can expand, perhaps by taking over less successful schools. And they seem to have ended twenty years of exam grade inflation by insisting on higher marking standards, accepting the first ever declines in A level and GCSE results in 2012. All of which should be welcomed.

The pursuit of excellence in state schools will also boost social mobility. By closing the achievement gap with private schools, it will level the playing field for those millions of children whose parents cannot afford school fees. But first, there's a prickly nettle we need to grasp.

WE CAN'T HAVE IT ALL

Right across the world, under all education systems, children from higher socio-economic groups *always* do better on average than those from lower groups. It holds in every single one of the sixty-five countries studied by the OECD, even in countries like Denmark and Sweden, with much higher social mobility than us. Whether it's down to nature or nurture remains hotly contested, but there's no avoiding the stark fact.

The left have always thought this unfair, which is why fifty years ago they imposed comprehensive education. By ending segregation at eleven, they hoped the performance of those at the bottom would be lifted by mixing with more able pupils.[149]

Clearly, it hasn't worked, and we still have the same 20 per cent of hard-core underachievers now as we had back in the 1960s – just in different schools. But the idea of unfairness is still very much alive. And however we dress it up, a market-based strategy for getting better value for money could leave children from lower socio-economic groups trailing even further behind.

The problem is that parents from the lowest-income groups are generally less capable of jostling their children into the best schools, and less capable of supporting them thereafter. Yes, choice and competition would soon get education in the leafy suburbs delivering better value, with committed parents demanding and getting improvement. But those notorious inner-city comps could sink further behind.

Of course, there are things that can and should be done in mitigation, including the allocation of extra cash for schools admitting seriously disadvantaged children (the coalition's Pupil Premium). Indeed, it was an unfair allocation of cash that did much to undermine the old secondary modern schools.[150]

And there's much to learn from overseas. The OECD reckons that the three countries performing best in terms of educational equity are Korea, Finland and Canada, countries that are also top performers in terms of overall PISA results. The proportion of their fifteen-year-old boys unable to read properly averages just 12 per cent – half our own 23 per cent and the OECD average of 24 per cent. Moreover, all three of those countries have cheaper schools than we do. So it's clearly possible to have better performance for both top *and* bottom, and to do so while spending less.

But while we can realistically expect to cut illiteracy among school leavers – which would be a huge step forward from now – market-based reform will in all likelihood widen the gap between top and bottom.

Which gives us a choice. Either we muddle along with our high costs, low overall attainment and 20 per cent illiteracy, or we accept a widening performance gap between top and bottom as the price of improvement. We probably can't have it all.

This is the classic choice between prosperity and equality. In today's globalised knowledge economy, our prosperity increasingly depends on having clusters of bright, highly educated people who can keep us at the forefront of new ideas and industries. But we can only produce such people if we accept that our education system cannot deliver prizes for all. Pushing ever greater numbers through dumbed-down exams and university degrees will never make anyone rich.

For well over a century, tax-funded education has been sold to us as an investment. With 6.3 per cent of our national income now going into it, it's time we demanded a better return.

SEVEN

FROM DESTITUTION TO DEPENDENCY

Labour has honoured the pledge it made in 1945 to make social security the birthright of every citizen. Today destitution has been banished.
– Labour election manifesto, 1950

We need to get rid of the slovenly, vicious, idle wasters of the community. Unfortunately the Welfare State is only too likely to encourage their increase.
– The Right Rev. E. W. Barnes, Bishop of Birmingham, 1948

Welfare is the most contentious area of government spending, and it has been ever since the first compulsory Poor Law tax was levied in 1572. The poor may have been with us always, but it was only when governments got involved that supporting them became compulsory under penalty of law. And although welfare spending has increased hugely since Tudor times, the awkward questions have remained unchanged and largely unresolved.

It's a classic head-and-heart issue. As we'll discuss later, these days most of us support the idea of a tax-funded safety net, certainly for the old and the sick. And in general we'd extend the net to include the unemployed. None of us wants to see personal destitution return to Britain – or anything even close to destitution – and tax-funded welfare seems to be the fairest and surest means to prevent it.

 But while our hearts may say that, our heads recognise that the costs have become insupportable. Welfare is already by far the biggest item in the government's budget and by far the heaviest burden on taxpayers. It accounts for nearly one-third of all spending, with the annual bill running at a colossal £230 billion (2010/11). That's 16 per cent of our national income, a bill of £9,000 for every single British household. Worse, on current policies, the burden is projected to go on increasing for as far as anyone can see. The inexorable growth in pensioner numbers and working-age welfare dependency means that tough decisions are unavoidable.

And that has turned up the heat under some deeply emotive issues of fairness that have always surrounded welfare. Is it fair that the hard-working and thrifty should have to support those who may choose not to work? Is it fair that taxpayers should fund other people's children? Is it fair that welfare recipients can enjoy better housing than work-ers? And is it fair that foreign migrants can claim benefits?

The questions come a lot more easily than the answers, but we'll start with something that is absolutely key to understanding the issues, yet is often forgotten.

HOW THE POOR STOPPED BEING POOR

For most of our history, being poor meant going without the basic necessities of life, such as food, clothing and shelter. It was the grim grinding poverty we read about in Dickens, and which still colours our perception of poverty today. But the establishment of the welfare state in the 1940s transformed the landscape. As the Labour Party boasted in its 1950 election manifesto, under their new social security system, destitution had been banished. For the first time ever, the poor no longer needed to live without life's necessities. It was a tremendous and historic achievement.

And it didn't stop there. Over the next half-century, welfare spending went on growing and the poor not only escaped destitution, they started to get a whole lot richer.

Let's take a snapshot in 1961. That was the year Yuri Gagarin became the first man in space, Kennedy was sworn in as US President, and *West Side Story* won the Oscar for best movie. Closer to home, the average British family had never had it so good. Incomes were rising and the ownership of consumer durables like fridges, washing machines and TVs was spreading fast. For middle Britain, this was the affluent society (a term coined just three years previously).

1961 is also the first year for which we have reliable and consistent national figures on the incomes of the poor, assembled and published by the Institute for Fiscal Studies.[151] The figures relate to standardised two-adult households with no children, are net of direct taxes (that is, income tax and national insurance) and, to make the comparisons meaningful, have all been adjusted to 2009/10 prices.

What the figures show is that 1961's typical never-had-it-so-good British family – a family halfway up the income distribution – had a net income of just under £200 per week in today's money. In contrast, a poor family – only one-tenth of the way up the income distribution – had an income of just over £100 per week.

The figures also show that over the next fifty years, both types of family experienced a huge uplift in their real incomes. But here's the really striking thing: the incomes of our poorest families increased so much that they caught up with and surpassed 1961's typical middle-income family. The incomes of the poor doubled in real terms, lifting them to what in 1961 would have been considered never-had-it-so-good affluence. The following chart shows how it happened.

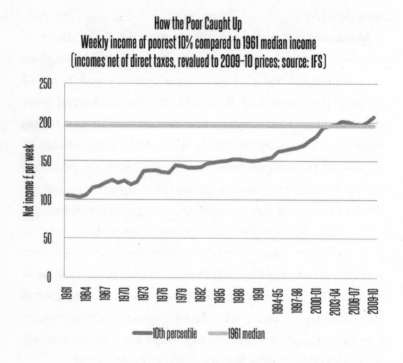

How the Poor Caught Up
Weekly income of poorest 10% compared to 1961 median income
(incomes net of direct taxes, revalued to 2009-10 prices; source: IFS)

And if we stretch the definition of the poor to encompass those who are one-quarter of the way up the income distribution, we find something truly astonishing. Because those in that position today are actually richer than those who were *three*-quarters of the way up the distribution in 1961. Put simply, many of those counted among the poorest 25 per cent today are actually richer than many counted among the richest 25 per cent fifty years ago.[152]

Now it is true that there are one or two wrinkles in

this historic comparison. In particular, over the last half-century the price of housing rose more than prices generally, and that impacted the poor more than higher-income groups. But even taking account of that, a poor family one-tenth of the way up the income distribution has still seen its real net income increase by around two-thirds since 1961.[153]

Moreover, although housing costs have risen, the real price of many other things has fallen. Consumer durables are cheaper, and today's poor have access to a wide range of goods that were still considered luxuries in the early 1960s. Among the poorest tenth today, 90 per cent have washing machines – owned by less than a third of 1961 households.[154] Almost all their homes now have at least one TV, probably with a huge colour screen unavailable even to the richest families fifty years ago. And 90 per cent of their homes have central heating – a rarity for everyone back then.

So to summarise, poverty as traditionally defined – the grinding destitution of Dickensian England – had been banished by 1950. But welfare benefits went on rising after that, lifting the poor well clear of any meaningful poverty line. In material terms, many of today's poor are as well off as comfortable middle Britain in the affluent 1960s.

NOT POOR YET STILL POOR

So the poor are no longer poor. Yet according to the official count, millions of our fellow citizens live below the poverty line. How can that be?

The answer is that during the 1960s, the official definition of poverty was changed.

Traditionally, the poverty line had always been defined by reference to how much cash people required to supply their essential needs – food, clothing, housing etc. But in the 1960s, the poverty line was redefined in terms of *relative income levels*. It's currently set at 60 per cent of median household income, and any household with an income below that level is classified as poor. In other words, the classification of poverty changed from an absolute measure to a relative measure.

The choice of an absolute or relative measure has a huge effect on the poverty count. For example, we've just seen how much richer the poorest 10 per cent have become since 1961. But according to the relative measure of poverty, far from getting richer, the poorest 10 per cent have actually got poorer. Back in 1961, the income of a household one-tenth of the way up the income distribution was 54 per cent of the median income.[155] Fifty years later, the corresponding figure has fallen back to 50 per cent.

The difference between the two versions of poverty is crystallised by taking today's official poverty line and comparing it against incomes back in 1961. Today (2009/10), the poverty line is £250 per week. But back in 1961, that level of income (adjusted for prices) would have been in the top 30 per cent of all incomes.[156] In that age of affluence, a family now classified as scraping by on the verge of poverty would have been considered very comfortably off.

Defining poverty relative to median income is a very different concept of poverty to the one most of us carry in our heads. It means the poverty line is less about ensuring access to life's key necessities, and more about keeping up with everyone else, or the Joneses as they used to be known. As the median Joneses get richer, their neighbours automatically get poorer; unless they get more welfare.

In terms of traditional poverty, it's also counter-intuitive.

It means that as the country gets more prosperous, unless benefit levels are raised, poverty automatically increases. Even more preposterously, it means that if the economy collapses, poverty declines. So, as GDP plunged between 2008 and 2010, the Office for National Statistics recorded a decrease in the proportion of households living in poverty, from 19 to 17 per cent.[157] At that rate, if we could just get ourselves back down to 1961 GDP levels, we'd abolish poverty altogether.

In truth, we'd probably all accept that the definition of key necessities does change over time. In the twenty-first century, our necessities have moved beyond basic food, clothing and shelter, and might well now include some of those 1961 luxuries we listed earlier – central heating, washing machines, fridges and even TVs.

But even if we accept that welfare support levels should take some account of contemporary living standards, mechanistically linking them to average incomes is going way beyond what most of us think of as poverty relief.

In reality, of course, today's official definition of poverty isn't measuring poverty at all: it's measuring inequality. And, as we'll discuss later, it forms part of a broader socialist agenda to impose more equality right across the income range.

We can have differing views on that agenda, but it is undeniable that income inequality has increased since 1961. The following chart shows how it happened, with the poorest 10 per cent falling a bit further behind the median, and the richest 10 per cent pulling further ahead (see overleaf).

In summary, the poor are no longer poor in the traditional sense, but they haven't been getting richer at the same rate as the rest of society.

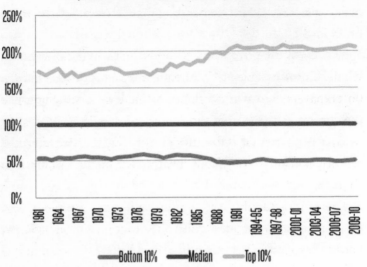

Richer but Less Equal
Incomes of top and bottom 10% relative to median 1961 to 2009-10
(equivalised household incomes, decile points: source: IFS)

THE SOARING COST OF WELFARE

If we hadn't changed our definition of poverty, we might
reasonably have expected our welfare bill to fall over the
last half-century. After all, greater prosperity has meant
more jobs, higher wages and greater opportunities for individuals to put something aside for a rainy day. Even the
poorest among us ought to have found it easier to support
themselves rather than relying on welfare.

But instead we've experienced the opposite. As we've
got richer, the cost of welfare has increased, not just in
absolute terms but also as a percentage of our growing
national income.

The decades since the end of the Second World War have
brought us growth and prosperity on an unprecedented
scale, with national income increasing more than fourfold.

But the new definition of poverty has led governments to widen the range and level of benefits way beyond anything envisaged when the welfare state was planned. In consequence, social security spending has grown nearly three times faster.

That kind of divergence between costs and resources is wholly unsustainable. It is already placing a severe burden on taxpayers, and if it continues to increase at anything like the current rate, then by mid-century, welfare will be costing us over a quarter of our national income. By the end of the century, it will be consuming nearly six pounds in every ten we earn.

There is no doubt that we face a serious problem, and it's a problem that also confronts our neighbours. Right across Europe welfare spending has reached unsustainable levels, and in several countries national budgets are already in meltdown.

Moreover, despite all the spending, income inequality has also been rising virtually everywhere. According to the OECD:

> Over the two decades prior to the onset of the global economic crisis, real disposable household incomes increased by an average 1.7 per cent a year in OECD countries. In a large majority of them, however, the household incomes of the richest 10 per cent grew faster than those of the poorest 10 per cent, so widening income inequality...[158]

And the OECD has a compelling explanation for this. Widening income inequality seems to have been driven by the very same forces driving global development and prosperity – market globalisation, the spread of new technologies and deregulation. These forces go way beyond anything an individual country's politicians can control, and they're foolish to try. Because ultimately *everyone* can benefit, including the poor – whose incomes, let's not forget, have doubled over the last fifty years.

So rather than attempting to contain economic development, the OECD's prescription is to tackle inequality through education. Skills and knowledge count more than ever today, and it's essential for countries to ensure that their entire populations have access to the very best educational opportunities – something we'll come back to.

But the OECD warns against attempts to impose equality through more income redistribution. It says such policies 'would be neither effective nor financially sustainable'. Not only would there be 'counterproductive disincentive effects', but social spending in most countries is already unsustainably high. More redistribution means less prosperity.

A top finance official from the world's new economic superpower, China, makes the same point more bluntly. Commenting on the fiscal and economic crisis in Europe, he tells us: 'The root cause of the trouble is the over-burdened welfare system, built up since the Second World War – the sloth-inducing, indolence-inducing labour laws ... People need to work a bit harder, they need to work a bit longer ... We (the Chinese) work like crazy.'[159]

Something clearly has to give. The unpalatable truth is that we are actually going to have to make some of those tough choices our politicians are so fond of mentioning, but which they rarely spell out in detail.

We'll be looking at those choices in the next chapter. But first we need to make a list of the problems with our current system. And we'll start with pensions. Because, adding up all the various benefits paid to pensioners, they account for over half of all social security spending.

PROBLEM ONE: TOO MANY PENSIONERS

In 1950, the average male retiring at age sixty-five could expect to live for another eleven years; today, he can expect to live for twenty-two.[160] So he'll be drawing his pension for twice as long, as will the average woman.

And today's 65-year-old is good for many more miles than her counterpart in 1950. Britain's top septuagenarian film starlet tells us:

'I don't buy into you're on the slagheap when you're forty or fifty or sixty or seventy or whatever ... Age is just a number. It's totally irrelevant unless you happen to be a bottle of wine.'

As Joan Collins vividly demonstrates, sitting by the fire with a cup of cocoa is still years away for today's typical sixty- or even seventy-something. Travel, salsa classes and online dating are much more compelling activities. Retirement is a chance to catch up on all those things there wasn't time to do while working.

Which is terrific in every respect. Except the cost. Because however we do the sums, there's no avoiding the fact that paying pensions for an average of twenty-two years is twice as expensive as paying them for eleven.

Moreover, the fact that we're living so much longer means that we now have many more pensioners to pay those pensions to. Their numbers have nearly doubled since the Second World War and currently stand at 13 million, or one in five of the entire population. They've increased by over 1 million just in the last six years, and there's little sign of a slow-down.[161]

Now, when Bismarck launched the modern world's first state pension scheme in the 1880s, he set the pension age at seventy. But since at the time the average life expectancy for a Prussian male was under fifty, the number of people who lasted that long was pretty small. Later, in an attempt to boost morale during the Great War, the German government cut the pension age to sixty-five, but most still never made it.

Lloyd George introduced Bismarck's pensions to Britain in 1908, complete with the qualifying age of seventy. In 1925 that was lowered to sixty-five, again following the German lead, and in 1946 lowered further to sixty for women.

And that's how things stayed for the next six decades, despite our massive rise in life expectancy. Successive governments were told of the growing cost problem, but, since the crunch was always some way off, it was easy to leave the tough choices for their successors.

At least our politicians didn't make things worse by cutting the pension age still further, which is what the French Socialists did.[162] And they have now finally begun to grasp the nettle, with the younger pension age for women abandoned, and plans to increase the unified state pension age to sixty-seven by 2028, and sixty-eight by 2046.

Unfortunately, it's not enough. Even when we get to 2046, the male pension age will still be only three years higher than it was in 1950, against that increase in life expectancy of eleven years. And by the time we get to 2046, life expectancy will almost certainly be even higher and an awful lot more unaffordable benefit spending will have flowed under the bridge in the meantime. Problem One remains at the top of our list.

PROBLEM TWO: WE'RE (NEARLY) ALL ON WELFARE

There are 26 million households in Britain. So how many do you reckon get welfare benefits?

Five million?

Ten?

According to the government statistics, a staggering 19 million British households are in receipt of at least one welfare benefit. Seven million of those are pensioner households, and the other 12 million are working age.[163] That leaves just a quarter of British households still standing entirely on their own two feet.

We've already seen how pensioner numbers doubled since 1950, but the increase in working-age welfare dependents has been even greater. The number claiming unemployment benefit is up from around 300,000 in the early 1950s to its present 1.6 million recipients of jobseeker's allowance, as it's now called. Incapacity benefit (and similar) claimants are up from only a few hundred thousand to 2.6 million. And lone-parent claimants – almost unheard of in the 1950s – now number 600,000.

Overall, the number of working-age welfare dependents has increased from well under a million sixty years ago to 5.7 million today. The economy may be four times bigger, but it seems there are six times as many working-age people who cannot support themselves within it.[164]

Moreover, people who are by no stretch of the imagination poor now receive substantial amounts from the state. We've all read stories of millionaires getting child benefit and the winter fuel allowance, and they're not one-off anomalies. The following chart ranks households across ten groups according to their net income, from the poorest to the richest, and shows what percentage of their income they get from cash welfare payments.[165]

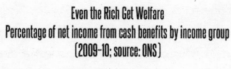

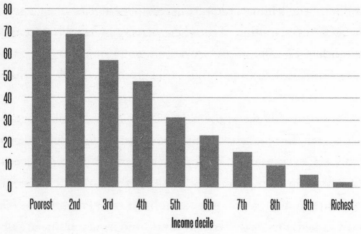

So *all* income groups now get benefits, irrespective of how rich they are. Households on middle incomes – well clear of poverty – on average get between a quarter and a third of their income from state benefits. It's become known as middle-class welfare.

And neither should we gloss over the relatively small percentage received by the richest tenth. Despite the fact that their annual incomes average over £100,000, we're *still* paying them benefits costing nearly £5 billion annually.

Overall, the think tank Reform has estimated that middle-class welfare costs taxpayers £31 billion per year, or 15 per cent of the entire benefits bill.[166]

And the nonsense is actually worse than that. Because it's the middle class and the rich who pay the taxes to fund the benefits. They are being taxed with one official hand, only to get some of it paid back with the other official hand. It's what's known as fiscal churn, and it means our expensive tax and benefits bureaucracy is robbing Peter to pay Peter. The administrative and leakage cost of that pointless circularity has been estimated at 5 per cent or more of the amount churned, which runs into billions annually.[167]

Of course, there is that deprived one-quarter of households who get no hand-outs at all. They turn out to be the workers. Well, more specifically, they're the workers who are either childless, or whose children are too old to qualify for child benefit. And as they toil away and pay their taxes to fund everyone else's welfare cheques, they might well ponder why they're being forced to subsidise people who are already living way above any traditional and credible definition of poverty.

PROBLEM THREE: WORK DOESN'T PAY

If you're one of those hardworking taxpayers, it's very easy to get angry with people who apparently make no effort to support themselves. They are surely abusing your willingness to contribute more than you receive, and, if they have the ability to support themselves, then they must have the responsibility for doing so. Their entitlement to welfare can't simply trump your entitlement to keep what you earn.

And from a moral perspective you could be right. But you do need to ask yourself how you'd actually behave if you were the one caught in the jaws of the notorious welfare trap.

The welfare trap is simple but deadly. Because so many benefits are means-tested, the more of their own income they earn, the more the poor lose in benefits. In fact, benefit withdrawal rates are so steep that many of the poor face effective marginal tax rates far above those confronting even the fattest of City fat cats (the effective marginal tax rate being the percentage of each additional pound earned that is lost through benefits withdrawal plus income tax and national insurance payments).

According to the Department for Work and Pensions (DWP), in 2011, over 600,000 of the unemployed were facing a Participation Tax Rate in excess of 90 per cent.[168] That is, if they got a job and started earning, more than 90 pence in every pound they earned would be lost in benefits withdrawal and tax.

It was nearly as bad for those already in work, given the opportunity to increase their earnings. The Department reckoned 130,000 of them were facing marginal rates above 90 per cent, with nearly 2 million facing rates of at least 60 per cent. That is far higher than the top rate of 47 per cent paid by an investment banker on a million a year.

As a specific example of how the trap works, the Department quoted the case of a couple with two children. As long as they are both unemployed, they receive benefits of around £330 per week, comprising a complex cocktail of child benefit, child tax credit, jobseeker's allowance, income support, housing benefit and council tax benefit. The case shows what happens if one of them gets a job and starts earning at the minimum wage.

The figures are shocking. If the new earner works up to fifteen hours per week, the family's net income increases hardly at all. Having lost jobseeker's allowance, their income support is also scaled back almost one-for-one against earnings.

Once working hours hit sixteen per week, then there is an uplift in net weekly income, to just under £400, because at sixteen hours per week an additional further benefit called working tax credit kicks in. However, extending working hours beyond sixteen brings very little further net income uplift, as more and more benefit gets withdrawn. Even if the worker puts in fifty hours a week, net weekly income barely nudges above £400.

What this means is that for much of the week, this unfortunate worker's effective marginal tax rate exceeds 90 per cent, and each additional hour's work nets him just 44 pence.

Forty-four pence an hour. To knowingly and voluntarily accept those terms, you'd either have to be an incurable workaholic or a saint.

Moreover, in reality you'd find it very difficult to be sure that you'd even be left with 44 pence. The benefits system has become so complex and unwieldy that you'd be justifiably concerned you could get less, or that you might even lose money. Even worse, your new entitlement could get miscalculated, resulting in an overpayment that you would later have to repay *after* you'd already spent the money – that's a perennial and nightmarish problem for people moving into work or increasing their hours.

PROBLEM FOUR: COMPLEXITY AND FRAUD

After seventy years of the welfare state, the benefits system has become mind-bogglingly complex. In 2010, it was estimated that there were fifty different benefits available, all with their own individual rules and application forms.[169]

The Department for Work and Pensions' benefit procedures manuals run to fourteen volumes and 8,690 pages. Yet the DWP doesn't even administer all the benefits. Child benefit and the various tax credits are administered by HMRC, while housing benefit and council tax benefit are administered by literally hundreds of individual local authorities. All have their own voluminous procedures manuals to follow, forms to complete and files to maintain.

For the honest poor, this complexity is an impenetrable thicket that not only acts as a powerful disincentive to taking paid employment, but also seriously hampers them in claiming their legitimate entitlements.

And it's also a big problem for taxpayers. The system has become hugely expensive to administer. Working-age benefits alone are estimated to cost £3.5 billion a year to administer, and adding in pension-age benefits takes the total to well over £5 billion.[170]

On top of that, although many of the rules are there supposedly to prevent abuse, the system's very complexity leaves it wide open to fraud and error.

Barely a day passes without some shocking new benefit fraud hitting the headlines. Current headlines report a mother of five who fraudulently claimed £112,000 in income support, housing benefit and council tax benefit; a bingo caller who defrauded us out of £43,000 in incapacity benefit; a bank manager and her partner who took £105,000 and, most scandalous, a Nigerian gang who attempted to defraud DWP of £1.7 million, albeit they 'only' got away with £270,000. And the scandalous thing about that case is that the plot only worked because three of the gang had actually been employed as benefits officers by DWP – which was by no means the first such inside job.

Annual losses are officially estimated to be running in excess of £5 billion, and jobseeker's allowance alone has an estimated fraud and error rate of 6.5 per cent.[171] But that's just an estimate: we don't know what we don't know, and nobody knows how much is actually going astray. That's why the National Audit Office has refused to sign off the

DWP's accounts for twenty-two consecutive years, 'because of the material level of fraud and error in expenditure on state benefits'.[172]

In the light of all these problems, the coalition government has embarked on an ambitious programme to simplify the entire system. From 2013, it will replace a vast swathe of the existing working-age benefits with a single payment – what it's calling the universal credit. At the same time, it will reshape the entitlement rules with the aim of ensuring work always pays. Their reforms are pointing in exactly the right direction, but getting them to work properly will entail some extraordinarily difficult and unpopular decisions, as we'll see in the next chapter.

PROBLEM FIVE: INCENTIVISING DEPENDENCY

Always and everywhere, state welfare systems have suffered from perverse incentives and abuse.

If people can live off welfare without working, then some will choose to do so even if they're able to work – especially if work pays barely more than benefits. Some may have children in order to benefit from family housing and support. And some will abuse the system's generosity through deliberate fraud. However noble the intentions of those establishing the system, benefits can twist and distort the behaviour of recipients and potential recipients alike. And the more generous the benefits, the more twisting there's likely to be.

The original Tudor Poor Laws recognised these issues and tackled them in a number of ways. First, they made a sharp distinction between those seen as the deserving poor, such as the old and infirm, and the undeserving poor, such as the idle able-bodied. The latter were set to work for their benefits, and could be consigned to the workhouse or even a house of correction to make sure that they did.

Second, the system was local, taxpayers in each parish being responsible only for their own local poor, and not those from elsewhere. And because of that localism, parish overseers were able to use their local knowledge to target relief very precisely on those deemed to deserve it.

Third, the penalties for persistent idle scroungers were severe, including flogging, branding and even execution.

Today's welfare system is a world away from that. To start with, it's national rather than local, removing any chance of using local knowledge to target relief and prevent abuse. Second, the penalties for abuse are pretty mild. Nobody would suggest a return to the harsh Tudor regime, but today, only around 6 per cent of *detected* fraud is even prosecuted, let alone punished.[173]

And third, our system has avoided making any distinction between the deserving and undeserving poor. Instead, our 6 million working-age welfare dependents have been viewed as victims – victims of the market, or of incapacitating illness, or perhaps of finding themselves with children they can't afford to maintain. And, as victims, they are entitled to support from the rest of us.

Of course, blaming the markets and capitalism has always been a favourite theme of the left, but, with the development of Keynesian economics in the 1930s, it acquired a coherent intellectual framework that for decades silenced the right as well.

Keynesianism said that markets don't necessarily oper-ate to provide jobs for everyone who wants them, and economies can get stuck for prolonged periods with a defi-ciency of demand and high levels of unemployment. In that situation, individual workers can't be expected to find jobs, and while the government conducts the necessary 'pump priming' operations to get the economy moving, the unemployed deserve to be given a decent level of welfare support. The unemployed are thereby absolved of personal responsibility for their own situation.

As we know, the simplistic certainties of post-war Keynesianism were blown sky-high by the economic crises of the 1970s. But the view of the unemployed as victims persisted. True, the Thatcher government did make an attempt to change it, epitomised in Employment Secretary Norman Tebbit's much-quoted remark after the inner-city riots in 1981: 'I grew up in the '30s with an unemployed father. He didn't riot. He got on his bike and looked for work, and he kept looking 'til he found it!'

But against that, it was the Thatcher government that presided over a huge growth in the number of working-age people on invalidity benefit, which comprises the other main group of jobless who can't be held responsible for their dependence on welfare.

Indeed, there's a widespread belief that the Thatcher government encouraged the switching of jobless from unemployment benefit to invalidity benefit to disguise the true extent of joblessness. And although there's no actual proof of that, it is a fact that from the early 1980s to the early 1990s, the number of people on invalidity benefit more than doubled and real expenditure trebled.

Today, there are 2.6 million people of working age on the current version of invalidity benefit, compared to less than half a million in the mid-1970s. Nobody seriously believes that's because we now have five times as many people who are absolutely unable to work through physical and mental incapacity. But it does mean we have five times as many people who've been absolved of responsibility for supporting themselves, by reason of 'incapacitating' illness.

In 2007, a Freedom of Information request obtained details of the specific incapacities involved.[174] They included a wide and bizarre range of vaguely defined complaints ranging from 'malaise and fatigue' (16,000 cases), to 'dizziness and giddiness' (8,000), to 'headaches' (4,000). Sixty people had been signed off with 'nail disorders', and another fifty with 'acne'. An astonishing £4.4 billion had been paid to people deemed simply 'too fat to work'.

As the Labour MP and redoubtable poverty campaigner Frank Field commented:

> It is a racket, which governments have allowed to exist for far too long. I do not blame people for working the system, it is the job of politicians to stop them doing it.
>
> The big change over the last decade has been into illnesses which largely defy a clear medical classification: depression, dizziness and such. It is a move from the tangible illness to the intangible.

Clearly, that's not to say that everyone on incapacity benefits – or indeed unemployment benefits – is lead swinging. But it is saying that our benefits system has seriously twisted people's behaviour. It has incentivised dependency, encouraging millions of people to drop out of the labour market and imposing a huge cost on everyone else.

PROBLEM SIX: NURTURING THE UNDERCLASS

In 2008, the country was horrified by the case of a Dewsbury woman who arranged for her own daughter to be kidnapped.

The girl spent twenty-four days drugged and tethered inside a divan bed while the police and public combed the local area in an increasingly desperate search for her. Fortunately, she was released with no physical harm, but it then emerged that it was her mother who'd arranged it – the very woman who'd been on TV tearfully appealing for her daughter's safe return. She'd done so in an attempt to extract money from the newspapers and public, having apparently got the idea from the huge donations that had flowed into the Madeleine McCann fund.

It turned out that the woman had seven children by five different fathers, and by all accounts the children were badly neglected. Moreover, although she was entirely dependent on £20,000 of child-related benefits – including a free council house – that didn't apparently stop her smoking sixty cigarettes a day and drinking freely.[175]

But if all that wasn't bad enough, as the media dug into the local background, they discovered an even more disturbing picture. The entire neighbourhood seemed somehow to have gone wrong. We learned that a quarter of its working-age households were jobless and living on benefits (well before the recession took hold). Nearly one-third of households with children had no breadwinner and were entirely dependent on welfare. Crime was 70 per cent above average, drugs a serious problem, educational attainment low, and personal health and lifestyles so bad that the typical resident could expect to be dead three years ahead of the rest of us.[176]

Officially, the area is classified as 'deprived'. According to the Department for Communities and Local Government, it ranks in the most deprived tenth of all areas in England.[177] Yet despite that, it can't really be described as poor. True, its average income is lower than the national average, but after taking account of all those welfare payments, the shortfall is only 15 per cent.[178] And money almost certainly goes further, with, for example, property prices less than half the national average.

Moreover, the term 'deprived' doesn't properly capture the dysfunctional behaviour and attitudes we saw on our TV screens. David Cameron seemed closer when he described the area as 'an estate where decency fights a losing battle against degradation and despair' and 'a community whose pillars are crime, unemployment and addiction'.[179]

What we saw felt much more like what influential American political scientist Charles Murray describes in his theory of the underclass. He sums it up thus:

> By underclass, I do not mean people who are merely poor, but people at the margins of society, unsocialised and often violent...
>
> My fundamental thesis is that large increases in ... three indicators – drop-out from the labour force among young males, violent crime, and births to unmarried women – will be associated with the growth of a class of violent, unsocialised people who, if they become sufficiently numerous, will fundamentally degrade the life of society.[180]

That's a very scary prospect, and not just for the unfortunate residents of Dewsbury. It's made even scarier by the possibility that by providing generous welfare benefits, we may have inadvertently promoted labour force drop-out and births to unmarried women. On Murray's argument, our very generosity may have nurtured the growth of an underclass.

What the Dewsbury kidnap case highlighted was that, while tackling poverty by increasing welfare benefits may reduce income inequalities, it doesn't solve the real problems of deprivation. On the contrary, by allowing large sections of the working-age population not to work, and by incentivising workless single women to have children, it makes many of those problems worse. It sets up and funds an inter-generational spiral of decline.

This echoes a point long made by Frank Field, once Director of the Child Poverty Action Group. He argues that simply giving more money to poor families does nothing to improve the life chances of their children. As he put it in a report for the coalition government:

> Even if the money were available to lift all children out of income poverty in the short term, it is far from clear that this move would in itself close the achievement gap.
>
> … there is much more beyond just improving short-term family incomes in determining the life chances of poor children. A healthy pregnancy, positive but authoritative parenting, high-quality childcare, a positive approach to learning at home and an improvement in parents' qualifications together, can transform children's life chances, and trump class background and parental income. A child growing up in a family with these attributes, even if the family is poor, has every chance of succeeding in life.[181]

In other words, sorting out the problems of today's poor is not about pumping up their benefits still further – as Blair's headline-grabbing pledge to abolish child poverty sought to do. It's about the much more difficult task of somehow changing their behaviour.

THE PROBLEMS BEFORE US

So to summarise, our benefits system has succeeded in lifting the poor out of poverty, but it's costing more than we can afford. And we've identified a list of six underlying problems with the current system:

1. The pension age is too low.
2. Too many benefits go to those who aren't poor.
3. Work doesn't pay.
4. The system is over-complex and open to fraud.
5. It incentivises dependency.
6. It nurtures an underclass.

We simply can't go on like this. In the words of King Edward VIII, shocked by the poverty and distress he encountered on a visit to South Wales in 1936, something must be done. In the next chapter we'll lay out what that something might look like.

EIGHT

TOUGH ALL OVER

Tough decisions lie ahead on welfare, and they will not be popular. I will take them in the long-term best interests of the country.
– Tony Blair, writing in *The Sun*, 1998

We have to take tough decisions and we have to do it in a way that is fair and we have to try to take the country with us at the same time.
– David Cameron, speaking to *The Sun*, 2011

If we're ever to control the ballooning cost of our welfare system, our politicians are going to have to make – and stick to – some of those tough decisions they tell us about. Everyone agrees on that. But in practice, tough decisions on welfare have turned out to be a whole lot tougher than even the toughest of politicians have had the stomach for.

That's because reining back welfare always creates losers. And unlike spending cuts in our public services, there's no way of offsetting those losses through improved efficiency. There are outright losers and they make a lot of noise, a noise unfailingly amplified by the media. For any politician, that's as tough as it gets.

But the taxpaying public are ready for change. Over the last two decades, support for benefits spending has plummeted, with only a quarter of us prepared to countenance further increases, compared to 60 per cent back in the early 1990s.[182] Support for redistribution is also down sharply, and over half now think unemployment benefits are too high. An overwhelming 84 per cent believe that the key to getting ahead in life is hard work, not relying on state welfare.

So with the majority firmly behind them and with the leading tabloids urging them on, the coalition government has the best reforming chance since the Second World War – if they can just step up to those tough decisions.

In the previous chapter we identified six problems with our current system. We'll leave the first – the state pension age – until later, but the other five all relate to working-age benefits. And the issues they raise are almost identical to those we faced the last time our welfare system got into serious difficulties.

WE'VE BEEN HERE BEFORE

In the early 1800s, the old Tudor Poor Laws had been in place for more than two centuries. Poor relief was still administered by each individual parish and funded by local taxpayers. And to keep costs down and incentives sharp, the system still made a distinction between the deserving poor, such as the old and infirm, and the undeserving poor, such as the idle able-bodied. The latter were expected to work. By the standards of today, provision for even the deserving poor was minimal and conditions were harsh. But of course, the country as a whole was much poorer and cost was always an issue.

The crisis sprang from the French Wars at the end of the

eighteenth century. Food prices had shot up and the poor were hit hard. Amid much concern about starvation and civil unrest, some local magistrates had begun increasing the relief available, even to the able-bodied poor and even when they were in work.

In 1795, magistrates meeting at the Pelican Inn in Speenhamland, Berkshire, had pronounced that 'the present state of the poor law requires further assistance than has generally been given'. They'd therefore devised a scale of additional reliefs based on the price of bread. The idea was that labourers would go on working hard for whatever they could earn, but if it wasn't enough to feed themselves and their families, the parish would provide a top-up. In effect, it was a wage subsidy.

In those hungry years, the Speenhamland system and similar schemes had spread to many other parishes. However, serious problems had emerged. For one thing, the system allowed employers – mainly farmers – to cut wages and rely on the parish to keep their workers in food. For another, it depended on workers striving hard to earn as much as possible for themselves, keeping the required top-ups as low as possible. In other words, the system was based on some pretty naive assumptions about human behaviour.

Unsurprisingly, costs had escalated rapidly, especially in the depressed economic conditions following the end of the Napoleonic Wars. And as increasing numbers of the poor fell back on parish relief, the burden on local taxpayers had become insupportable. Something had to be done.

In 1832 the government responded by setting up the Royal Commission on the Operation of the Poor Laws. And it confronted the same fundamental issue we face today: how to provide welfare support for the poor, without undermining their incentive to support themselves, and without spending more than taxpayers can afford.

After due deliberation, and after consulting the leading economists of the day, the Commission spelled out two key recommendations, both quickly accepted by the government.

First, to save money and make sure that work would always pay, it proposed to cut the level of welfare benefits for the able-bodied to *below the minimum* such people could earn for themselves. And since there was no minimum wage, that meant the level of earnings even the *least productive* worker could achieve, which it reckoned ought to be around subsistence level. In the report's own famous words:

> ... as the condition of any pauper is elevated above the condition of independent labourers the condition of the independent class is depressed ... Such persons therefore are under the strongest inducements to quit the less eligible class of labourers and enter the more eligible class of paupers ... Every penny bestowed, that tends to render the condition of the pauper more eligible than that of the independent labourer, is a bounty on indolence and vice.[183]

Second, to deter malingerers, the Commissioners proposed to make all welfare *conditional*. The condition was that relief would only be available on entry to a workhouse, where the regime was to be made deliberately harsh. Workhouses were placed under a duty to provide food, shelter and clothing – and indeed some medical care – but they were designed to be unappealing to all but the desperate. The message was that everyone was expected to work, and *any* job would be preferable to falling back on the parish.

In practice, this requirement came to be observed

more in the breach, since so-called outdoor relief (that is, providing assistance to the poor in their own homes) was much cheaper than putting people into the relatively expensive workhouses. For example, in 1871 there were just over a million people receiving poor relief, and less than one in seven was in a workhouse.[184] But the mere existence of the workhouse and the risk of ending up there undoubtedly served to concentrate the minds of anyone tempted to malinger. The conditionality of welfare shaped behaviour.

In terms of keeping welfare rolls low, the Commission's policies were spectacularly successful. Throughout the Victorian period, the numbers drawing relief never rose much above 5 per cent of the population. And in an age before state pensions, that included not just the jobless, but also the elderly and infirm. The comparable figure today – including state pensioners – is about 30 per cent.

Of course, conditions for the Victorian poor became a national disgrace, and nobody wants them to return. Nobody today would deliberately consign Britain's poor to subsistence welfare, and the workhouses are long gone. Nevertheless, the Commission's decisions clearly signpost the two tough choices we again confront today:

1. We must decide between keeping a high level of welfare benefits on the one hand, and saving money and making work pay on the other: we can't have all three. This is the iron triangle of welfare reform.[185]
2. We must decide between welfare available to all, however they behave, and welfare *conditional* on recipients behaving in a certain prescribed way – such as working for the dole.

Our politicians rarely spell things out like this because both choices unavoidably entail losers. And although the coalition government started out being more explicit than its predecessors, they stirred up such a storm of opposition that the debate got smothered. So let's see if we can summarise the real options.

MAKING WORK PAY

There are broadly three ways to make work pay.

First, we could cut benefits, as the Poor Law Commissioners did. Second, we could abolish means testing and allow people to keep *all* of their benefits *on top* of anything they earn. Or third, we could increase what people get paid in work.

Taking them in reverse order, increasing what people get paid in work was pretty well what the Blair government tried when it introduced the national minimum wage in 1999. By making employers pay more to their lowest-paid workers, low-paid jobs would immediately become more financially attractive relative to benefits.

Except that, sadly, legislating for higher wages doesn't change the underlying economics. If it's unattractive to employ someone on £3 an hour, it's even more unattractive to employ her on £4 an hour.

Moreover, wages are only part of the cost of employing someone. The national minimum wage for an adult is currently £6.19 per hour. But to that has to be added the employer's national insurance contribution, plus the cost of the workplace, uniform, subsidised catering and a string of other items attached to employing an extra person. It can easily add 50 per cent on top of the wage, pushing the annual full-time employment cost towards £20,000.

That £20,000 might be covered comfortably by what

an extra worker could bring in for an employer in central London. But a similar employee in South Shields might struggle. Average labour productivity in the north east is barely 60 per cent of London levels, and the jobless are very likely to be below average productivity for the area.[186] But if our South Shields worker can't deliver output worth £20,000, she won't be employed – because employers are not in general permitted to employ people at below the minimum wage. The national minimum wage may thus have made the welfare trap worse.

The official position is that the minimum wage has not damaged employment. But that's based on evidence from the boom years, when jobs were plentiful.[187] And much of the evidence boils down to the fact that employment in low-paid jobs continued to expand even after the introduction of the minimum wage. However, since we know many of those jobs went to migrants rather than jobless low-productivity Brits, that's no real comfort.

As a strategy for getting our jobless into work, the current minimum wage is more of a hindrance than a help. If we're serious about boosting employment, it should be abolished. At the very least it needs to be cut, or frozen.

Of course, a much surer way of increasing what people get paid in work is to cut income tax and national insurance, ideally through raising the tax-free allowance. And indeed, that is exactly what the coalition has done. But apart from being very costly, it only helps those who are earning more than the allowance, which may not apply to many part-time jobs.

SURF'S UP

The second way of breaking the trap is to abolish means testing. If welfare recipients could keep all their benefits *on top* of anything they earned, work would be a lot more attractive. Indeed, for the unemployed thinking of taking a low-paid job, the withdrawal of benefits is generally a greater disincentive than income tax and national insurance, which only kick in above the tax-free earnings band.

One of the most radical proposals for reforming our welfare system sweeps away means testing entirely. It goes by the name of the Citizens' Basic Income (CBI), or alternatively the Basic Income Guarantee (BIG).[188]

The idea is very simple and very appealing: we sweep away the current impenetrable tangle of welfare benefits in its entirety, and use the money saved to make a regular flat-rate payment to every adult in the country. The payment is guaranteed whether or not the recipient also has other sources of income, such as earnings from work. The BIG is completely tax-free, but all personal earnings and other income get taxed at the standard rate. For those in work, the untaxed BIG takes the place of the personal tax allowance.

From the individual recipient's perspective, she now knows she can take a job without worrying about losing entitlement to any benefits. There is no means testing of any kind and anything she earns on top of her guaranteed basic income is hers to keep, subject only to paying income tax and national insurance. Suddenly the world of work, and earning to support herself and her family, looks a whole lot more attractive. All she has to do is climb aboard and ride the wave.

Taxpayers also gain, because not only are the billions spent on administering the current complex benefits system largely saved, but there are now more working taxpayers around to share the overall cost burden. The opportunities for fraud are also greatly reduced.

In one heroic leap we've escaped the welfare trap. It's so brilliant you wonder why nobody thought of it before.

Except, that is, for a couple of treacherous cross-currents.

The first is what's known as the Malibu Surfer Effect. What if, instead of taking a job to top up their BIG, recipients decide instead to give up the idea of work altogether and become Malibu surfers? Or, perhaps more realistically in Britain, Bournemouth beach bums. We might not want to pay tax to support them, but we'd have to because the basic income is guaranteed to all unconditionally.

The second problem is that the sums don't work. We certainly can't afford to spend any more than now, yet if we're going to sweep away every other welfare benefit, our basic income needs to be set high enough for an adult to live on. Moreover, since many adults have children, it needs to be set high enough to support them as well.

The social security budget currently stands at £200 billion. We can throw in the £65 billion cost of personal tax and national insurance allowances, plus £5 billion of administration savings, and we end up with a maximum overall pot of £270 billion.[189] With a population of 50 million adults, that means we could fund a Citizens' Basic Income of up to £5,400.

It's not enough. While a no-strings £5,400 might be pretty neat for our Bournemouth beach bum, it's very low for those with several children, especially since it would also have to cover housing.

Advocates of the Basic Income argue that that's part of its attraction. People shouldn't have children they can't afford to support, and those who already have would need to get a job or seek help from charities.

But even if we go along with the thrust of that, we'd surely

need some careful – and expensive – transition arrangements
to safeguard children who are already with us. Moreover,
£5,400 feels low for other groups as well, groups even
the Poor Law Commissioners would have recognised as the
deserving poor.

For example, a poor elderly person living in rented accommodation anywhere round London would struggle, because
there'd be no housing benefit. Similarly, a disabled person
dependent on paid carers would struggle because there'd be
no disability living allowance and no attendance allowance.
Indeed, anyone poor and unable to work, with dependants
and/or rented accommodation, would find life grim on £5,400.

So while our Basic Income Guarantee has cracked the
welfare trap, it's done so only at the expense of consigning millions of children, the old and the sick to much lower
living standards. There certainly isn't the money for an
income that leaves everyone at least as well off as they are
now. And while we could augment it with special allowances
for children and so on, that would immediately undermine
its simplicity.

Surfing may be a solution, but by no stretch of the
imagination would it be painless.

CUTTING BENEFITS TO MAKE WORK PAY

While the Citizens' Basic Income turns out to be more problematic than it first appears, it does at least point us towards
a real solution.

To begin with, surfing makes things very simple. It sweeps
away all the complexity of fifty different benefits and 20,000
pages of rules, in favour of one universal benefit paid to all,
irrespective of colour, creed or cohabitation arrangements.
And it leaves no doubt that work *will* pay.

And second, it directs us to the third way of breaking the welfare trap, which is to cut benefit levels, and use some of the cash to weaken the trap's hold.

Cutting benefits weakens the welfare trap at a stroke, because even the lowest level of earnings now looks more attractive relative to benefits. But in addition, the cash saved can be used to mitigate the high effective marginal tax rates that give the trap its bite. By saving money on the basic level of benefits, we can afford to withdraw those benefits at a much slower rate as individuals begin to earn their own income.

For example, suppose we dropped the official poverty line from 60 per cent of median income to 50 per cent, cutting the base level of benefits accordingly. For a household wholly dependent on benefits, that would cut their targeted income by 17 per cent. But against that, we'd release enough cash to ensure that nobody faced an effective marginal tax rate above 55 per cent.[190] That would be a vast improvement on the existing marginal rates of 90 per cent and beyond. For many of the jobless, it would make getting a job look at least halfway sensible. True, that's not as powerful as the surfers' Basic Income Guarantee, because we couldn't afford for the poor to keep *all* their benefits irrespective of how much they earned for themselves. But the taper rate would be nothing like as savage as under the current arrangements.

Of course, cutting basic benefit levels for the jobless poor is never going to be easy. The poor may be living at an income level that would have seemed pretty comfortable not that long ago, but as Beveridge himself predicted, they've got used to it. Winding things back is inevitably problematic both for them and for the politicians attempting it.

Nevertheless, this is roughly the approach being attempted

by the coalition government, albeit in a less ambitious form. Under their planned universal credit system, they are aiming to ensure that nobody faces an effective marginal tax rate higher than 76 per cent.[191] And to fund that, they're cutting benefits previously paid to certain groups. They include people who live in expensively subsidised rental accommodation (cuts to housing benefit), and families previously getting more than £26,000 of benefits in total (the benefits cap). They are also axeing some middle-class welfare, including child benefit entitlement for richer families.

The opposition from those who will lose has naturally been intense. But however hard, something like it is unavoidable. We'll come back to this later.

WE EXPECT YOU TO WORK

Let's now look at the Poor Law Commission's other big idea – making benefits subject to tough conditions.

Back in the Golden Age – those fifteen unbroken and unprecedented years of growth from 1992 to 2007 – the British economy created a net 4.7 million new jobs. It was far more than had been created in any previous fifteen-year period in our entire peacetime history. Yet despite that, at the end of 2007 we still had well over 5 million people of working age living entirely on benefits. Something had gone seriously wrong.

Part of the explanation is the welfare trap, and we've just looked at the options for springing that.

But at the same time, the welfare trap only operates because we allow it to. For some reason, we have accepted that the working-age jobless can continue a life on benefits even when there are plenty of jobs available.

The Poor Law Commissioners tackled this problem by

ensuring that welfare was only available subject to onerous conditions. In particular, recipients were to leave their homes and move into the workhouse. And once in the workhouse, they would have to work for their benefits. For the able-bodied, welfare was to be strictly conditional on working for it.

The welfare state established by Attlee's post-war Labour government never incorporated this kind of conditionality. Sure, eligibility for national insurance benefits was made conditional on having worked and paid contributions, but since those who hadn't contributed were always eligible for non-contributory national assistance, that had little practical effect. Making the totality of benefits conditional on working was felt to have no place in the New Jerusalem.

The great William Beveridge – the father of our welfare state – had not wanted this. In his path-breaking 1942 report, he recommended that after six months, unemployment benefit should be conditional on attending a work or training centre.

He argued that benefits 'which are both adequate in amount and indefinite in duration' brought with them the danger 'that men, as creatures who adapt themselves to circumstances, may settle down to them'. He wanted the 'enforcement of the citizen's obligation to seek and accept all reasonable opportunities of work ... [and] to cooperate in measures designed to save him from habituation to idleness'.[192]

Habituation to idleness – there's more than an echo there of the Poor Law Commissioners' Report. Both Beveridge and the Commissioners fully understood the dangers of unconditional welfare. Unfortunately, Attlee's government – and, in fairness, most governments since – chose to ignore those dangers.

Today, a leading proponent of the Beveridge view is
Professor Lawrence Mead of New York University. He's
closely associated with the US policy of workfare, under
which many benefits are time-limited and welfare recipients
have to earn them by actively participating in programmes
designed to get them into paid employment. Those
programmes can include training, rehabilitation and unpaid
work experience. They can also involve longer-term place-
ment in low- or unpaid jobs with community projects, even
just sweeping up leaves.

According to Mead, the big message to everyone on
welfare should be *we expect you to work*.

Mead points to the huge success of workfare in cutting US
welfare rolls. It started to be widely introduced just before
the Golden Age, and whereas Britain's welfare dependency
remained broadly unchanged through that boom, US rolls
fell by an astonishing 70 per cent. And of those who moved
off welfare, 60 per cent moved into paid employment.

Mead describes the approach as 'new paternalism', a
strongly interventionist system that 'helps and hassles'
people back to work, and which 'enforces values that had
broken down'.[193] Even where people are made to work
in unpaid community jobs, the experience gives them a
bridge to the world of paid employment: 'You put people
in those jobs and they rather quickly leave and get jobs in
the private sector. Turns out they could have worked
all along.'

The pay-off is obvious, both to taxpayers and the new
workers themselves. There are costs in terms of additional
administration, but the potential welfare savings are
immense, and Mead's ideas are known to have influenced
the coalition government's thinking.

Inevitably there is a snag. As critics constantly point out, 40 per cent of those who've dropped off the US welfare rolls aren't actually in work. And many are now dependent on US government food stamps to survive. They're certainly not left to starve, but they are worse off than before. Mead says: 'I am concerned about those who do not go to work and that they appear to be worse off. But the critics have not found evidence to say that people are in difficulties.'

There's no way round this. Setting tough new conditions on welfare may persuade the majority of recipients to get a job, but a significant minority are going to fall by the wayside. Some people do not respond to a tougher regime by moving into work as hoped, and we need to acknowledge that.

Clearly, nobody would start from here. But, judging from experience in the US, Australia and elsewhere, welfare reform will make little progress unless we impose tougher conditionality. Mead and the new paternalists reckon that British reformers have spent too much time on the complexities of the welfare trap, and not nearly enough time on hassling the jobless back to work.

That is now finally starting to change, even if the coalition government has steadfastly maintained it has no plans to introduce US-style workfare.

It will not be easy. In welfare reform – as opposed to welfare itself – there are, sadly, no free lunches.

A HARD POUNDING: THE STRUGGLE FOR REFORM

Getting all 6 million of our working-age welfare dependents to support themselves is never going to happen. However much we reform our welfare system, there are people who are genuinely too sick to work, people who are between jobs and lone parents with very young children. Nobody knows how many that might add up to, but most estimates put it at around 2 million or so.

Let's agree that we are not going to walk away from them: they are what used to be called the deserving poor. But for the rest – the other 4 million – we have to reform our system and try to get them into work.

As we've seen, there are no easy fixes. Effective reform means taking those tough decisions the Poor Law Commissioners highlighted two centuries ago:

- We must cut benefits so that work always pays.
- We must make welfare conditional on working.

And once we've taken those decisions, we have to follow through. Our politicians will have to find some way of facing down the opposition that has derailed every previous attempt at reform over the last forty years.

It is encouraging that the coalition government has shown a willingness to grasp some notoriously painful nettles. In their first year, they announced cuts to high-profile working-age benefits, including housing benefit and child benefit. They also changed the basis on which many benefits get uprated for inflation, linking them to the consumer price index (CPI) rather than the retail price index (RPI) – something that will erode their value over time.[194]

But the opposition has been intense and emotional. A cap on housing benefit rates – which during the Labour years had soared – was greeted with accusations of Balkan-style social cleansing. *The Guardian*'s Polly Toynbee foresaw 'a mass exodus of the poor ... all abruptly ejected from their homes, forced to move to the lowest rent, poorest zones all over the country. This is social cleansing on an epic scale.'[195]

Never mind that the previous rules had resulted in taxpayers being fleeced by private landlords, and that most of the properties concerned would not easily find other unsubsidised tenants. Those points got lost in the noise.

Even more radically, the coalition is sweeping away an entire swathe of working-age benefits, replacing them with a single benefit that continues even after the jobless move into work. It's called universal credit, and from 2013 it replaces the previous jumble of working tax credit, child tax credit, housing benefit, income support, income-based jobseeker's allowance and income-related employment and support allowance.[196]

Under the universal credit, work will *always* pay, so the jobless are guaranteed to be better off when they move into work. And the scope for individuals to earn without paying tax will be reinforced by boosting the tax-free personal income allowance to £10,000.

It's a great idea, echoing some of the attractions of the Citizens' Basic Income. But, as always, there will be losers. According to the Institute for Fiscal Studies, they could number 1.4 million families, despite an additional £1.7 billion of taxpayers' cash injected to smooth things along.[197]

More fundamentally, the universal credit still tapers off as the poor earn more for themselves. Someone entering work from joblessness will face an effective marginal tax rate of 65 per cent – that is, she loses 65 pence for every pound she earns, which on the minimum wage leaves her working for £2.12 per hour (2012). And once she's earning enough to pay tax and national insurance, she'll lose 76 pence out of every additional pound, which will leave her working for just £1.46 pence an hour. That's a marked improvement on the current arrangements, but it will still dampen the financial incentive to work.

We're back to the iron triangle of welfare reform. To weaken the welfare trap, we need to leave people with a bigger slice of the cash they earn for themselves. But that costs money – serious money – and the only realistic way of raising it is to cut the basic level of benefits people receive without working.

To get the effective marginal tax rate down to, say, 50 per cent, we'd need to reset the basic level of benefits down from a target 60 per cent of median income to *below* 50 per cent.[198] In a world of fiscal austerity, the trade-off really is that cast-iron.

Two hundred years ago, the Poor Law Commissioners didn't hesitate. They made the sums add up by slashing the level of basic welfare benefits right back to the bone, and beyond. That isn't going to happen today, and nobody suggests it should. But the failure of the universal credit to get marginal tax rates down below the 65-to-76-pence range means that the welfare trap will retain a powerful bite.

Which places a lot of weight on the other leg of the coalition's reforms – helping and hassling the jobless back to work and making welfare conditional on cooperation.

NO, WE REALLY *DO* EXPECT YOU TO WORK

The centrepiece of the coalition's approach to employment is the Work Programme. It replaced all existing welfare-to-work programmes in 2011, and was expected to deal with 3.3 million claimants over the next five years.[199]

It works by using mainly private contractors – such as Ingeus, Serco and Avanta – to help and hassle welfare claimants into jobs. The contractors direct job search, CVs, interview preparation and preparation for a life in work rather than on benefits.

A key feature is that the contractors don't start to make money unless their assigned claimants find and keep a job. Depending on the claimant type, contractors then get between £3,000 and £14,000 for each one who remains in employment for a prescribed period, with further possible incentive payments on top of that.

The government expects contractors will succeed with 36 per cent of claimant referrals. However, the National Audit Office reckons it could be substantially less, and overall success will obviously depend on recovery from the Great Recession.

For claimants, the Work Programme requires their full and active participation. If they fail to comply – for example, by failing to show up for work – they can be 'sanctioned' by having their benefits stopped. And it will no longer be acceptable for claimants to turn down every single job opportunity simply on the basis that it doesn't pay enough, or that it's not the claimant's dream job.

This is nothing like the workhouse, but it is most certainly conditional welfare. And it has naturally generated fierce opposition.

For example, the Mandatory Work Activity Scheme requires claimants to do a month's unpaid work experience if it's felt they're failing to 'demonstrate the focus and discipline necessary to seek out, secure and retain employment opportunities'. Claimants failing to complete their assignment have their benefits stopped for thirteen weeks for a first failure, and six months for a second.

The scheme was greeted with rage across the left-wing media. Requiring claimants to undertake unpaid work experience was branded 'slave labour', especially after it emerged that some of Britain's biggest and most profitable companies were involved. One *Guardian* commentator wrote:

... it's about people effectively working for nothing, not only in charities and the public sector, but in huge retail chains ... Tesco, Poundland, Asda, Boots, Argos, TK Maxx and the Arcadia group (including Topshop and Burton) are involved ... it clearly represents a boon to the kind of multinational giants whose profit margins must be creeping upwards thanks to the plentiful supply of people ... effectively paid a pittance to work for them by the taxpayer.[200]

On the face of it, the accusation sounds plausible enough: companies clearly make more profit if they don't have to pay their staff. But the temporary staff involved here were only assigned to these jobs because they'd already failed to demonstrate focus and discipline. They were not people the companies would have rushed to recruit under normal circumstances, but jobless drifters being given a last-ditch chance to show they were employable. Far from enslavement, these one-month assignments represented a golden opportunity to break into the world of paid employment.

Inevitably, several of the big-name companies offering these opportunities got so rattled by the adverse publicity that they walked away. It closed off a promising avenue for the jobless to get into work, and gave us a vivid demonstration of why conditionality programmes are so difficult to implement.

The difficulty has been even more acute in tackling the 2.6 million on incapacity benefit, the system Frank Field describes as a racket. The coalition has introduced a requirement for claimants to undergo a personal capability assessment with a healthcare professional. And unlike in the past, the focus of the assessment is on the functional effect of the individual's medical condition, rather than the condition itself. The aim is to identify what work a claimant *is* capable of doing, since there is now a 'body of evidence which demonstrates that work can be beneficial for individuals with health conditions and disabilities and may even promote recovery'.[201]

Once again, if claimants refuse to cooperate, they risk losing benefits. And that's difficult, because subjecting genuinely sick people to the stress of reapplying for benefits could make some conditions worse. As a grieving relative said of one man who tragically died from a heart attack shortly after having been passed fit for work, 'the worry put so much pressure on him'.[202]

The problem is that pressure is an essential ingredient of conditionality. With no pressure, there's no hassle, and no overcoming the welfare trap. All that can be done in the case of claimants undergoing these capability assessments is to ensure that those with truly life-threatening conditions are properly identified and dealt with appropriately.

And that is precisely why these decisions are so tough.

WILL WE EVER SORT OUT WELFARE?

Of all the areas where government spends our money, welfare is the most difficult place to save it. Unlike in, say, health or education, we cannot expect to make meaningful savings through improved efficiency. Savings in welfare *always* entail outright losers.

When we increase the pension age, that's an outright loss to those whose pensions are deferred.

When we cut middle-class welfare, that's an outright loss to people who pay huge amounts of tax and get so little in return.

And when we cut welfare for the poor, that's an outright loss to people who already have less than everyone else.

But because the welfare bill is now so large, and because it will go on growing unless we act, cuts are unavoidable.

That is why we somehow have to get the jobless into work. Quite apart from the financial and other benefits they earn for themselves, having them in work cuts the welfare bill, boosts tax revenue and goes a long way towards making our overall tax burden sustainable.

Weakening the welfare trap will not be easy, requiring a prolonged and painful squeeze on basic benefit levels. Helping and hassling the jobless back to work will be even harder, demanding extraordinary resolution in the face of raw emotion.

The decisions are tough, and the road distinctly stony, but given where we're starting from, there really is no alternative. That is, there is no alternative other than ignoring the problem and hoping somehow, sometime, something will turn up ... before we go bust.

NINE

CRIMINAL INJUSTICE

Labour is the party of law and order in Britain today. Tough on crime, tough on the causes of crime.
– Tony Blair, 1997

It's getting dangerous – teenagers are walking up and down the streets, drinking, hiding in corners … people are afraid to leave their own homes, because of what they'll meet … they're too afraid to phone the police, because if the police are seen at their door, word gets back.
– Council estate resident, Lanarkshire, 2012[203]

The maintenance of law and order is a core duty of the state. Indeed, as the political philosopher Thomas Hobbes pointed out four centuries ago, the state's very legitimacy rests on its ability to protect us citizens and our property. If it fails in that, it forfeits our loyalty and loses its right to tax us.

Politicians of all parties have long recognised this as a touchstone issue for electors, and talking tough on crime is a staple of electioneering sound bites. Yet many of us believe our political class and the entire criminal justice system are soft on crime. And despite official statistics apparently showing crime rates falling, nearly two-thirds of us reckon it's rising.

In this chapter we'll look at why we feel that way, and how well we're being served by the police, the courts and our penal system. We'll look at what the government spends and whether we get value for money. And we'll ask how taxpayers could get a better deal.

THE MOST EXPENSIVE SYSTEM IN THE WORLD

You may be surprised to learn that we have the most expensive system of law and order anywhere in the developed world. According to the OECD, government spending on Public Order and Safety costs us 2.6 per cent of our GDP, against an international average of 1.6 per cent. And we not only spend a lot more than our European neighbours, we even spend more than the supposed crime capital of the world, America.[204]

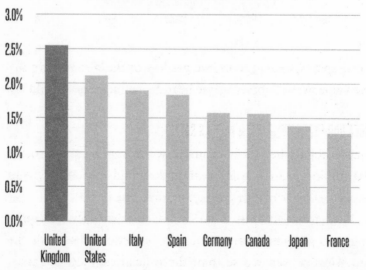

Our Expensive Law And Order
Government expenditure on Public Order and Safety as % of GDP
(2008; source: OECD Government at a Glance)

Our spending has grown rapidly over the years, increasing by nearly 50 per cent in the decade prior to the 2008 crash. And by far the biggest expense is the police, costing us over £19 billion annually, equivalent to £750 per household.[205] But although we now have the world's most expensive system, we have far fewer police officers than most of our neighbours.[206]

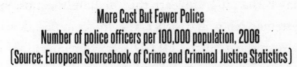

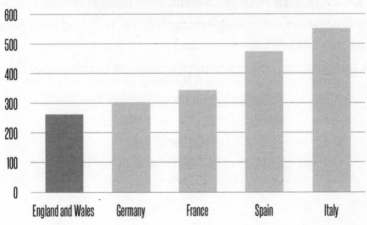

So despite spending most, we get less of the resource we say we value most: bobbies on the beat. Something doesn't add up.

DOES OUR EXPENSIVE SYSTEM KEEP US SAFE?

According to the official estimate, we currently suffer around 10 million crimes every year in England and Wales. And every year, our risk of falling victim is one in five.[207]

Now, for most of us, a one-in-five risk probably feels quite high, so the simple answer to our question is no. But the situation is even worse than the official estimate suggests, because the survey on which it's based – the British Crime Survey (BCS) – doesn't cover all crime, as we'll discuss later.

We're also a lot less safe now than we were back in the days when PC Dixon patrolled Dock Green. The BCS figures don't stretch back that far, but we do have figures for crimes recorded by the police going back over a century.

We should note that the police-recorded crime figures run at less than half the BCS figures, mainly because people don't bother reporting most crime to the police. Moreover, the basis of recording the police statistics changed in the late 1990s. Nevertheless, we can still look back at the long-term trend through the twentieth century up to that point. And it's pretty alarming.

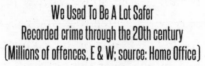

We Used To Be A Lot Safer
Recorded crime through the 20th century
(Millions of offences, E & W; source: Home Office)

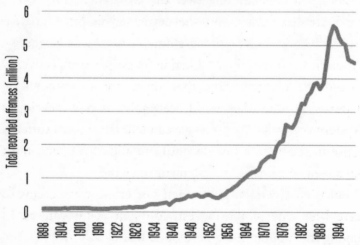

After a long period of stability, crime levels began climbing in the 1930s and continued to rise through the Second World War. But something dramatic happened in the late 1950s to move us onto a wholly different trajectory. In just thirty-five years from 1957 to 1992, police-recorded crime increased *tenfold*.

Of course, there was some population growth through the period, but nowhere near enough to explain that kind of increase. And as the years went by, the police do seem to have recorded a somewhat greater proportion of the offences reported to them. But the big picture is all too clear – in the lifetime of anyone over forty, crime has got a whole lot worse.

Our expensive system of law and order seems to have let us down badly. Taxpayers are suffering a criminal injustice.

THIS IS THE MODERN WORLD – GET USED TO IT

Defenders of the current system often argue that higher crime is a fact of modern life, so we'd better just get used to it. Whether because we invented rock and roll, or TV, or we stopped going to church, or any of the many other standard sociological explanations, over the last half-century, crime has increased right across the developed world. Our own crime rate simply reflects these international trends, and we should learn to put the problem in its proper perspective.

And it's perfectly true that there are some common patterns around the world, certainly among developed Western countries. As far as we can tell, all of them suffered a rise in recorded crime up until the mid-1990s, and most have seen some modest abatement since then.

But even if we allow for that, our crime wave seems to have been one of the biggest. And our crime rate ranks among the highest in the developed world.

For example, in 2010 the United Nations Office on Drugs and Crime published statistics on crime rates across more than 100 countries.[208] It looked at police-recorded crime for six major groups of offences – assault, rape, robbery, burglary, vehicle theft and kidnapping. The results were stark: for all six crimes, it placed England and Wales in the top quartile (that is, the crime rate in England and Wales was among the highest 25 per cent of all countries worldwide). Scotland was little better, being in the top quartile for five of the six offences.

Now, there are difficulties in comparing crime rates across countries. Not only do the definitions of crime vary, but recording and reporting standards also vary, especially as between developed and underdeveloped countries.

But even if we confine the comparison to our near neighbours in Europe, the statistics suggest our crime rates are high. The Council of Europe has a large-scale project that collects and publishes European crime statistics.[209] And out of thirty-six European countries, it currently places Scotland fourth highest for overall crime, with England and Wales close behind in fifth place. Here's how we compare to some of our nearest neighbours:

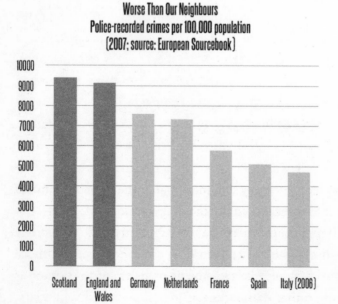

Worse Than Our Neighbours
Police-recorded crimes per 100,000 population
(2007; source: European Sourcebook)

So, while crime has increased everywhere since the 1950s, among comparable nations we seem to suffer more than most.

WHY DON'T WE BELIEVE THE GOVERNMENT'S CRIME STATS?

It's a constant frustration of Home Secretaries that most of us don't believe their official crime statistics. According to the official version – the British Crime Survey – crime has halved since its peak in 1995, and is now back lower than it was thirty years ago.[210]

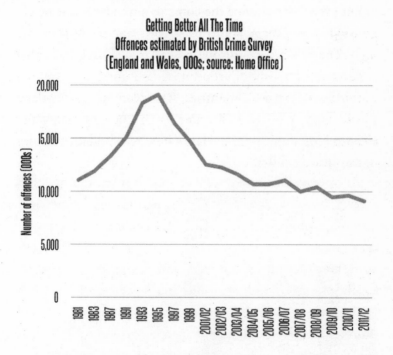

On the face of it, governments and the criminal justice system have succeeded in tackling crime, and, while not complacent, they are to be congratulated for delivering. But we don't believe it. According to the very same official survey, something like two-thirds of us think that crime is increasing rather than falling.

How can that be? How can so many of us believe crime is rising, when the official statistics tell us it's falling?

The liberal media reckons it's because we've been misled by ... well ... the media. As *The Guardian*'s Polly Toynbee put it:

> ... crime has plunged by more than 40 per cent over the last decade. The BCS finds that the chance of being a victim of crime is now at its lowest since the survey began...
>
> ... And yet Britain is more alarmed by crime than the rest of the west, with the least confidence its government is 'cracking down' ... Fear stoked by the media impels politicians to distort priorities and waste a fortune on what doesn't work.[211]

These commentators claim we're deluded about the extent of crime. We're suffering from what they term a 'moral panic', and we haven't grasped the real facts, which unequivocally show crime is falling.

It's a patronising view of our intelligence, and a rather trusting view of the survey figures. Media reports certainly help shape our perceptions, with 59 per cent of BCS respondents citing TV and radio as sources.[212] But few of us believe everything we see on the telly, and we surely place more weight on our own observations and experience.

Over recent years almost everyone has personally suffered from crime. In the case of our own household over the last ten years, that's meant three burglaries, one theft from a vehicle, one assault and numerous instances of antisocial behaviour. The neighbours have had similar experiences, and just down the road there was a cold-blooded murder that remains unsolved to this day. It feels like a lot of crime, especially since we live in what's officially a low-crime area.

And even if we accept there's been some reduction since

the peak, that's not a lot of comfort. To start with, much of the fall can be ascribed to one-off factors, such as better vehicle security, or home electronics getting too cheap to burgle, which cannot be extrapolated into the future. More fundamentally, any fall in headline crime over the last fifteen years is nowhere near enough to reverse the surge over the previous thirty. Many of us can recall when crime was *very* much lower than it is today.

And it isn't just us dumb victims who think the official figures understate the true extent of crime. Having reviewed both the police-recorded crime statistics and the figures from the British Crime Survey, the government's own National Statistician – the top statistician in the land – concluded: '... neither series produces, nor can they ever produce, a count of "total" crime'.[213]

Although the British Crime Survey is more comprehensive than the police statistics, it too understates the true extent of crime. It's based on an annual poll of 50,000 adults, where respondents are asked about their experiences as victims of crime – whether or not those crimes have been reported to the police. But it has several serious gaps.

For one thing, it limits the number of offences recorded for any one respondent to six, even if the victim has actually suffered more. Second, it doesn't cover those living in communal establishments such as hostels and student halls of residence, even though such people are especially likely to be victims of crime. Third, it doesn't cover crimes against businesses or commercial premises and vehicles, a category that includes, for example, shoplifting.

The fast-growing area of cyber crime is also reckoned to be under-recorded, and, until recently, crimes against children were missed out altogether. Finally, the BCS excludes those most serious crimes of all – murder and manslaughter – on account of the victims not being available to answer the survey questions. Overall, it's likely that the BCS understates the true number of crimes by millions.

As for the police-recorded crime statistics, there is evidence of manipulation by police chiefs under pressure to deliver results. For example, the offence of being drunk and disorderly does not get reported in the violent crime statistics, whereas its close relative, the so-called Section 5 Public Order Offence, does. So chiefs under pressure to cut violent crime have in the past encouraged their officers to opt for the unreported offence. It's called 'gaming the system'.[214]

It's hardly surprising we don't trust the crime stats.

THE COST OF CRIME

We should never underestimate the cost of crime in terms of personal distress and fear, but we can also look at it in terms of cash. And that's useful in evaluating what the government spends on protecting us.

Back in 2000, the Home Office published an estimate of the overall cost of crime in England and Wales.[215] It was based on a detailed calculation of costs for each main type of crime, including the emotional and physical cost to victims, the value of lost output, health service costs, loss and damage to property, security and insurance costs and, of course, costs to the criminal justice system itself. The estimated price tag on individual crimes ranged from £1.1 million for homicide, right down to £100 for theft from a shop.

Overall, based on the number of crimes estimated by the British Crime Survey in 1999, the annual cost of crime was put at £60 billion.

Unfortunately, the Home Office has not published an

updated total figure since 2000. If we believe the British Crime Survey, the cost ought to have fallen because crime has come down. But against that, we know that the Home Office has revised upwards its cost estimates for crimes inflicted on individuals and households.[216] And, factoring in the inflation we've had since 2000, the best guess is that the comparable figure today stands somewhere in the range of £60–£80 billion.

Which suggests that, on average, crime costs every family in the country something like £3,000 every single year. And even if an individual family has a crime-free year, it will still be paying the price in terms of higher home and car insurance premiums, higher prices charged by shops and, of course, higher taxes to pay for our criminal justice system.

THE THIN (BUT EXPENSIVE) BLUE LINE

So far we've seen that, despite spending more on law and order than any other developed country in the world, crime remains a serious problem. Recorded crime has increased hugely over the last half-century, our official statistics substantially understate the true extent of crime, and our crime rate is higher than any of our near neighbours. Crime costs the average family around £3,000 per year.

It's a familiar picture. Yet again the government is spending our money but failing to deliver results. And we need to know why.

We'll start with the police. The thin blue line is widely believed – not least by the police themselves – to be our strongest defence against lawlessness. Most of us feel safer with a visible police presence, and for years we've been pleading for more 'bobbies on the beat'. Yet, as we've seen, compared to other countries we have relatively few officers.

The last Labour government tried to address this by

ramping up police budgets. Between 1996/7 and 2009/10, spending rose by nearly 50 per cent in real inflation-adjusted terms. Yet the extra money did not get reflected in increased police visibility on the streets.

To start with, despite the 50 per cent budget boost, the number of police officers increased by only 13 per cent (England and Wales).[217] Police chiefs reckoned they could get better value by adopting a new staffing model known as 'mixed economy policing', under which they switched from real police officers to cheaper, less trained civilian staff. So, between 1997 and 2010, the proportion of officers on the payroll fell from nearly 70 per cent to under 60 per cent.

Moreover, from 2002 onwards, police forces began replacing real officers (known as sworn officers) with a new breed of cheaper semi-police, known as Police Community Support Officers (PCSOs). They are uniformed to look roughly like real police, but they don't have the same powers of arrest and detention. And neither do they have the same level of training. Their police colleagues reportedly refer to them as 'numpties in yellow jackets'.[218]

The driver behind these changes was cost: police officers are very expensive. The average annual pay up to the rank of sergeant is now nearly £40,000, around 50 per cent higher than average earnings across the country. Add in the cost to employers of generous police pensions and employers' national insurance contributions, and the final price tag comes to nearly £55,000.

On top of that, the police have long enjoyed terms and conditions that have been the envy of workers elsewhere. These limit police flexibility and increase costs, with numerous reports of officers having to be paid extra for doing things that most people would take as a normal part of the job (for example, answering the phone while off-duty).[219] Inside the force they're known as Ts & Cs, but to outsiders they bear a striking resemblance to the old 'Spanish practices' that once hobbled entire swathes of British industry.

With civilian staff and PCSOs cheaper and more flexible than traditional officers, it's hardly surprising that the thin blue line is getting thinner. Our policemen and women charge far too much for their services, and they're being replaced by cheaper – though not necessarily more effective – alternatives.

WHERE ARE ALL THE COPS?

We may have fewer police than other countries, and they may be getting replaced by cheaper staff, but we've still got nearly 140,000 of them in England and Wales.[220] Surely we'd expect to see more of them pounding the beat.

One reason we don't is the age-old problem of 'paperwork'. That's been the bane of a policeman's lot ever since Robert Peel, but under the last Labour government it got a lot worse. Complex new Whitehall targets required complex new record keeping, with ambitious programmes to rid the police of institutionalised racism, sexism and homophobia generating yet more paperwork. It's officially estimated that officers now spend around 20 per cent of their time on it.[221]

But much more disturbing than paperwork is that the proportion of officers available on the frontline is extremely small. According to Her Majesty's Inspectorate of Constabulary (HMIC), out of the 155,000 police officers and PCSOs employed in England and Wales, on average, fewer than 19,000 are 'visible and available' at any one time – a mere 12 per cent of the workforce.[222]

So where are all the others? Where are the other 136,000

police employed by us but not 'visible and available' to protect us? What on earth are they all doing?

To start with, around one-third of the workforce is employed in back-office support roles well away from the frontline.

Second, to provide 24/7 cover – as the police are required to do – they currently have to employ five officers for every one officer actually on duty. Basic police shift hours are just thirty-seven hours per week, and availability is further reduced by holidays, rest days, sick leave, training and court appearances.

Everybody agrees there's scope for substantial efficiency improvements. Even the chairman of the Police Federation – the police trade union – acknowledges that 'efficiency savings can be made and we could operate with ... 12 per cent cuts'. Not only could more police officers be deployed on the frontline rather than in the back office, but also shift patterns could be reformed to make better use of the officers already on the payroll. And in fairness, budget cuts are forcing many police forces to do precisely that: for example, North Yorkshire recently introduced a new shift system that cut the number of annual rest days by fourteen.

But Ts & Cs mean it's a long hard struggle, and the problem isn't simply one of getting more of our police visibly onto the streets. There's also the small matter of what they do when they get there. As we all saw graphically illustrated during the August 2011 riots in London and elsewhere, a mere police presence on the streets is no longer enough to deter crime. They also need to act robustly. Whether it's called 'zero tolerance' or 'early intervention', the police need to be seen to nip crime in the bud before it escalates.

And then we come to the thorny issue of detecting crime once it's happened.

LOW DETECTION RATES

According to the Home Office, the detection rate for police-recorded crime is currently 28 per cent.[223] That is, of the 4 million or so crimes recorded by the police, just over 1 million were 'cleared up' with the offender receiving what's known as a sanction.

This measured detection rate has increased somewhat over the last ten years, but a 28 per cent rate is still not impressive. Even taken at face value, it implies offenders have only around a one-in-four chance of being caught and punished. But since the police-recorded crime statistics seriously understate the true extent of crime, the real detection rate is even lower – certainly less than half the official figure.

Moreover, the results are flattered by certain crimes that more or less solve themselves. For example, drugs offences have a stunning 94 per cent detection rate, but that's because most offences only come to light when the police apprehend the offender. If we exclude drugs offences, the overall 28 per cent detection rate immediately falls to 24 per cent.

It's a similar case with crimes of violence, where the detection rate is put at 45 per cent. In many cases, the police have been called to the incident and easily identified the offenders, or the victim may know the perpetrator. If we exclude crimes of violence as well as drugs offences from the calculation, the overall detection rate falls to just 18 per cent.

So for the three-quarters of recorded crime excluding drugs and violence – largely crimes against our property – the average detection rate is less than one in five. As a burglar, your chance of being caught and punished is no more than one in eight, and that's assuming the householder bothers to report the crime to the police in the first place.

It's generally accepted that detection rates used to be much higher. The current Home Office statistics go back to 1988, when the rate was 35 per cent. Fifty years ago, it's reckoned the rate was 50 per cent or more. This is another crucial government service that's been heading in the wrong direction.

CRIME AND NOT MUCH PUNISHMENT

Let's suppose you commit a crime. It's not murder, it's not the Brink's-MAT robbery, and it's not recklessly obstructing access to a bat roost.[224] It's an average kind of crime – maybe one of the 5 million-odd thefts that take place every year. What are your chances of getting caught and punished?

As we've seen, there's a greater than 50 per cent chance your victim won't even report it to the police. And even if they do, there's only a one-in-four chance you'll be tracked down and apprehended. So nine times out of ten – *nine times out of ten* – you'll never hear another word about it.

But let's suppose you're unlucky, and you get collared. There's still a very good chance you'll get let off with a police caution, a warning or a fixed penalty notice – otherwise known as a mild slap on the wrist. In 2009, only 55 per cent of police-detected crimes led to a charge or summons.[225]

But again, let's assume you're unlucky and you're in that 55 per cent. You're formally charged and your case is passed onto the Crown Prosecution Service, who decide whether to prosecute. In over a third of cases they decide against proceeding, so only about one-third of the original police detected crimes end up court.

You're really unlucky now, because you're one of those cases. And worse, you're then among the four-fifths of court cases ending in a guilty verdict. Which means the fates have really got it in for you, my friend, because *well* under 5 per cent of crimes end in a court conviction.

So now you're standing in the dock, awaiting sentence. Maybe it will be ten years' hard labour in HMP Dartmoor. Not a chance. Just a quarter of convicted criminals standing in the dock receive custodial sentences, which in 2009 meant 80,000 receiving average sentences of about sixteen months.

To summarise, of the nearly 10 million offences estimated by the British Crime Survey, less than 1 per cent end up being punished by custodial sentences.

And even that's not the end of it. While you might assume your sentence of sixteen months means you'll stay in prison for sixteen months, it doesn't. The astonishing reality is that offenders sent to prison for less than four years are released automatically *and unconditionally* after serving just half their sentence in custody. So for most prisoners, sixteen months actually means eight months.

Even prisoners serving longer sentences for more serious crimes are generally eligible for automatic parole after serving two-thirds of their sentence. And they can be released before then if they manage to convince the parole board they aren't a threat to the community outside – something that many dangerous criminals have managed to do with ease, only to offend again after release.

This issue was brought into sharp focus by the horrific murder of City financier John Monckton on his own doorstep on 2004. His killer had been released early from a twelve-year sentence for attempted murder, even though he had been assessed as 90 per cent likely to commit more violence. And that wasn't a one-off aberration: it later emerged that there had been ninety-eight murders by dangerous criminals out on licence in the community just in the two years around Mr Monckton's death.[226]

Even convicted murderers are routinely released back

among us. They may have been given what are termed mandatory life sentences, but in reality they're out and about in an average of fourteen years, with many released even earlier.[227]

So we've ended up with a criminal justice system that catches very few criminals, and those it does catch generally escape with little punishment.

Now, we all have our own ideas about the morality of punishment, and we're never going to agree on that. But one thing we should all agree is that lighter punishments mean less deterrence.

And deterrence surely ought to be a key function of our criminal justice system. The penalties for crime should be sufficient to act as a deterrent for anyone tempted to offend. True, we also need proportionality: nobody thinks we should hang people for parking offences, or even stealing a sheep. But we do expect the law to impose deterrent sentences, and we expect the penalties to increase markedly for persistent offenders.

Deterrent sentences are particularly important when the chances of being caught and convicted are so small. After all, if you know your chance of being punished is small, we should surely counterbalance that with the certain knowledge of a heavier punishment if you do get unlucky. It should be like the National Lottery – a small chance of your number coming up, but a big result if it does.

Which is why the current system seems so wrong. And why, despite spending more than everyone else, we still have more crime. In terms of keeping us safe, the cash is being misdirected.

PRISON WORKS

As a crime fighter, by far the most successful Home Secretary in our lifetimes was Michael Howard, who held the post from 1993 to 1997. When he took over, crime was soaring:

according to the British Crime Survey, it had increased by over 50 per cent in a decade. But in just two years he turned the tide, and, by the time he left office, crime rates were firmly on a downward track.

His basic formula was straightforward, and he spelled it out right at the start:

> Prison works. It ensures that we are protected from murderers, muggers and rapists – and it makes many who are tempted to commit crime think twice ... This may mean that more people will go to prison. I do not flinch from that. We shall no longer judge the success of our system of justice by a fall in our prison population.[228]

To back his policy, Howard initiated a major prison-building programme, and prisoner numbers increased sharply. It was a spectacular success.

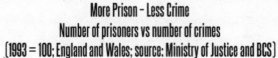

More Prison – Less Crime
Number of prisoners vs number of crimes
(1993 = 100; England and Wales; source: Ministry of Justice and BCS)

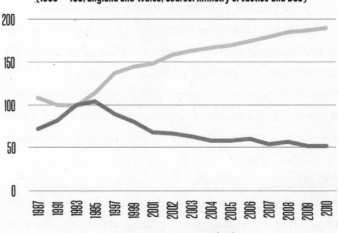

We really couldn't ask for a more powerful demonstration of prison's effectiveness. In terms of keeping us safe, it looks like the proverbial no-brainer. For most of us, the obvious question is: why don't we lock up even more criminals and cut even more crime?

But, amazingly, that isn't how everyone sees it. Despite its obvious success, Howard's policy outraged the liberal media and, more worryingly, the legal profession. He was excoriated for pandering to the 'hang 'em and flog 'em brigade' (that's the electorate, by the way), and accused of dragging British justice back to the Dark Ages. He was especially targeted by the BBC, culminating in a notorious interview with Jeremy Paxman when he was asked the same question twelve times in an apparent attempt to impugn his integrity.[229]

So let's look at the arguments against prison.

ARGUMENT ONE: PRISON COSTS TOO MUCH

Anti-prison campaigners argue that putting criminals behind bars is an expensive and ultimately ineffective way of tackling crime. It is expensive because prison places are costly ('dearer than Eton' is a common benchmark). And it is ineffective because prison fails to reform and rehabilitate, with many released prisoners reoffending within months.

Far better, it is claimed, to focus our major effort on non-custodial community sentences. Not only are they a lot cheaper, but a good probation service has a much better chance of reforming offenders if they remain part of the community at large.

Well, we must accept that our prison places are expensive – appallingly so. According to the Ministry of Justice, each one costs an average £45,000 annually, which makes Eton fees a snip at £31,000. It also seems a lot compared to our cheapest prisons: many of them cost far less than the average, and one high-profile US sheriff accommodates his prisoners in army surplus tents, cutting costs considerably.[230]

But even if each additional prisoner does cost us £45,000, we need to set that against the estimated £60–£80 billion overall annual cost of crime.

Ten years ago, the Home Office published some very interesting research showing how imprisoning more criminals could cut crime.[231] Drawing on their own detailed record of everyone convicted of a serious offence since 1963, they worked out that half of all serious crime is committed by just 100,000 hardcore repeat offenders. The group evolves over time, with fresh 'recruits' replacing those who 'retire', but it seems to remain at around 100,000.

Now, with multiple convictions, these people are all well known to the authorities. And they're responsible for half of all serious crime. Yet despite that, at any one time, only 20 per cent are in prison. The vast majority are out and about among us, free to carry on offending. It makes no sense.

Let's do the arithmetic. To lock up 100 per cent of these hardcore criminals would require an additional 80,000 prison places. At £45,000 per place, that would cost £3.6 billion annually. But against that, we could expect a huge reduction in crime. If the Home Office research is right, crime would halve, and we'd save £30–£40 billion.[232]

It's no contest. Whatever anti-prison campaigners may claim, the cost argument against prison simply doesn't hold water.

ARGUMENT TWO: PRISON DOESN'T REHABILITATE

Anti-prison campaigners argue that prison fails to rehabilitate prisoners. Getting on for half of them are reconvicted of new offences within just twelve months of release, so prison has failed.

And that's undeniably true. But the real question is whether the alternative of probation is any better.

On the plus side, it does appear that reconviction rates are a bit lower for offenders given community sentences compared to those sent to jail. According to the Ministry of Justice, it's around 10 percentage points lower than for those sent to prison.[233]

However, that still leaves nearly 50 per cent of those on community sentences reconvicted of a new offence within two years. And over nine years the reconviction rate is a shocking 70 per cent (2000 to 2009). That's not effective rehabilitation. Moreover, there's a danger of comparing apples and pears: we'd surely expect the reconviction rate for community convicts to be a bit lower because they tend to be the ones who are selected by the courts as being less likely to reoffend in the first place.

And then there's the credibility of the £1 billion per annum probation service being able to deliver the promised community rehabilitation. Its record is not good, as highlighted in the National Audit Office (NAO) report on community orders (the flagship scheme under which offenders are ordered to undertake unpaid community work, such as painting and decorating, gardening, environmental clean-up projects, graffiti removal or work with charities).[234]

Clearly, such a scheme can only succeed if offenders actually turn up to do the work, and in theory the probation officers (or 'Offender Managers' as they're now known) are supposed to see that they do. Yet in practice, the NAO discovered that non-attendance is rife, with officers apparently being prepared to accept any old excuse, including oversleeping and self-certified 'sickness'. Enforcement standards are hugely variable and record keeping shambolic.

The reality is that both prisons and the probation service do an equally shocking job of rehabilitating criminals. Whether they've been sent to jail or given a community sentence, the vast majority of convicts sooner or later reoffend.

And there's a very good reason why rehabilitation is such a flop – nobody actually knows how to do it. The NAO report looked at ten widely used rehabilitation programmes, and found little evidence of success for *any* of them. To be sure, some drug treatments can help people off drugs, but whether they help people off crime is another matter entirely.

Whatever campaigners may claim, we simply don't know how to reform habitual criminals. Until we do, the law-abiding majority would be much better off and much safer if we simply locked such people away for good.

COST-EFFECTIVE JUSTICE

Getting on for half of all newly released convicts are reconvicted of a new offence (or, more likely, several new offences) within a year.[235] After eight years, more than 80 per cent have been reconvicted.[236] And that just relates to *convictions*, which, as we've already seen, are far fewer than the offences actually committed.

So why take the chance? Why do we release these people back into the community knowing that the vast majority will inflict yet more grief on us?

One argument is that not everyone who gets sent to jail is necessarily a habitual criminal. We all make mistakes, and everyone surely deserves a second chance. That's a fair point, especially when an offender is young, and the offences non-life-threatening. But repeat offenders put themselves into an entirely different category. By reoffending after release, they show that they're unable to control their own behaviour.

'Three strikes and you're out' is a sentencing policy that took off in the United States during the 1990s. The idea is that once someone has been convicted of a serious offence three times, they've shown that they cannot be trusted out on the streets, and the safest thing for everyone else is for them to spend the rest of their lives behind bars.

According to our own official statistics, someone who has already received three previous jail sentences is nearly 60 per cent more likely to be reconvicted within one year of release.[237] That's a risk the rest of us should not be made to run. A three-strikes policy would ensure that we didn't.

As we've seen, our current justice system is not cost-effective. It's more expensive than other systems yet delivers worse results.

Part of the explanation is that our police are high cost and inefficient. There's no easy fix for that, because, unlike with other public services, we can't easily open policing to choice and competition. But we can at least make the police more accountable to the communities they serve, which should help concentrate minds. And that is the idea behind the recent introduction of elected police commissioners.

But our fundamental problem is that we allow persistent criminals to remain in the community. We could get much better value by keeping them locked up, and a straightforward way to implement such a policy would be 'three strikes and you're out'.

Of course, the prison population would expand, and that would cost us – perhaps £3–4 billion annually, as we discussed earlier. But we could recoup the bulk of that cost by cutting the £25 billion we currently spend on the probation service, our courts and the police. And any net addition over and above that would be a small fraction of the prospective tens of billions of savings we'd make from having less crime.

We can no longer afford the luxury of having 100,000 persistent criminals roaming free among us.

TEN

SPENDING MORE THAN WE NEED

Of all the vulgar arts of government, that of solving every difficulty that might arise by thrusting the hand into the public purse is the most illusory and contemptible.
– Sir Robert Peel, nineteenth-century Prime Minister

We've now reviewed three-quarters of government spending, and we've found massive waste and inefficiency throughout. From healthcare to education to welfare to law and order, the waste is everywhere.

We've also seen how our government often spends more than its international counterparts yet gets worse results. Overall spending is higher than the average across the developed world, higher than Germany and considerably higher than the United States and Japan.[238] And even if you believe that all governments are wasteful, ours seems to be more wasteful than others.

The obvious conclusion is that our government is spending more than we need. If we could emulate the world's government efficiency leaders we could get better results for less cash. And we can start by recognising that size really does matter.

BIG IS BAD

Over recent years, a number of studies have compared the costs and performance of governments around the world.

On the cost side they've looked at government spending as a percentage of national income. But on the performance side there's no readily available single measure, because, despite all the money governments spend, they've been singularly reluctant to produce meaningful measures of their output. They've asked us to take it on trust.

So the authors of these studies have gone back to first principles and asked: what are the key things government is trying to achieve? Once that's decided, they measure success in each of those areas individually and produce an overall average performance score for each country.

A widely quoted study from the European Central Bank identifies seven main government objectives: economic growth, economic stability, a fair income distribution, an educated population, a healthy population, good public administration and good public infrastructure. For each of those objectives, the authors identify one or more statistical measures of achievement. For example, fair income distribution is measured as the income share of the poorest 40 per cent, and education is measured as secondary school enrolment rates combined with educational attainment levels.

What the study finds is that countries with small governments – defined as governments spending less than 40 per cent of national income – tend to outperform those with big governments (those spending 50 per cent or more) across most areas, especially on economic performance. The only area where most countries with big governments substantially outperform is in having a more equal income distribution.

Comparing performance against costs points to a clear conclusion on the relative efficiency of big and small governments.

> 'Small' governments post the highest efficiency amongst industrialised countries. Differences are considerable as 'small' governments on average post a 40 per cent higher score than 'big' governments.
>
> In summary, we find that differences in efficiency are much more pronounced than in performance across countries, with 'small' governments clearly outranking the others. This illustrates that the size of government may be too large in many industrialised countries.[239]

We can see the pattern by charting each country's public sector efficiency score against the cost of its government relative to GDP: the more government spends, the less efficient it is.[240]

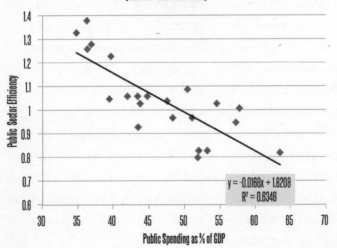

Big is Bad
Public sector efficiency vs public spending across 22 developed economies
(Source: OECD and ECB)

$y = -0.0166x + 1.8208$
$R^2 = 0.6346$

As spending increases, output of things like health and education does not increase commensurately, and the higher tax to pay for the spending starts to undermine economic performance quite seriously.

Now, nobody is saying this is a mechanistic relationship, and the authors of these studies present their results as indicative. Moreover, overall performance differences will clearly reflect other factors as well as government spending. But the big picture on value for money is pretty clear: big is bad. Very bad.

£140 BILLION OF WASTE

According to these international studies, the world leaders in government efficiency are the US, Japan, Australia and Switzerland. Their governments are on average around 20 per cent more efficient than ours. If our government could somehow match those leaders, we'd save something like £140 billion annually. That's over £5,000 for every single family. Or, put another way, it's enough to abolish income tax for everyone earning less than £50,000. It's cash we're effectively wasting because our government's efficiency falls short of what others achieve.

So, if it can be done, how come our government fails to do it?

One factor leaps out: all four of these top-performing governments spend a lot less than ours. On average over the last ten years they have spent 36 per cent of GDP, whereas our government has spent 46 per cent.[241] To match their performance we need to radically downsize our government.

And that's the key message from these international studies. To cut the waste, we have to cut the proportion of GDP spent by the government.

In broad terms, taking one year with another, we need to get spending down well below 40 per cent of GDP, back to where it was in the late 1990s. And unfortunately, with no meaningful economic growth in sight, that means cutting spending – by around one-fifth from current levels.

Of course, that's easy to say and much harder to do. There would be losers, and they would resist fiercely. And there'd be cutbacks in our public services, with the most inefficient operations closing. We'd all have to get used to government doing less.

The real issue is what we'd have to give up. We'd have more efficient services, but would there be enough to go round? To answer that, we have to take a closer look at why the government currently spends as much as it does. And we'll start with public services.

GOVERNMENT AS A SERVICE PROVIDER

The idea of government as service provider goes back to the English Civil War. With the monarchy overthrown, there was an urgent need to find some new basis for political legitimacy, and the philosopher Thomas Hobbes came up with the notion of a service contract. As we saw in the previous chapter, this says that the state and its citizens have entered into an implied contract, under which the citizens give up some of the freedom they enjoyed 'in a state of nature' in exchange for the state protecting them. The citizens accept the impositions of the state – including its taxes – but the state must maintain law and order and keep the country safe from foreign foes. The state's legitimacy rests on its success in providing those services.

In the case of law and war, they are clearly services only the state can provide, and for the following 200 years that's pretty well all it *did* provide. But in Queen Victoria's reign, governments extended their reach significantly. Industrialisation and the rapid growth of cities threw up new challenges in areas like public health and working conditions. The emergence of strong new competitors – especially Germany – raised fears that Britain was slipping behind in education and science.

It was then that governments began building what we now refer to as the public services. A civilian police force was established, government schools were opened, school attendance was made compulsory and existing educational provision increasingly brought under central control. Local government was hugely strengthened, and its responsibilities widened to include roads, sanitation, water supplies, energy supplies, housing, education, healthcare, poor relief and a host of others things. In the twentieth century the process gathered pace, with many local services – including healthcare – centralised, and the addition of state pension and insurance services.

Today, most of us see such services as vital to our lives, and we could not imagine life without them. But what we don't always grasp is that wanting the service does not imply that the government has to provide it. Government doesn't provide our food or insure our cars, and it doesn't automatically follow that it should provide our education and healthcare.

Indeed, back in the nineteenth century, many of our so-called public services already existed before government got involved. From education to healthcare to incapacity benefits, a lot was already being done by churches, charities and individuals. And there's every reason to think they'd have done more if they hadn't been crowded out by government.[242]

On top of that, many public services are also available from competing private sector suppliers. A substantial minority of us already buy private health insurance, private education, private pensions and private redundancy insurance. Private security services are booming and more than 40 per cent of us subscribe to Sky TV as a supplement to the state broadcaster.

Moreover, many of these private services are miles better than their public sector equivalents. Hospitals are cleaner, waiting lists are shorter, exam results are better and Sky offers sports and movies not available on the BBC.

In fact, the only thing that holds us back from buying more privately is that we can't afford to pay twice. We have to stick with the state services because the taxes to pay for them leave most of us without enough cash to go private. In effect, the government locks us into its services, whether we want them or not. Instead of allowing us to choose our own providers, like we choose our preferred supermarket, it has imposed an effective monopoly.

Monopolies are rarely in the interests of consumers, having little incentive to deliver good service but every incentive to charge extortionate prices. And that's why we have a raft of rules and regulations to control them and protect consumers from abuse. But the rules only apply to private sector monopolies: the government permits *itself* to be as monopolistic as it likes. Or, more precisely, it charges us for its services whether we use them or not, something private sector monopolists can only dream about.

We need to ask how this can possibly make sense for *us*, the paying customers. We need to know how the government can justify its monopoly services.

STATE MONOPOLY IS GOOD BECAUSE...

Over the years we've heard a range of justifications.

Some argue that public provision is cheaper and more efficient. They reckon the state can do things more cheaply than the private sector because the state can achieve really big economies of scale. Or rather, there are big economies of scale to be had, and only the state can be trusted to run the monopoly required to achieve them. That was the argument for our old nationalised industries, like British Telecom, which were often described as 'natural monopolies'. Yet as soon as we dismantled them, we discovered that services improved and we no longer had to wait years for a new phone line.

The modern variant is that state monopolies avoid all the wasteful duplication we get with competing private sector suppliers. And by excluding private suppliers we also avoid our cash being 'plundered for private profit'. This is an argument often made for the NHS.

It's not convincing. Those supposedly inefficient, profit-plundering private healthcare providers routinely supply services to the NHS more cheaply than the NHS can produce them for itself. And even if government provision does cost less than competing private provision, that doesn't mean it's a better deal. Lower cost often means lower provision, and the size of the bill tells us nothing about quality and value for money. Whatever might be theoretically possible, in practice the public sector is hugely inefficient.

Another traditional justification is that the state *has* to provide certain things, because left to ourselves we'd end up buying less than we need. For example, Hobbes's core functions of defence and law and order are difficult to charge for individually. As individuals we might decide not to buy any, hoping to free ride on the backs of fellow citizens who have. And if we all did that, we'd be left with neither defence, nor policing, nor street lighting, nor a number of other things.

Economists label these things public goods, and it's long been accepted that they have to be provided by government and paid for out of taxation. However, the range of true public goods is pretty limited, and defence and law and order amount to just one-tenth of current government spending. The argument certainly cannot justify anything like the current total.

A related justification says that government should provide certain things free because we all benefit if everyone has them. Classic examples are immunisation against infectious diseases, and public health measures like sanitation. We can extend the argument to state education – at least up to lower secondary level – because we all benefit if everyone has a shared level of literacy and other basic skills.[243]

Then there's the nanny-knows-best justification. Nanny says that her services are so valuable that everyone should be forced to partake of them, whether or not they'd choose to do so. Again, education is the usual example, with the government overriding short-sighted parents who might deny their children school. But while nanny is right to protect children against negligent or abusive adults, that's not the same as protecting adults against themselves. She's over-reaching herself when she orders us to take a daily dose of castor oil – especially if she pays for it out of our taxes.

The fact is that none of these arguments comes close to justifying the current level of state spending. Few of us believe that government delivers services more efficiently than the market sector, and while we can agree on the need for public goods like defence, government immunisation programmes and some level of support for educational provision, we could get all of that for a fraction of what government currently spends.

No, the real justification for the present scale of spending is nothing to do with cost saving, or public goods, or shared benefits, or nanny-knows-best, or any of the other points we've just been through. And it's certainly not about the delivery of outstanding service. The real justification is what Tony Blair used to call 'social justice in action'.

GOVERNMENT SPENDING AS SOCIAL JUSTICE

A century ago, when Lloyd George introduced Bismarck's state benefits scheme to Britain, his Cabinet colleague Winston Churchill memorably described it as being like a safety net, below which none should fall, but above which all could rise.

A tax-funded safety net was controversial at the time, but these days almost all of us support it. We don't want to live in a society where the old and the sick, or the unemployed, can fall into destitution. But today's welfare state has moved a long way beyond the safety net and it's been driven by a very different philosophy.

The left's justification for welfare spending is rooted in Marx's famous slogan 'from each according to his ability, to each according to his need': we stand or fall in equality and solidarity, and what you consume should be based on need not earning power. Of course, as last century's events horrifically demonstrated, Marxism doesn't actually work in the real world, so today's left promotes a gentler message. It emphasises the benefits we all get from living in a fair and decent society, and our collective responsibility for maintaining it.

For example, the left-wing commentator Polly Toynbee has likened society to a caravan trekking across the desert: to survive the journey we must stick close together, nobody falling too far behind and nobody moving too far ahead. Equality matters, and the state must manage things by taxing the rich, redistributing to the poor and having us all share the same cradle-to-grave public services.

On this view, high public spending is a mark of a healthy society, as exemplified by modern-day Sweden. It's one element in a much wider agenda encompassing progressive taxation and pay caps for the richer members of society, especially greedy people like chief executives and bankers.

This left-wing case for public spending draws heavily on a redefinition of poverty developed by Labour academics in the early 1960s. As we've seen, traditional absolute poverty had been banished well before then and relative poverty was a concept developed to replace it.

The academics said that poverty 'can be defined only relative to the material and emotional resources available at a particular time to the members either of a particular society or different societies'.[244]

That's a bit of a mouthful, and something defined in terms of 'emotional resources' hardly sounds like a workable basis for government policy. But the Labour Party seized on it. They'd realised that announcing the banishment of poverty had not been smart electorally: the word 'poverty' is highly emotive, and campaigning to abolish poverty is a lot easier than campaigning to impose socialist equality.

So they redefined poverty. In future, it would be defined not in absolute consumption terms (based on having enough food, clothing, shelter and so on), but in relative income terms, calibrated against the national average. The poverty line was arbitrarily set at 50 per cent of the average income, later revised to an equally arbitrary 60 per cent of the median. Thus, when Tony Blair made his famous pledge to end child poverty by 2020, the small print told us the measure of success would be no child living in a household with an income less than 60 per cent of the national median household income, whatever that might turn out to be.[245]

The thrust of this is clear. While Blair and others may present their approach as fighting poverty, what they're really pursuing is equality. And the implication for benefits spending is that no matter how well-off the poor may become, unless they're within 60 per cent of middle-income Britain, their benefits will have to be increased. Or, to put it another way, any success middle-income Britain has in raising its own earnings will be subject to a tax surcharge in order to ensure those on lower incomes do not get left too far behind. Indeed, from the left's perspective, extra taxation on the richer members of society is a good thing in itself because it reduces inequality.

Similarly, our public services must ensure equality, with nobody allowed to pull too far ahead. So, in education, state grammar schools were abolished because it was reckoned they allowed middle-class children to pull ahead. It was better for all children to be held back together, a line of thinking that later drove the dumbing down of exam standards.

This is why the left opposes private alternatives to state monopolies. If those with deep enough pockets are allowed to contract out of the collective equalising experience, they can buy advantage. Private education is especially condemned – even though many of the left's most strident voices (including caravaner Polly Toynbee) have had their own children privately educated.[246]

But if we're going to justify high public spending on the basis of equality, then we need to understand precisely how equality benefits us. Arabian Nights tales of caravans trekking across the sands are fine around the campfire, but if you're a taxpayer being stung for half your income, you need a bit more than that.

EQUALITY BENEFITS US BECAUSE...

It's easy to see how equality might benefit the poor. As long as the damage inflicted on the economy by high taxes and pay caps for wealth creators is not too devastating, the poor should come out ahead.

And it's easy to see how equality would benefit the politicians promoting it. The politics of envy may not make for an attractive spectacle, but it's a tried-and-tested stratagem for electoral advantage, long deployed by the left. Moreover, the creation of a large client group dependent on state employment and welfare has clear attractions for politicians able to position themselves as representing that group – a point Bismarck recognised when he launched state benefits back in the 1880s.

But how does equality benefit the rest of us – the ones who have to pay for it?

Historically, the left ignored this question – or at least, they asserted the wider benefits of equality as a self-evident truth, not requiring empirical evidence. But following the collapse of communism and the general failure of high-tax societies to deliver prosperity, they've been casting around to come up with some proof. Two recent and widely promoted attempts have been so-called Happiness Economics and a book entitled *The Spirit Level*.[247]

According to Happiness Economics, we now have considerable evidence that getting richer doesn't make us happier.[248]

Well, when we say considerable evidence, what we mean is that we have a collection of opinion polls with answers to questions like this:

Q. Describe your current happiness state. Are you:
1. Unhappy
2. Fairly happy
3. Very happy

So how do you rate? Typically people rate themselves at 2, although the overall average comes out slightly higher at 2.2 – a bit happier than fairly happy.

Now, it turns out that the average score doesn't change very much over time. Come rain or shine, boom or bust, on average we're 2.2. Yet we know we've been getting richer for years. And that – according to Happiness Economics – tells us that getting richer doesn't make us happier.

The socialist policy conclusion is that governments should be less concerned with economic growth and more with the wider aspects of social wellbeing. It doesn't really matter if the economy stops growing – we're rich enough already and more of the same will not make us happier.

Needless to say, that conclusion is heavily contested, not least because simple opinion polls cannot possibly capture the highly subjective and multi-faceted nature of happiness. Moreover, the material goods that made for 2.2 happiness fifty years ago would almost certainly not deliver 2.2 happiness today. As we've got richer, our expectations and benchmarks have been transformed, so happiness comparisons over time are pretty flimsy.

In terms of equality, Happiness Economics is on even shakier ground. Because the evidence from these polls is that, at any given time, richer people are on average happier than poorer people: on average, money *does* buy you happiness. As one researcher put it, 'there's no one single change you can imagine that would make your life improve on the happiness scale as much as to move from the bottom 5 per cent on the income scale to the top 5 per cent.'[249] So taxing the rich to fund welfare is going to make the rich less happy, thereby cancelling out any happiness gains made by the poor.

Happiness Economics attempts to get round this by wheeling out an argument long used by socialists to justify redistribution. It's called the diminishing marginal utility of income, and it says that the richer you are, the less each additional pound of income is worth to you. For example, a man who already has half-a-dozen cars will value an additional car much less than a man who has no cars. So when governments redistribute income from rich to poor, the poor gain more in happiness than the rich lose.

To put it in its traditional form, redistribution delivers the greatest happiness of the greatest number.

Except that there's no evidence that it's true. Happiness is so subjective that mine cannot possibly be weighed against yours. Even if I accept that the greatest happiness of the greatest number is a legitimate reason for the government to forcibly cut my happiness – which is highly contentious in itself – there is no reason to think my loss will be outweighed by your gain.

TURNING TO SPIRITS

With Happiness Economics looking like a dud, the authors of *The Spirit Level* tried a different approach to justify equality-based policy. They argued that inequality has seriously pernicious effects on the whole of society by 'eroding trust, increasing anxiety and illness, [and] encouraging excessive consumption'. And they attempted to demonstrate that by using a mass of international comparative statistics on such things as physical and mental health, violence, drug abuse, obesity, imprisonment and social mobility.

The idea certainly avoids the problems involved in measuring happiness, and when the study was launched it generated a wave of publicity and support from the left. BBC Home Affairs Editor Mark Easton's enthusiastic report caught the mood:

> [The study] shows that greater inequality is linked to more kids dropping out of school; more violent crime; more people ending up in prison; more babies dying and more mental illness. There is also a strong correlation between greater inequality and less social mobility as well as less trust. It seems that the more equal a society, the happier it tends to be.[250]

At last the left had some hard and persuasive evidence for equality-based welfare.

Or at least, they had if the study could stand up to scrutiny. Somewhat predictably, it couldn't.

For example, the authors claimed to have established a statistical relationship between income inequality and life expectancy, suggesting that high levels of inequality literally shorten lives. If true, that would constitute a pretty powerful case for income redistribution, since few would argue that the property rights of the rich should outweigh the poor's right to life itself.

But when others attempted to replicate the study's results they failed.[251] And not just on the supposed relationship between inequality and life expectancy, but also on very many of the study's other claims. In fact, the more others probed the study, the less convincing it became.

Even people sympathetic to *The Spirit Level*'s intentions were dismayed at its cavalier and unconvincing use of statistics. Professor John Kay, a respected economist and popular *Financial Times* columnist, wrote:

> The evidence presented in the book is mostly a series of scatter diagrams, with a regression line drawn through them. No data is provided on the estimated equations, or on relevant statistical tests. If you remove the bold lines from the diagram, the pattern of points mostly looks random, and the data dominated by a few outliers.[252]

The overall conclusion is that the equality case for high public spending remains very much one of socialist faith. The empirical evidence that it increases the sum of human happiness, or that it reduces all those social ills set out in *The Spirit Level*, is to all intents and purposes non-existent.

SPENDING MORE THAN WE NEED TO

With the equality case for public spending no more than a matter of faith, we're back with the idea of the public sector as a service provider. And on that basis, it's pretty clear that government is spending far more than we really need it to.

One way of calibrating how much more might be to consider which services we absolutely need the government to provide from taxation, and which ones we could in principle buy for ourselves if our taxes were lower. Because, as we discussed earlier, for many services the case for public sector monopoly supply is not compelling.

We could immediately put together a long list. Many of us already buy private health and education services, and alternative suppliers would multiply if government withdrew. Similarly, there are already plenty of private suppliers for pensions, sickness and unemployment protection. The entertainment business is well furnished with commercial suppliers, so we could privatise the BBC and abolish cultural and sports subsidies. We could be left to donate our own cash to international aid charities, and pay industrial and agricultural producers direct rather than subsidising them via government.

However, while this approach is conceptually appealing, in practice there are some problems. In particular, our calculation would need to take account of those who would be unable to afford essential services even if taxes were cut. Unless we were prepared to let them sink – or at least become wholly dependent on possible private charity – we'd need to allow for some continued tax-funded support. And it's very uncertain how much that would be.

A simpler and more practical approach is to look at how much other countries spend, or more precisely how much those global efficiency leaders spend. Because all of them provide tax-funded support for the poor in respect of essential services.

We've already calculated the answer: over the last decade, the world's efficiency leaders spent an average 36 per cent of GDP, whereas ours spent 46 per cent. Which suggests that our government is overspending by around 10 per cent of GDP – a huge amount.

As seen in previous chapters, much of that overspending reflects inefficiency in the way our public services operate. So if we can somehow reform those services to improve efficiency, we can cut the overspend without sacrificing anything in terms of results. Clearly that would be the preferred solution for taxpayers, which is why governments of left and right focus so much attention on efficiency drives of one kind or another. Unfortunately, their efforts to date have barely scratched the surface – something we'll come back to.

As for income inequality, we might expect that cutting back welfare spending would increase it. However, it's by no means clear that the overall effect would be as great as the left often claims. We've already discussed the poor targeting of many benefits, with large sums going to those who don't really need the help. And according to the OECD's figures, only one of those world efficiency leaders – the US – has an income distribution significantly wider than ours. The others achieve more or less the same distribution as us, while spending a great deal less.[253] With better targeting, it seems it can be done.

After a detailed international survey of public spending and performance over the last century, two eminent economists from the IMF and European Central Bank concluded:

> ... countries with small governments have performed as well, or even better ... than countries with large governments ... we believe that much of what governments want to achieve through public spending could be achieved by levels of spending ranging from 25 to 35 per cent of GDP.[254]

Spending a good 10 per cent of GDP more than that is not something we need to do, and certainly not something we can afford to do any longer.

ELEVEN

THE DARK ART OF STEALTH TAXATION

There is no art which one government sooner learns of another than that of draining money from the pockets of the people.
– Adam Smith, *The Wealth of Nations*

The art of taxation consists in so plucking the goose as to obtain the largest amount of feathers with the least possible amount of hissing.
– Jean-Baptiste Colbert, finance minister to Louis XIV 1665–1683

So government spends half our national income, wastes well over £100 billion a year, and forces us to take services we could better obtain elsewhere. The obvious question is: why do we put up with it?

One possible explanation is that we somehow think our government delivers great value for money, just as supporters of big government would have us believe. But we surely can't be that stupid. We can't really believe we're getting great value when the results are so much worse than those achieved by our main competitors, and the costs very often higher.

A much more plausible explanation is that although we may have serious concerns about the quality of our public services, we don't get too exercised because they're free. Or, to put it another way, we think that someone else is paying.

THE 'SOMEONE ELSE IS PAYING' DELUSION

The 'someone else' in question is generally taken to be a rich social reprobate. A plutocratic landowner, a wedged-up banker or a footballer's wife in her gas-guzzling 4x4 would all fit the bill very nicely. Nobody likes people like that, it's only fair that they pay, and frankly it makes us much happier to know that they're being dragged down to the same level as everyone else.

There's undoubtedly something in this, which is why politicians go on so much about taxing greedy bankers and rich foreigners (or non-doms as they're now called). But in reality, there's a serious problem. Because when you move beyond the rhetoric and do the sums, it turns out that someone else doesn't have nearly enough cash. There simply aren't enough rich social reprobates and foreigners to go round.

Let's suppose we define the undeserving rich as anyone with an annual income over £150,000: that's approximately what the Prime Minister gets paid, and is widely viewed as a benchmark above which a public servant becomes a public sector fat cat. And let's suppose we squeeze these appalling people until their pips squeak and their wallets run dry. How much tax could we raise?

The answer is: not nearly enough. The sad fact is that there are only about 300,000 such people in the entire country, and their total combined income is only around £120 billion.[255] So even if we slammed each one with a 100 per cent tax rate – casting them penniless into the gutter to starve – we'd still only raise about one-sixth of what the government spends in a year. Moreover, we might not be able to repeat the tax in subsequent years, by reason of the undeserving rich having expired.

That's not to say that it hasn't been tried. Indeed, twice in living memory, Labour governments have imposed taxes on the rich that actually went *beyond* 100 per cent – that is, for every extra pound of gross income received, the government tried to extract more than one pound in tax. In 1967, Harold Wilson's government imposed a special 45 per cent charge on annual investment income over £8,000. Combined with income tax at 41.25 per cent and surtax at 50 per cent, that meant a total tax rate on the idle rich of 136.25 per cent.

Of course, in the real world beyond the politics of envy, such preposterous taxes raise nothing. The rich simply defer their income – thereby paying nothing at all in tax – or emigrate, taking their disgusting billions with them.

The fact is that the rich already pay a lot more tax than the rest of us, and quite right too. Those 300,000 people on incomes above £150,000 may comprise only 1 per cent of income-tax payers, but they pay a quarter of all income tax. It's just that they can't possibly fund more than a fraction of our government's massive spending.

In reality, the bulk of tax has to come not from our relatively small number of super-rich, but from us, the much larger number of people in the middle. According to the Office for National Statistics, 60 per cent of taxes are paid by the 50 per cent of households with annual incomes between £20,000 and £60,000.[256] To put it bluntly, for all but the poorest, the belief that someone else will pay is a sad delusion. Whatever politicians may suggest to the contrary, most of the government's bills end up being paid by those in the middle. The middle has to pay because that's where the money is.

However, if our rich benefactor is a delusion, and if we're actually paying most of the bill ourselves, that raises another question: how come we don't notice? After all, we're talking a pretty chunky bill here.

WE NEVER SEE THE FINAL BILL

The celebrated London hairdresser Michael Van Clarke has coiffed more supermodels, rock stars and royals than *Hello!* magazine has had celebrity photo spreads. And none of them leaves his salon without a detailed bill, showing exactly how much they've paid to him and his staff, and exactly how much they've paid to the government.

It's much more than just VAT. Mr Van Clarke would not have reached the pinnacle of his profession without being a stickler for detail, so his bills also identify all the other taxes the salon has to pay – the ones you as a customer don't normally see. They include business rates, insurance premium tax, climate levy and landfill tax. Crucially, he also shows the income tax and national insurance payments he has to deduct from his staff pay.

The result is shocking: on a typical bill, around half is accounted for by tax. Or, to put it another way, if it wasn't for the taxes, Van Clarke and his colleagues could provide their services for only half what they currently charge. Tax *literally* doubles the price.

Seeing the breakdown for the first time, new customers can hardly believe they've been paying all that tax without even realising it. Yet we're all in the same position. As we go through our lives, we just don't realise how much tax we're paying. With scores of different taxes, many of them highly complex, and many hidden from view, we simply can't keep track. We never see the final bill.

And that would be a pretty good reason why we don't complain more. With no final bill we just don't realise how much government is costing us. We may know how much we're paying in council tax, and perhaps income tax, but the rest is usually quite vague. Moreover, the individual tax payments are separated and we never sit down to add them all up.

This is a similar charging technique to that employed by budget airlines. They've become notorious for luring customers in with low headline fares, but failing to mention all the additional charges that have to be paid in order to make an actual booking – airport taxes, baggage charges, fuel surcharges, administration fees and various other additions they dream up. The final bill obviously comes out much higher than the initial headline fare, but the airlines hope that by splitting the charge across a slew of separate items they can bamboozle customers into not noticing.

Now compare that to the way various politicians have misled us in presenting their tax policies. Most blatant was New Labour's 1997 pledge that 'there will be no increase in the basic or top rates of income tax'. Because, while they delivered on that specific pledge, what they'd slyly failed to mention was that they were going to increase a whole raft of other less understood taxes, including those on our pensions.

This headline pricing technique depends on what behavioural psychologists call compartmentalisation – the human instinct to think about the world as a set of separate compartments rather than taking a holistic view. Apparently we evolved that way because it helps us simplify problems and makes us less anxious about the world. But when it comes to finance, it means we can all too easily get distracted by detail and fail to assemble the big picture.

Of course, in the case of budget airlines, they have a problem. No matter how many distracting compartments they split their fares into, eventually they have to present the buyer with a final bottom line. The buyer can then see the real bill and make a fully informed judgement.

But with tax, we're never presented with that bottom line. We never see the final bill. The individual taxes we pay remain in their separate compartments – many hidden – and we carry on in ignorance of the total.

WE CAN'T WORK IT OUT

It was 1966 and George Harrison was doing pretty well. He was twenty-three years old, at the top of his profession and one of the most adored people on the planet. But then he got a nasty shock:

> I discovered I was paying a huge amount of money to the taxman. You are so happy that you've finally started earning money – and then you find out about tax. In those days we paid nineteen shillings and sixpence out of every pound (there were twenty shillings in the pound), and with supertax and surtax and tax-tax it was ridiculous … Anybody who ever made any money moved to America or somewhere.[257]

Of course, there had been angry taxpayers before him. Some had overthrown governments, and some had written to *The Times*. But Harrison was a gifted songwriter, and he channelled his anger into a song for the Beatles' new album *Revolver*. The result was 'Taxman', which immediately became the world's most memorable blast against high taxation and the only tax analysis ever to go multi-platinum.

If you're of a certain age, this iconic song will now be playing inside your head. It is a brilliant summary of how taxes weigh us down through our entire lives. But the song also highlights the extreme difficulty of working out how much we're actually paying.

In the song, Harrison complains he only keeps one pound for every nineteen taken by the taxman. But he's underestimating, because, in reality, 'nineteen shillings and sixpence out of every pound' means he keeps just one for every *thirty-nine* taken. All that stress and sweat, all those screaming girls, and he's ended up with just one-fortieth of what he's earned.

He also underestimates the taxes on what he buys. He mentions taxes on driving, sitting, heating and those essential Cuban-heeled Beatle boots. But he clearly hasn't a clue how much tax, and his list merely scratches the surface – although, in fairness, back in 1966 there were so many taxes that listing them all would have left him still singing the song when the Beatles broke up four years later.

Harrison ends his song with death duties. He doesn't even attempt to unravel them – all he knows is that he must be spending his entire life working for the taxman.

Now, in theory, the tax system has been simplified since 1966, and it ought to be easier for us to calculate our own personal tax bills. The vast ragbag of purchase taxes has been replaced by a unified system of VAT and the income tax system is also now unified, with the separate surtax abolished.

But is it any easier? Let's see if we can work out what you're paying, because you almost certainly don't know.

HOW MUCH TAX ARE YOU PERSONALLY PAYING?

We'll start with the taxes you come up against in your every-day life. According to the official count, there are seventeen of them:

- Income tax
- National insurance
- Council tax
- VAT
- Motoring taxes – fuel duty and vehicle excise duty
- Sin taxes – beer and cider duty, wine and spirits duty, tobacco duty, betting duty, National Lottery tax
- Capital taxes – stamp duty, capital gains tax and inheritance tax
- Other – TV licence fee, air passenger duty and insurance premium tax

Most are familiar. But some we encounter only occasionally, when we can be shocked by their severity. For example, anyone buying the average detached house in south-east England today gets whacked with a £20,000 bill for stamp duty.

And a couple of the taxes you may not even have recognised as taxes, although the government itself certainly counts them that way. The £145.50 TV licence fee is a lump sum tax on TV use, whatever the BBC likes to suggest about it being a subscription for watching *Doctor Who* and *Hotter than my Daughter*. Similarly, a big slice of National Lottery ticket sales goes towards funding government spending on projects like the London Olympics that would otherwise need funding from general taxation. Combined with betting duty, that means 40 per cent of your National Lottery stake is effectively tax.

So let's see what each of these seventeen taxes cost you.

Some are fairly easy to pin down. You should be able to get what you pay in income tax and national insurance (entirely missed by George Harrison) from your printed pay slips or pension advice notes or your self-assessment demand from HM Revenue and Customs. Similarly, you know exactly how much council tax costs because the demand drops onto the mat every spring. All your other separately billed taxes should also be fairly easy – if tedious – to track.

The problems come with the taxes hidden inside the price of what you buy (so-called indirect taxes). For example, you can only calculate how much VAT you're paying if you keep a detailed record of all your purchases. And detailed means detailed. Because VAT is not applied at a neat uniform rate across all items, your record will need to differentiate between all the various items subject to each different rate. But the rules are complex and arbitrary, so you won't necessarily know which items attract which VAT rate.

For example, the great pasty tax debacle revealed that while hot takeaways are subject to VAT and cold takeaways aren't, tepid takeaways may or may not be, depending on whether they're 'above ambient temperature'. So to track your VAT payments you'll need to keep a detailed temperature record.

And while many of us believe supermarket food is zero-rated, any food classified as confectionery attracts VAT at the full rate. Thus, plain digestive biscuits are zero-rated, but chocolate digestives are charged at 20 per cent because the chocolate is deemed to make them confectionery. But then Jaffa cakes, which also have a chocolate coating, *are* zero-rated (something you might want to remember next time you find yourself in the biscuit aisle). And contrary to popular belief, full-rate VAT applies to many household essentials, including detergents and that most essential of all essentials, toilet paper. On the other hand, domestic energy attracts a lower VAT rate.

In reality, working out your VAT payments will likely prove impossible. You may have better luck with your motoring taxes, but your sin taxes will again prove problematic. Booze duties come in a whole variety of different flavours, and you'll need to have kept meticulous records of precisely how you indulged during every single one of those weekend benders. Which, let's face it, is unlikely.

The bottom line is that calculating a personal tax bill will probably defeat even the most persistent and pernickety accountant. And for the rest of us, life is simply too short. You don't know how much you pay because it's just too hard to work out.

But there's something even worse than that. Your ignorance reflects the fact that today's taxes are difficult to disentangle not by accident but by design. Six millennia of experience have taught the taxman that your ignorance is his bliss.

YOUR IGNORANCE IS NO ACCIDENT

As far as anyone knows, the world's very first taxman set up shop 6,000 years ago in the city-state of Lagash, now part of Iraq. He levied his taxes on property, and he doesn't seem to have been very popular. A clay tablet records a citizen of Lagash as saying, 'You can have a Lord, you can have a King, but the man to fear is the tax assessor.'

A few thousand years later, the ancient world's most famous taxman proved just as unpopular. 'And it came to pass in those days, that there went out a decree from Caesar

Augustus, that all the world should be taxed.'[258] Augustus is widely considered to be the father of modern taxation, but he clearly had a lot to learn. Sending out decrees that all the world should be taxed is not something any modern ruler would consider: it could stir up no end of trouble.

One thousand years after that, the Normans adopted similar in-your-face techniques in their newly conquered lands in England. In 1085, William the Conqueror commissioned the Domesday Book specifically to document wealth and taxable capacity, so he could fleece his new subjects more comprehensively.

In fairness, none of these early taxmen had to worry overmuch about public opinion. And neither the Roman Army nor the Sheriff of Nottingham felt obliged to stand on ceremony when it came to collecting tax arrears.

But despite those advantages, as government's ambitions and costs grew – especially in the military field – collecting sufficient revenues proved increasingly difficult. And rulers discovered that taxpayers can be very dangerous if pushed too far.

Thus, in the England of Robin Hood, a cash-strapped King John got into serious difficulty when he unilaterally ramped up a slew of levies, fees and fines. His barons revolted, and he only clung on by surrendering his divine right of taxation without consent. Today, the signing of Magna Carta in 1215 is remembered as a key moment in the long march of personal liberty, but it was actually driven by the need to placate revolting taxpayers.

In 1381, a skint Richard II got into serious trouble when he tried to impose a third poll tax in four years. His final demand went down so badly it triggered the famous Peasants' Revolt, led by Wat Tyler. And while the revolt was quickly and brutally suppressed, it gave the rulers a very nasty fright. In fact, it was six centuries before a British government tried another poll tax – and when it did, it immediately triggered another revolt.

Fast-forward 250 years, and yet another bankrupt king ran into even greater trouble over tax. Charles I seized on the ancient tax of Ship Money – which had previously been levied only on coastal towns in times of war – and tried to impose it across all towns in time of peace. Big mistake. Imposing such a highly visible tax on people who'd never agreed, and never previously had to pay, provoked a massive backlash. In the end it fomented a Civil War, with Charles literally losing his head.

It was around then that things began to change. Right across Western Europe taxmen were coming under pressure to raise substantially more cash. Whole new taxes were required because the old ones no longer produced nearly enough revenue for high-spending rulers like French monarch Louis XIV, the self-styled Sun King. The problem was wars. Rulers would keep fighting them, and wars were getting a lot more expensive.

At the forefront of the new tax thinking was Louis' legendary finance minister Jean-Baptiste Colbert. Not only did he develop a number of new revenue sources, but, more important, he was the first taxman to articulate the absolutely essential principle of modern taxation: stealth. His famous analogy about hissing geese precisely captures the idea – to give taxpayers a right royal plucking without having them notice quite what's going on.

Stealth taxation is all about keeping taxes hidden from view. The ideal stealth tax is invisible to those who end up paying it. Failing that, the next best thing is to spread the taxes around so that taxpayers never quite fathom out how much they're paying overall. Stealth taxation is the art of keeping taxpayers in ignorance.

In seventeenth-century England it was clear that many traditional taxes failed the stealth test dismally.

Poll tax had been a disaster, and Ship Money had fomented a Civil War. Property tax remained in place and had been the bedrock of taxation since ancient Greek and Roman times. But property tax is not stealthy. It involves billing property owners each year for the amount due, and pursuing them when they fail to pay. It's a highly visible process and owners can get angry. Today's council tax regularly tops opinion surveys as Britain's most hated tax, and even ruthless medieval autocrats found limits to how much they could squeeze from property owners alone.

New sources of tax revenue were desperately needed.

THE TAX HIDDEN INSIDE

If taxes can be hidden inside the price of what we buy, there's a sporting chance we won't really notice. And in the seventeenth century, taxmen began to milk that idea for all it was worth.

During the English Civil War, Parliament funded its army by imposing the first ever excise duties on domestic goods. The duties were applied not just to beer and whisky, but also to a range of basic commodities. And over the next 150 years, as the cost of war spiralled, successive governments taxed an ever-widening range of goods. They included basic necessities like salt, candles, leather, beer, soap and starch, right through to luxuries such as wine, silks, gold and silver thread, silver plate, horses, coaches and hats. Yes, if you bought a man's hat between 1784 and 1811, you had to pay a graduated hat tax.

Many of these new imposts were driven by the need to finance the nation's interminable wars. But all too often they were not rescinded after the wars ended – there was an upward ratchet effect. And that's a repeated theme throughout the history of taxation. Taxpayers are persuaded to accept new burdens during the exigencies of war, but then somehow get stuck with them forever afterwards. It happened on a large scale in both the world wars last century.

The burden of new duties certainly soared during the eighteenth century. It's been estimated that total revenue from customs and excise duties tripled between 1700 and 1820, from around 5 per cent of national income up to nearly 15 per cent.

But as the taxes increased, they lost their stealthiness. Resentment grew. Smuggling and evasion became a big problem, with the dreaded Excise Man a popular hate figure. And certain taxes provoked violent resistance, such as the Smithfield meat tax riot of 1647 and the West Country cider tax riots of 1763.

By the time Napoleon had been defeated, virtually everything people bought seemed to be taxed, and there was a further raft of taxes on property and capital transactions (although the notorious window tax had actually been introduced long before, in 1696). In 1820, the clergyman and writer Sydney Smith memorably surveyed the multitude of taxes then in force:

Taxes upon every article which enters into the mouth or covers the back or is placed under the foot. Taxes upon everything which it is pleasant to see, hear, feel, smell or taste. Taxes upon warmth, light and locomotion. Taxes on everything on earth or under the earth, on everything that comes from abroad or is grown at home. Taxes on the raw material, taxes on every fresh value that is added to it by the industry of man. Taxes on the sauce which pampers man's appetite, and the drug which restores him to health; on the ermine which decorates the judge, and the rope which hangs the criminal; on the poor man's salt and the rich man's spice; on the brass nails of the coffin, and the ribbons of the bride; at bed or board, couchant or levant, we must pay.

The schoolboy whips his taxed top; the beardless youth manages his taxed horse, with a taxed bridle, on a taxed road; and the dying Englishman, pouring his medicine, which has paid 7 per cent., into a spoon that has paid 15 per cent., flings himself back upon his chintz bed, which has paid 22 per cent., and expires in the arms of an apothecary who has paid a licence of a hundred pounds for the privilege of putting him to death. His whole prosperity is then immediately taxed from 2 to 10 per cent. Besides the probate, large fees are demanded for burying him in the chancel. His virtues are handed down to posterity on taxed marble, and he will then be gathered to his fathers to be taxed no more.[259]

Smith wasn't alone in his anger. In the aftermath of the massively expensive Napoleonic Wars, Britain had been lumbered with huge government debts, and the consequent burden of taxation was threatening the old order. Spending taxes – far from being stealthy – were now fuelling a lurch towards the kind of revolutionary mood that had overwhelmed France. There were fears that the oppressed over-taxed masses would rise up, just as they had done so recently across the Channel.

Some new source of revenue was required – and fast.

TAXING WHAT WE EARN – STEALTHIER THAN YOU THINK

In 1798, Britain had been at war for nearly half the previous century, and the national debt had ballooned. Worse, the ongoing struggle with revolutionary France had turned very nasty, with invasion a real possibility. Caught in a desperate squeeze, Prime Minister William Pitt the Younger took the drastic step of introducing Britain's first ever income tax.

It was never going to be popular. Income tax seems the very antithesis of a stealth tax – it is highly visible, highly personal and highly provocative. The Chinese emperor who'd imposed the world's very first income tax had been overthrown, and his hated tax abolished.

Pitt could only get away with it because Britain was facing possible national annihilation, and even then he had to promise it was a purely temporary emergency measure, describing it as 'aid and contribution for the prosecution of the war'. And indeed, once Napoleon had been defeated, it was abolished – reportedly 'to a thundering peal of applause' – with the individual tax records physically destroyed (although not before the sneaky taxman had taken secret copies).

But that left subsequent governments with a serious problem. By the end of the war, income tax had been contributing around 20 per cent of total government revenue. Its abolition meant the entire weight of taxation now fell back on spending and property taxes – the ones Sydney Smith railed against in 1820, and which fuelled such resentment across the land.

So, as the opposition to spending taxes increased, governments eyed the substantial revenue that income tax had already shown itself capable of raising, and looked for a chance to bring it back.

It was Prime Minister Robert Peel in 1842 who reintroduced it, despite having personally opposed such a move during the preceding election. And just like Pitt before him, he presented it as a purely temporary measure. But even though both Gladstone and Disraeli later made explicit election pledges to abolish it, this temporary tax stayed. Indeed – incredible though it may seem – according to the strict black-stockinged niceties of Parliamentary procedure, it remains 'temporary' right up to this day – getting on for two whole centuries later.

Its longevity would probably have amazed Pitt and Peel. Such a visible and personal tax seems designed to set the geese at the government's throat. Yet in practice, income tax has turned out to have some powerful stealth features, unappreciated at its launch.

Consider Peel's original tax. Back in 1842, he set the annual income threshold at £150, which meant his new tax only caught rich people with incomes above that level. In today's terms, the equivalent income would well be in excess of £100,000. Yet today, tax is actually payable on incomes well under £10,000. So what started out as a tax on rich men has become a tax on virtually all working adults, and many pensioners besides. And the striking thing is that it's happened without governments having to raise a finger.

How? Through successive governments systematically failing to increase the tax threshold in line with inflation and the growth of incomes. In 1842, average earnings were about £30 per annum. Today, they are over £23,000. If Peel's threshold had been kept in line with the growth of earnings, it would now be about £115,000, and nobody earning less than that would be paying income tax.

So, as price levels and incomes have increased, governments have been able to capture more and more of us in their income tax net simply by doing nothing. That's much less provocative than announcing an actual tax increase, and we may not even notice what's going on. It's classic stealth taxation.

And it's been spectacularly effective, especially through the periods of high inflation we've experienced since the Second World War. At the end of the 1930s there were around 4 million income-tax payers, compared to over 30 million of us now caught in the net.[260]

The same stealth technique has been applied just as successfully to the higher rates of tax.

It was Lloyd George who first imposed a higher tax rate in his much trumpeted People's Budget of 1909. He called it super-tax (later surtax), yet despite some fiery rhetoric, by later standards it was actually rather light. It was levied as an additional income tax of 2.5 per cent on anyone with an annual income of £5,000 or more, which in 1909 caught just 10,000 of the super-rich. Adjusted for the growth in average earnings since then, today's equivalent of £5,000 would be well over £2 million. But today's actual higher-rate threshold is under £45,000. So, today, you start paying higher-rate tax at a relative income level a mere 2 per cent of the level originally set by Lloyd George.

This decline in the relative level of the threshold has pulled millions of middle-income earners into the higher tax brackets. In the last twenty years alone, the number of higher-rate taxpayers has virtually doubled, from 1.7 million in 1990/91 to 3.3 million in 2010/11. All of that reflects the operation of stealth.

And today's income tax incorporates a second powerful stealth feature: PAYE – Pay As You Earn – which helps government pick our pockets without us really noticing.

Under the PAYE system, employers withhold income tax and national insurance from our wages and salaries before we get them and pay those deductions direct to the government. And because we never get to hold the bird in our hand, there's much less chance we'll miss it as it gets dragged off into the fiscal bush.

PAYE was yet another tax device that got slipped in under cover of war. Before the Second World War, many taxpayers had paid income tax as lump sums, literally writing cheques and painfully watching as the money drained from their bank accounts. It was a process guaranteed to concentrate minds on just how much was being taken, and to make life tricky for the taxman.

But as income tax got hiked to fund the war, many people found themselves paying it for the first time. Whereas in the late 1930s there had been only 4 million taxpayers, by 1944 there were 15 million. It was an administrative nightmare, especially since most people didn't even have bank accounts back then.

So the government introduced PAYE, arguing it would make life easier for everyone, especially taxpayers. One of their tax inspectors was so enthused he later claimed 'it was an example of service to taxpayers, the goodwill from which still survives'. However, the Chancellor responsible, Sir Kingsley Wood, seems to have been seriously stressed about it, and on the very day of the announcement he suffered a heart attack and died. Either way, PAYE has subsequently proved to be an invaluable stealth tool in the hands of high-taxing governments.

THE TAX THAT WON'T ADMIT IT'S A TAX

National insurance is a tax so stealthy it doesn't even admit it's a tax. It prefers to be known as a 'contribution'.

Another of Lloyd George's new taxes, 'contributions'

were supposedly to fund pensions, unemployment benefits
and, later, healthcare. But although the payments were
channelled into a separate national insurance fund, there
was never enough to finance all the benefits being paid out.
It had to be heavily supported by general taxation, and
soon became little more than an accounting fiction. These
days, the revenue is simply another gigantic tax flow pouring
into the Treasury's big black money pit.

Not that it stopped Tony Blair trying to persuade us
that raising national insurance rates was somehow different to raising income tax. And that the increase in national
insurance after the 2001 election was something other than
clawing back the income tax cut made before the election.[261]

In reality, of course, national insurance is simply an
additional tax on what we earn, and appears as such in
the national accounts. Both employees and employers have
to pay it, as do the self-employed. It is a tax because it is
mandatory, albeit with a range of different rates.

And contribution rates are a lot higher than is generally
realised. As of April 2011, the main contribution rate for
employees has been 12 per cent, with a further 13.8 per cent
paid by the employer. That's a combined tax rate actually
higher than the 20 per cent standard rate of income tax.

So the overall tax rate – the so-called tax wedge – for
the typical employee is now 40.2 per cent. That is, for every
pound the employer has to shell out for an extra hour's
work, the employee only actually takes home 59.8 pence.
The rest is taken by the government.

This makes national insurance a very attractive stealth
tax. Whereas most of us know the headline income tax rate,
few of us know the national insurance rates. And even fewer
realise that our employer effectively has to dock a hidden

13.8 per cent from our pay packet to cover the employer's contribution.

TAXES HIDDEN EVEN DEEPER INSIDE

It's a common and comforting belief that we ordinary people don't need to worry about company taxes, because we don't have to pay them. Company taxes are paid by companies, so they don't affect us, right? In fact, given their outrageous profits, big companies surely ought to pay *more* tax. Instead of letting them stash it away in some dodgy offshore tax haven, the government should make them pay their fair share.

This line of thinking has long made companies a tempting target for the taxman. Companies can't vote, and the very word 'profit' conjures up pictures of faceless corporations grinding the faces of the poor. Taxing them sounds like striking a blow for social justice.

The only problem is that, although companies can't vote, they can't pay tax either. They are simply legal constructs, and they can't pay tax any more than they can breathe. All company taxes ultimately have to be paid by us as individuals.

And we pay in three possible ways. To begin with, companies can pass on taxes in the form of higher prices charged to us as customers. That's the point Michael Van Clarke highlights so vividly with his hairdressing bills.

Second, companies pass on taxes in the form of lower wages paid to us as employees. For example, it is well established that the employers' national insurance contribution is a tax on jobs. It's a tax that makes it more expensive to employ labour, reducing both the number of jobs on offer and the wage rates companies are able to pay.

Third, company taxes reduce the returns paid to us as

investors. And in case you're thinking you don't care about the idle rich, remember that anyone with a private sector pension is an investor.

This is a critical point, so it's worth pausing to make sure we've got hold of it. When companies get taxed, it's their customers, employees and investors who end up paying. And that means us. Whatever anti-capitalist campaigners may say about taxing profit rather than people, all taxes ultimately get paid by people. There isn't anyone else.

Of course, the taxmen themselves have long understood this. When British governments started taxing company profits back in the nineteenth century, they actually presented it as a simple extension of personal income tax. The idea was that a company's profits constitute income for the owners, and they should therefore be taxed at the same rate as income tax. At the same time, there was no further tax charge on dividend distributions, since the profits had already been taxed once.

But while that original approach was straightforward and transparent, as time went by, the temptation to add stealth surcharges proved too much for governments to resist. During the First World War, Lloyd George imposed an additional 'excess profits tax', at rates up to 80 per cent. Later, the Second World War saw the corresponding tax hiked to an eye-watering 100 per cent. And when that war ended – as so often in taxation – the additional tax was retained, albeit in a different guise and not at 100 per cent.

Since the Second World War, company taxation has become fearsomely complex, and we're not going to unravel it here. But two features are worth highlighting.

First, successive governments have had a strong predilection for taxing dividend distributions more heavily than retained profits. It reflects a view that profits ought to be used for reinvestment in the business rather than 'wasted' on shareholders. And it's been bolstered by offering generous tax deductions against the cost of capital investments.

But government interference in business decisions has rarely been successful, and there's no evidence that these policies have boosted productive investment overall. Moreover, imposing an extra tax on dividends to shareholders increases the cost of capital to British companies, because shareholders quite rationally react to the higher taxes by demanding higher gross returns. What might seem like a tax on idle rentiers is actually a stealth tax on everyone involved, including customers and employees.

The most notorious stealth attack was Gordon Brown's 1997 decision to impose tax on company dividends paid to pension funds. Previously, the funds had been able to reclaim the profits tax paid by the companies in which they invest, and Brown's move cost them dear. So dear, in fact, that it proved the death knell for much of the private pension provision in this country. It was a perfect demonstration of how profits tax hits ordinary people and not just the rich.

The second point to highlight is the impact of globalisation. As business has gone multinational, it's become much more difficult to tax within national borders.

STEALTH MEETS ITS MATCH

In the good old days, companies were essentially trapped inside borders and wide open to being taxed by national governments. But now they're multinational, they can switch their operations and profits around the world, out of harm's way. These days, if national governments push their luck too far, the golden geese don't just hiss – they take wing and fly away.

Unsurprisingly, this has angered the supporters of big government. There are constant demands for tough new measures to clamp down on companies which manage their affairs to avoid tax, despite the fact that it's perfectly legal to do so. And governments have responded by making company tax codes ever more complex, loading them down with anti-avoidance provisions.

But multinationals turn out to be far smarter than your average goose. With the help of their well-paid advisors, they've proved highly adept at finding ways round even the most complex national tax structures. Indeed, they've often been able to exploit that very complexity to shield themselves from tax.

The truth is that stealth taxation has met its match. Modern multinationals can manage their financial affairs just as stealthily as governments, and they've found all sorts of inventive ways to limit their profits in high-tax countries and move them elsewhere.

Reluctantly, governments are being forced to accept this new reality, and many are cutting company tax rates in the hope of luring footloose international profits into their own tax net. Ireland is the best-known example, cutting its rate to just 12.5 per cent and attracting billions in foreign company investment and profits.

It's known as tax competition, and big-government advocates describe it as a destructive 'race to the bottom'. But they're spitting into the wind. The global economy is here to stay and, as far as multinational companies are concerned, the wholesale taxation of profits may soon be a thing of the past. Governments will be forced to raise revenue directly from their taxpaying citizens, rather than stealthily via companies.[262]

THE BURDEN ON MR AND MRS AVERAGE

Now we've seen how tax became so stealthy, let's return to your own tax bill. As we discussed earlier, you probably won't be able to calculate it directly, but we can at least look at Mr and Mrs Average's bill.

According to the Office for National Statistics (ONS), the average working-age family has an annual income of £40,000 before tax and benefits.[263] And taking account of all those seventeen personal taxes we identified earlier, 38 per cent of it goes in tax. That's an average £15,300 per family, or £290 per week.

For the average family, that's a lot of money. Thirty-eight per cent of income is well over twice what they spend on housing and household fuel combined. If they saw their tax payments in a single consolidated annual statement like this, most would be shocked.

But high though it is, this bill doesn't yet include all those hidden company taxes that ultimately have to be paid by us. According to the Treasury, total taxes – including those levied on companies – cost us £550 billion (2011/12). And if we spread that across Britain's 26 million households, it's equivalent to a total bill of £21,200 each.[264]

Thus, in one way or another, either as direct tax payments we can see, or as indirect tax payments via higher prices, lower wages and lower investment returns, British families pay an average of £21,200 to the government.

That may seem like an extraordinary burden to carry, and it is: it's getting on for the same amount as we spend on everything else put together. But £21,200 is *still* a long way short of the true overall cost of government. And that's because of government borrowing.

Unlike families, governments rarely balance the books.

Instead, they routinely spend more than their income, running up huge mountains of debt.

But all of that debt has to be serviced by taxpayers. Governments borrow in our name, and it's us on the hook both for the interest payments and the eventual repayment of the principal. Just as with company taxes, it's ultimately down to us – there isn't anyone else to pay it. As the economist and financier David Ricardo pointed out 200 years ago, government borrowing is no more or less than deferred taxation.

And if we take off those deferred taxes as well, the total tax bill on the average British family turns out to be a truly astonishing £27,000 per family – virtually *double* the taxes we actually see in our everyday lives.[265]

Of course, taxes deferred are not quite the same as taxes paid today. Because, if we can defer them long enough, it won't be us paying them at all – it will be our grandchildren. And it's our grandchildren who come closest to filling the role of that 'someone else' to pay for the services we're all enjoying. We'll come back to this in the next chapter.

FOOLED BY STEALTH

It's taken 6,000 years, but the taxman has become history's most highly skilled pickpocket. He's learned a whole bunch of tricks for lifting our wallets without us even realising.

He's learned about hissing geese and how to back off if the hissing gets too loud. He's learned how to tax where we can't see what's going on. He's learned how to increase taxes without lifting a finger. And he's learned how to tax across our entire lives – our property, our purchases, our incomes and our companies. He's even learned how to tax our children and our grandchildren.

We can get see how successful he's been by comparing
our current situation with that of Sydney Smith, the man
who complained so memorably about the tax burden 200
years ago. Back then, taxes were so high many feared they'd
trigger a revolution. Yet in total they only amounted to 20
per cent of national income. Today our bill is over twice
that, yet most of us just accept it. The following chart shows
what's changed.[266]

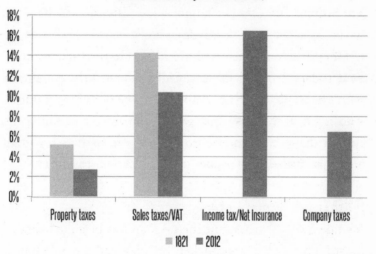

How The Tax Net Has Spread
Taxes as % of national income – 1821 and 2012
(Source: HM Treasury and Cato Journal)

So the tax net has spread much wider. In 1821 there was
no income tax, no national insurance contributions and no
company profit taxes. Together they now raise more than
the entire tax revenue in 1821.

On the other hand, the burden of taxes on what we own
and what we buy is actually lighter now. Dicing with near-
revolution taught governments that there are limits to how

much they can pile onto prices, especially the price of essentials. And we see clear echoes of that today in the zero-VAT rating of basic foodstuffs.

However, there is one further area of stealth taxation that is not included in our chart and was not even dreamed of back in 1821. And that is the disguised carbon taxation levied to support the government's green policies. The EU's Emissions Trading Scheme, which seeks to cap carbon emissions by businesses, is estimated to cost British consumers around £2 billion annually through higher electricity prices. And on top of that, there's a further £1 billion impost to meet the cost of developing renewable energy – the so-called Renewables Obligation.

The annual cost of these hidden green taxes is now running at over £100 per family, and is set to grow further. Yet they do not feature in official tax figures. It's something that we will need to watch very carefully.[267]

The reason we don't understand quite how much government costs us should now be clear: we've been duped. Worse, stealth taxation is only part of it. Unknown to most of us, government has been running up huge debts for the future – debts we will be hard-pressed ever to repay.

TWELVE

BORROWING, DEBT AND A FUTURE THAT DOESN'T ADD UP

Nothing is so well calculated to produce a death-like torpor in the country as an extended system of taxation and a great national debt.
– William Cobbett, 1804

Public finances must be sustainable over the long term. If they are not then it is the poor, the elderly and those on fixed incomes who depend on public services that will suffer most. So ... public debt will be held at a prudent and stable level over the economic cycle.
– Gordon Brown, Budget speech, 1997

Throughout history, governments have routinely overspent. That's to say, they've financed a slug of their spending by issuing IOUs.

In the old days, the big borrowing binges were to fight wars, often with little choice. But over the last six decades, the borrowing has been to finance welfare provision, over which there is a very definite choice. Despite that, and despite a generally benign economic environment, modern British governments have only managed to balance the books one year in ten. Even this year, after three years of supposed austerity, the government will *still* have to borrow one pound for every seven it spends.[268]

The fact is that, even equipped with the dark arts of stealth taxation, no government in the last half-century has managed to push taxes beyond 38 per cent of national income: for us here in Britain, that seems to be about the limit of what we and our economy will tolerate. However, few governments have limited their spending to that level, preferring to borrow instead. No household or business could live in such perpetual deficit, but governments carry on regardless.

Today's government IOUs are bonds, and the British variety are known as gilts. In return for a loan, these gilts obligate the government to pay interest at a specified rate for a specified number of years and then to repay the loan. Except that's a wholly misleading account of what's going on. The real obligation rests not on the government, but on taxpayers. When the government borrows, it borrows in our name, and it obligates all of us, and our children, and our children's children, to make those future payments of interest and principal through higher taxes. Government borrowing is deferred taxation.

Even in the best of times, deferred taxation imposes a burden on tomorrow. But the coming years are not going to be the best of times. Britain – along with many other countries – is suffering a prolonged and severe debt hangover. Between us, we've lived well beyond our means, we've borrowed far more than we can comfortably afford to service, and we'll be dealing with the consequences for years.

True, we can't blame it all on government overspending. In the bubble decade leading up to the 2008 crash, British households managed to increase their own debts by nearly three times.[269] And while much of that is secured against property, it still requires servicing, and sagging property prices have eroded the safety margin. Commercial companies also tripled their debt over the bubble years, substantially gearing up their balance sheets. In a classic case of unintended consequences, that dangerous trend was fuelled by Gordon Brown's stealth tax on pension funds, which increased the cost of equity finance for companies, encouraging them into debt.

And overshadowing everything were the banks, which took on colossal amounts of debt. From the mid-1990s through to the crash, the combined liabilities of UK financial institutions multiplied by a heart-stopping eight times: that is, what they owed to depositors, lenders and bond investors increased from a little over £2 trillion, to getting on for £20 trillion. It dwarfed our annual GDP of less than £1.5 trillion, and it was often said that the banks were turning Britain into a gigantic hedge fund. When the crash hit, we found out what that meant: we taxpayers were expected to pick up the losses. We had unwittingly ended up as guarantors for many trillions of bank debt.

Against that, you might think the government's own debts are the least of our problems. After all, the official measure of the debt, the one quoted by the Chancellor in the Budget, is 'only' £1.2 trillion, a mere 72 per cent of GDP (2012/13).[270] But that's hopelessly complacent. For one thing, annual debt interest payments are now running at £45 billion – more than the defence budget – and rising fast. Worse, the official measure of debt massively understates its true extent.

THREE CENTURIES OF THE NATIONAL DEBT

The national debt was established in the 1690s, at the same time as the Bank of England. The definitions have changed a

bit over the years, and these days the headline total goes by
the name of the public sector net debt (PSND). But there's
more than enough consistency to give us a broad historic
overview, which is summarised in the following chart.[271]

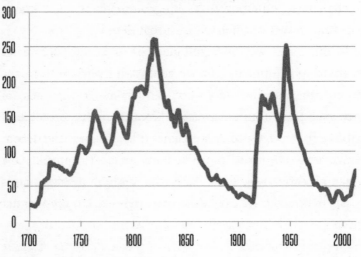

What we see are two giant waves, both reflecting the cumu-
lative cost of major wars.

In the immediate aftermath of the Napoleonic Wars, the
national debt exceeded 250 per cent of national income.
Already dangerously high after the several eighteenth-century
conflicts, the huge cost of fighting revolutionary France had
driven it up by a further 100 per cent in just two decades.

It then took the best part of a century to get the debt
ratio back down to 40 per cent, widely viewed as a safe and
sustainable long-term level (and the figure incorporated in
Gordon Brown's Golden Rules for fiscal stability).

In the twentieth century, the national debt again spiked. The cost of fighting two consecutive world wars meant that by the mid-1940s the ratio was back over 250 per cent of GDP. And, once again, it took decades – albeit not quite a century – for it to be brought back down to sustainable levels.

THE DOOMSDAY MACHINE

Napoleon's final defeat at Waterloo left Britain as the world's unchallenged superpower. Yet the country was on its knees. The reason was our massive national debt.

In this book we've steered clear of nightmare scenarios, but with government debt we can't. We must confront the doomsday machine. The doomsday machine operates on indebted governments just as it does on maxed-out credit card borrowers. Once debt reaches a level where the debtor is forced to borrow more just to pay the interest, the machine takes over. Each successive interest payment adds to the debt and, as the debt increases, lenders demand higher interest rates before they'll lend more.

Greece has reminded us what happens next. As the machine cranks up, credit is frozen. The creditors impose harsh repayment plans, forcing the debtor into extreme belt-tightening. The economy grinds to a halt and, with the government no longer in control, the battle takes to the streets. All bets are off. The nightmare scenario has arrived.

Two hundred years ago – long before EU bail-out funds – it very nearly got us. Government debt interest payments had reached 10 per cent of GDP, consuming half of all tax revenue. Ordinary families were being taxed to the hilt, only to see their money handed over to bankers and rentiers while decent hard-working people went hungry. When the battle moved onto the streets, the government deployed

armed troops against peaceful demonstrators. The Peterloo
Massacre in 1819 saw cavalry kill fifteen and wound 500.
Britain was on the brink.

Somehow the situation was contained, but, like Waterloo
itself, it was a damned close-run thing. Which is why cutting
the debt burden became the overriding fiscal priority for
governments throughout the subsequent century. And even
then, it took years to bring debt interest payments down to
a sustainable level.

The Burden of Debt Interest
Government debt interest payments as % of GDP, 1800-2012
(Source: ukpublicspending.co.uk; ONS; HMT)

In the twentieth century, debt from two world wars pushed
the interest bill right back up again. It never quite returned
to the previous doomsday levels, but 7 per cent of national
income was quite painful enough.

Today, the government's debt is once again increasing,

and at a rate never previously seen outside of a major war. Gordon Brown's worthless pledge to keep the national debt below 40 per cent of GDP was blown away as soon as it encountered its first proper test, with annual borrowing soaring above 10 per cent of GDP. And despite borrowing costs being artificially suppressed by the Bank of England, the debt interest burden is once again growing ominously.

LESSONS FROM HISTORY

There are those on the left who take comfort from this history, pointing out that today's debt remains far below previous peaks. They reckon we're much better placed than in either 1815 or 1945, and there's plenty of scope to borrow more to 'get growth going'. As for the long-term damage supposedly inflicted by government debt, they argue that even those historic peaks didn't stop the economy growing.

And that's true. In the thirty years after the Napoleonic Wars, per capita income in Britain grew by about 1 per cent per annum.[272] And in the corresponding period after the Second World War it grew by even more, at about 1.7 per cent. So it's certainly possible to have huge government debts and growth at the same time.

But debt is still a serious drag. During the thirty years from 1945 – the so-called Golden Age of Growth – our growth lagged far behind other countries, with Western Europe growing at 3.7 per cent. Of course, there were other factors, but it's very striking that Germany, France and Italy all had much less debt. Even in 1970, our public debt relative to GDP was still four times higher than Germany's, with debt interest costs *seven* times higher.[273]

So, while history tells us debt and growth are not

incompatible, working off a debt mountain is a long hard slog, and a big drag on prosperity.

Moreover, unlike its Victorian predecessors, today's government can't count on decades to work off its debt mountain. The globalisation of financial markets has fundamentally changed the landscape. Whereas the gilt market was once the centre of the financial universe – a dependable source of cheap finance for HM Government – it's now just one corner of the fast-moving and often fickle global bond and currency markets. And they give short shrift to over-borrowed governments, whoever they may be. As President Clinton's advisor James Carville famously put it: 'I used to think that if there was reincarnation, I wanted to come back as the President or the Pope ... But now I would like to come back as the bond market. You can intimidate everybody.'[274]

Market confidence demands that governments keep a close check on their debts at all times.

Finally, comparing today's official debt to the national debt in 1815 or 1945 doesn't capture anything like the full picture. For one thing, government debt now sits atop private sector debts far exceeding anything previously experienced. And, crucially, the government's official debt ignores huge swathes of its true liabilities – liabilities that did not exist in 1815, and barely existed in 1945.

THE REAL NATIONAL DEBT

The official public sector debt figure – the one quoted by the Chancellor – measures what's been borrowed in the financial markets, mainly gilts issues. But the government has massive additional liabilities that do not show up there, and which dwarf the official debt number.

Here are the most well known:[275]

Public sector pensions. The public sector has under-taken to pay pensions to millions of its employees. That's 12 million beneficiaries, more than 3 million of whom are already drawing pensions.[276] But the pensions are largely unfunded – that is, there are no funds put aside to make the pay-outs. The liability is a direct burden on taxpayers.

State pensions. The government has promised to pay us all – all 60 million of us – a state pension. But once again it's failed to put aside anything to pay for it, and our increasing lifespan makes that a huge liability.

PFI debt. The public sector has entered into more than 700 contracts under the private finance initiative. These commit taxpayers to more than £200 billion of payments over the next thirty years or so.

Liabilities of nationalised banks. RBS and Lloyds are effectively nationalised. Taxpayers are responsible for their liabilities.

Network Rail debt. This is a government liability kept off the official balance sheet only by a flimsy definitional fudge.

Nuclear decommissioning. The government has assumed full responsibility for decommissioning the old nuclear power stations.

For many years, successive governments steadfastly ignored these liabilities in calculating the national debt. Indeed, when Gordon Brown was Chancellor he made a speciality of it, encouraging the public sector to finance capi-tal projects with off-balance-sheet PFI contracts rather than official borrowing.

But manipulation on that scale is dangerous. It brings the official figures into disrepute, and, as Greece has demon-strated, countries that lie about their real debts can end up in serious difficulty.

So the government has started to produce broader and more realistic liability estimates alongside the narrow definition used by the Chancellor. The new figures are still emerging, but the Office for National Statistics has already published estimates for the items we've listed.[277] Put together with the Chancellor's figure – the public sector net debt (PSND) – they add up to a truly frightening total:

Liability	Amount – £ billion	Date of estimate
Official debt (PSND)	1,023	March 2012
Net bank liabilities	1,158	March 2012
Public sector pensions	1,165	December 2010
State pensions	3,843	December 2010
PFI debt	34	March 2010
Network Rail debt	24	March 2010
Nuclear decommissioning	57	March 2010
Total	7,304	

On this basis, the real national debt is £7,300 billion, seven times the official figure. More worrying still, it's five times the size of our national income. And even if you exclude the liabilities of our nationalised banks, the debt is still £6,150 billion, or four times the national income.

Moreover, this doesn't cover all the government's liabilities. There's a further slew of so-called contingent liabilities, including financial guarantees given to third parties, and things like potential medical negligence liability in the NHS. By their very nature they're impossible to pin down precisely, but the ONS has estimated them in excess of a further half-trillion.

Government liabilities of four or five times our annual

GDP puts us in wholly uncharted territory. They're around twice what we needed to defeat either Napoleon or Hitler, and they effectively land every household in Britain with a quarter-million pounds of debt. That's nearly *five times* what the average household risked borrowing for itself, even during that biggest debt bubble in history.

It is a catastrophic burden.

YES, BUT YOU'RE IGNORING THE GOVERNMENT'S ASSETS

Calculations like this are often dismissed on the basis that totting up the government's liabilities alone gives a grossly distorted picture. We're ignoring the fact that government has huge assets to back those liabilities.

For one thing, our nationalised banks have assets, and although they may not turn out to be worth quite what it says on the tin, they're worth much more than zero.

And that's true. But the problem is that nobody – including the banks – knows what they're actually worth, whereas the liabilities are now hanging round taxpayers' necks in their entirety. Indeed, the figure quoted in our table is not even the full liability, because the ONS has calculated it net of the banks' liquid assets – such as deposits with other banks. It's assuming their liquid assets *are* worth what it says on the tin, even in a renewed banking crisis.

The government also has assets, worth around three-quarters of a trillion pounds.[278] That's much better than nothing, even if it's nowhere near the government's liabilities. But those assets mainly comprise specialised facilities like motorways and hospitals, which are not only illiquid, but depend for their value on continued use in their specialist role. For example, an NHS hospital depends for its value on the purchaser being able to charge patients for its use as a hospital. But since it's the NHS paying for the patient, the government would be selling its hospitals only to have the NHS then pay a fee to use those hospitals in future. The net effect – the net burden on taxpayers – remains pretty much the same.

A more fundamental objection to our calculation says that we're counting the government's future payments while ignoring its future receipt of tax revenues. Government is an ongoing business, and our analysis gives a one-sided and misleading picture of the true fiscal position.

That's a good point, but it misses what our real national debt calculation is measuring. It's measuring the government's liability to make *future* payments in respect of loans or services it has received in the *past*. For example, the government's £1.2 trillion accrued liability to pay public sector pensions relates to the service and contributions that public employees have already delivered. It's the pension entitlement they've earned for past service, not for service they will deliver in future.

Of course, the government will have future tax revenues, and it can draw on them to meet its debt obligations. But the greater the payments in respect of past service and loans, the less of those future tax revenues will be left over to pay for future services.

And that's the key point. The massive growth in these obligations from the past jeopardises the government's ability to fund services in the future. Yes, it has revenue-raising powers and can always increase future tax rates. But that is *precisely* why taxpayers should be so concerned at the size of the real national debt.

A FUTURE THAT DOESN'T ADD UP

The government has huge liabilities in respect of past

overspending, liabilities that far exceed its assets. But far from reducing those liabilities, it's continuing to overspend and borrow into the indefinite future. Something doesn't add up.

The Budget's fiscal projections only go out five years, but we've got fifty-year projections produced by the independent Office for Budget Responsibility (OBR).[279] Of course, anything could happen in fifty years, and we can all quibble with their detailed assumptions, but their long-term projections are a stark demonstration of the problem we face.

Their main message is that the hotly contested spending cuts currently being implemented are not nearly enough. Unless government makes further substantial cuts, or imposes further tax rises, the official debt will go on growing. The safe long-term limit for government debt is traditionally reckoned to be 40 per cent of GDP. The government's official debt currently stands at 72 per cent of GDP, so it needs to fall. But, on the OBR's central projection, it rises, breaching 80 per cent during the 2050s. And note that this is just the *official* debt.

Moreover, this base case projection makes no allowance for disasters such as wars or bank collapses, of which there are bound to be one or two. And the OBR's key growth assumptions could easily be wrong, driving debt far higher.

Take NHS spending. The OBR's base case assumes that per capita NHS spending grows in line with the growth of per capita incomes. But, as we discussed in a previous chapter, NHS productivity lags way behind the rest of the economy so its services get relatively more expensive over time.[280] Therefore, unless we're now prepared to accept a long-term *decline* in healthcare provision – which seems highly unlikely – NHS spending will have to go on increasing faster.

The OBR itself has published an alternative projection that shows what happens to debt if NHS productivity continues to decline by 0.2 per cent annually, just as it's done historically since 1995. The result is alarming: the debt ratio shoots up to well over 350 per cent of GDP.

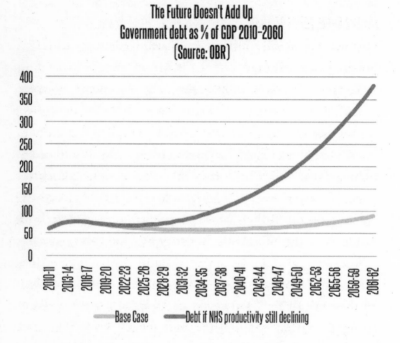

The Future Doesn't Add Up
Government debt as % of GDP 2010-2060
(Source: OBR)

Base Case — Debt if NHS productivity still declining

That's a picture of an unsustainable future. It's one thing to run up debts like that when a Napoleon or Hitler is trying to smash down the door. It's quite another to run them up in order to maintain welfare spending.

Of course, we'd never actually get to such debt levels because the financial markets wouldn't let us. Just like other big debtor countries, we'd find credit cut off – or at least only available on the harshest terms. We'd be well and truly stuck in the debt trap. As Napoleon himself put it: 'When a government is dependent upon bankers for money, they and not the leaders of the government control the situation, since the hand that gives is above the hand that takes ... Money has no motherland; financiers are without patriotism.'

Something clearly has to give before we get there, but the question is: what?

ESCAPE FROM THE DEBT TRAP

Historically, heavily indebted governments have had four possible escape routes:

Repayment – Nineteenth-century governments regularly repaid large amounts of debt: that is, they ran budget surpluses. And more recently we've had three repayment interludes: when Harold Wilson's government was forced to tighten fiscal policy following the 1967 devaluation; when Nigel Lawson was Chancellor in the late 1980s; and when Gordon Brown was temporarily cohabiting with Prudence in the late 1990s. But they were all soon reversed.

Default – HM Government proudly boasts that it 'has never failed to make principal and interest payments on gilts as they fall due'.[281] However, it doesn't mention a whole string of partial defaults through what's known as debt conversion. The most recent was in 1932, when the National Government converted £2.1 billion of War Loan, paying 5 per cent, into a new loan paying just 3.5 per cent, making all its holders significantly poorer at a stroke. These days, such conversions go by the picturesque name of 'haircuts', but they're still defaults.

Inflation tax – Prior to the 1970s, all HM Government's debt was denominated in fixed money terms, and even today, the bulk of it still is. What that means is that governments have been able to work off their debts by running the printing press and engineering inflation – effectively a gigantic stealth tax on debt holders. Of course, it doesn't work with the inflation-protected index-linked gilts introduced in the 1970s. And, crucially, it doesn't work if the markets get their retaliation in first by hiking interest rates to compensate for *anticipated* inflation.

Growth – GDP growth is the holy grail of indebted governments. Growth lifts tax revenue, cuts social spending, raises GDP and floats the government free. And it does so without making its creditors poorer: it's by far the best solution for everyone. The trouble is that highly indebted governments find it very difficult to stimulate and promote growth. They have little scope for tax cuts and find themselves boxed in by the very debts they're trying to work off.

In his book *The Cash Nexus*, historian Niall Ferguson investigates how important each of these factors was in working off those two historic debt mountains we looked at earlier.[282]

Up until 1914, the inflation tax played virtually no part, since Britain was on the Gold Standard and the government was unable to crank up the printing press. There were a number of debt conversions, but most of the work turns out to have been done by honest-to-goodness repayment and GDP growth.

Things were very different after 1945. With the Gold Standard ditched, governments of all complexions let rip with the printing press, and debt holders suffered horribly. In the half-century between 1948 and 1998, government debt increased by over 1,500 per cent in absolute terms. Yet because of inflation, in real terms the debt actually *declined* by 22 per cent, which is one big inflation tax. True, 250 per cent growth also helped, but with no net repayment and no outright defaults, the debt was mainly worked off through inflation.

From the government's perspective, the inflation tax is a much easier option than cutting spending, or raising taxes, or getting growth going. Just like all the best stealth taxes, it does its work without the government having to lift a finger.

Which is why many people believe it's being tried again, right now.

HERE COMES THE INFLATION TAX

In 2009 the Bank of England began its huge programme of quantitative easing (QE). Its aim was to inject cash into the economy by buying securities, and in the next three years or so the Bank bought £375 billions' worth. But virtually all of them were government gilts, which left one-third of the entire official debt held by the Bank – itself an arm of government. Whatever technical gloss is put on that, the government is once again funding itself by printing money.

Now, according to the official line, this isn't going to generate inflation because the economy is flat on its back, and the banks are sitting on the newly printed cash rather than lending it out. But in the first three years of the QE programme, UK inflation averaged 2 per cent higher than in the Eurozone and the US, and far exceeded the Bank's official 2 per cent inflation target. So the official line looks thin.

However, even if this isn't a deliberate attempt to bring back the inflation tax, the markets may not wait around to find out. And that's because of what happened in the 1970s.

The 1970s was when the inflation tax went seriously wrong. Fed up with being conned by ever-rising inflation, gilt investors went on strike – that is, they stopped buying. The gilt market no longer trusted the government to keep inflation in check, and demanded much higher interest rates to protect their returns. And to pay those higher rates, the government had to borrow even more.

The easy option had suddenly turned into a vicious circle. Once investors lost confidence in the government's commitment to low inflation, they pushed the cost of HMG's borrowing way beyond anything that had *ever* been seen before. The rate government had to pay on new borrowing peaked at well over 15 per cent, which applied to today's official debt would mean an annual interest bill in excess of £150 billion, or 10 per cent of national income.

Once again, we see the vital importance of retaining market confidence. For much of the nineteenth and early twentieth centuries, the government was able to fund its deficit at an average interest rate of 3 per cent or less. Investors trusted gilts because Britain was the undisputed hub of the global capital market, inflation was controlled by adherence to the Gold Standard and successive governments had demonstrated *by their actions* a strong commitment to fiscal discipline. None of those conditions holds today, and bond investors are far more sceptical.

The inflation tax is not an easy option.

THE REAL CHOICES

When we'd done with Napoleon and Hitler, although we were left with crippling government debts, the main driver of those debts was behind us. The worrying thing about our current position is that we can't say that. As far as we can see, despite the spending cuts and tax increases already announced, the debts look like increasing into the indefinite future.

According to the Office for Budget Responsibility, to get the debt ratio back down to that safe level of 40 per cent by

2060, a further annual cut of £17 billion is required. And that's under their base case, which, as we've already seen, looks pretty optimistic.[283]

Obviously growth is the most attractive way out – everyone agrees on that. But there's the crucial question of how we get that growth. The left's answer is for the government to borrow still more in the hope of kick-starting, or pump priming, or 'investing' the economy back to health. But German Finance Minister Peer Steinbrück spelled out the problem with that when a panicky Brown government took precisely that route in 2008:

> All this will do is raise Britain's debt to a level that will take a whole generation to work off. The same people who would never touch deficit spending are now tossing around billions. The switch from decades of supply-side politics all the way to a crass Keynesianism is breath-taking.
>
> When I ask about the origins of the crisis, economists I respect tell me it is the credit-financed growth of recent years and decades. Isn't this the same mistake everyone is suddenly making again, under all the public pressure?[284]

The real choices do not involve borrowing yet more, but finding ways to cut borrowing while stimulating sustainable growth. And the only known way of doing that is to cut spending sufficiently so that both borrowing *and* tax rates can be reduced. In other words, government must shrink.

We'll come back to this in our final chapter, but first let's consider the last of those classic debt escape routes: default.

DEFAULTING ON THE IMPOSSIBLE DREAM

As we've seen in the case of Greece, defaulting on market debt is not a great idea. It may eliminate the debt overhang, but it means the government will be cut off from any further borrowing for years – probably decades – to come. However, defaulting on those huge pension liabilities is another matter altogether.

Of all the items included in our calculation of the real national debt, the £3.8 trillion liability in respect of state pensions is both the biggest and the most tempting target for default. According to the government: '… state pensions are a liability that arises according to the circumstances and legislation prevailing at the time of the claim, which makes any estimate of future payments too uncertain.'[285]

Translation: the government can make and change the state pension rules whenever it wants to, and there's absolutely nothing pensioners and prospective pensioners can do about it. State pensions aren't real debt because the government can renege on its promises at any time.

And renege it certainly has. Back in 1980, it broke the promised link between the basic state pension and average earnings. Thereafter, pensions were only uprated in line with prices, and the basic pension subsequently fell from 26 per cent of average earnings in 1979 to just 16 per cent by 2000. True, the earnings link had only been in place since 1975, and before 1973 *any* uprating had been sporadic.[286] But it was still a broken promise to pensioners.

Today, the government has restored the earnings link – albeit from its lower base – but is now busy reneging on the pension-age promise. It's already announced increases to sixty-seven by 2028, and sixty-eight by 2046, and is sure to go further. Even the man who wrote the report recommending those increases now says: 'If I was redoing my report I would be more radical, arguing for an even faster increase in the state pension age.'[287]

Lord Turner now reckons we might need a pension age of seventy by 2030, which is the age and date many analysts light on.

The Exchequer savings will be substantial. Raising the pension age not only saves the cost of the pensions themselves, it also brings in additional tax and national insurance receipts from those who remain in work for the additional years. Merely raising the age from sixty-five to sixty-six will save an annual £5 billion, plus a further £1 billion from the additional tax receipts.[288] On top of that, the economy gains from having more workers, producing £8 billion of additional output. On that basis, raising the pension age to seventy could save something close to £25 billion, plus an additional £5 billion in tax revenues. £30 billion of annual Exchequer benefit makes it very easy to see why it's going to happen.

Understandably, those who've worked for forty years, dutifully paying their national insurance contributions, feel betrayed and angry. The deal was a pension at sixty-five – or sixty for women – and government is wrong to renege on it. People have been planning their lives on that basis, and they worry about their ability to carry on working to seventy: not everyone feels like Joan Collins.

On the other hand, the original deal assumed that the average pensioner would obligingly die at seventy-six, as agreed. Instead he's living to eighty-seven, and the entire pensions landscape has changed out of all recognition. We might fervently wish otherwise, but state pensions cannot be held immune, and it's surely better to concentrate our resources on providing decent pensions for the real elderly.

The truth is that the state pension is yet another example of the impossible dream. The first generation of pensioners got paid out without ever having paid in, and the system has been running to catch up ever since. Successive governments led us to believe we could have both a decent pension *and* retirement at sixty-five. And, let's be honest, we didn't take much convincing.

Reality has now caught up with us. We're standing in the cold hard light of dawn, nursing a serious debt hangover, and there are no painless remedies.

THIRTEEN

GETTING A GRIP

Because the public sector has invested £6 billion in new technology, modernising our ability to provide back office and transactional services ... I can announce a gross reduction in civil service posts of 84,150 – to release resources from administration to invest in the front line.
– Gordon Brown, 2004

Never put off until tomorrow what you can do the day after tomorrow.
– Mark Twain

Business as usual is no longer an option. The government's debts are already higher than we can sustain, and they're still growing. Economic growth is not galloping to the rescue and history tells us the aftermath of the financial crisis will drag us back for years. Inflation could erode existing debts, but only at the cost of making future borrowing even more expensive. We have to get a grip on the government's finances.

Raising taxes is a non-starter. For one thing, higher taxes would make economic recovery even more difficult. For another, peacetime Britain has never managed to pay anything like the amount of tax that would be needed to fund public spending at the current level. For the last fifty years, our total tax payments have *never* exceeded 38 per cent of GDP, far short of the 40 to 50 per cent spending we've experienced over the last decade, and less than the government currently plans to spend in future.

The only realistic way to make the numbers add up is to cut public spending, which is exactly what the coalition is attempting. But they face huge resistance, led by the powerful public sector unions and amplified by the BBC along with the rest of the big-government media. Electors are understandably worried about the reported destruction of our public services, and with an election only two years away, progress is slowing. Which is most unfortunate, because, as we saw in the last chapter, the cuts haven't yet gone far enough.

If only we could eliminate all that government waste. If we could eliminate the waste, we could cut the bill without cutting our services. Or, more precisely, we could achieve the results we need at a price that's actually affordable.

And it's within our grasp to do it. As we've discussed, many other countries get better results without their governments spending nearly as much as ours. If we could match the best, we could cut government spending by £100 billion a year or more, and close our fiscal gap at a stroke.

However, we'll need to be radical. Uncomfortably radical.

EFFICIENCY DRIVES ARE NOT ENOUGH

The Labour administrations of Blair and Brown were firmly wedded to big government. During their thirteen years in power, they increased public spending relative to GDP by a stonking 10 percentage points – far more than any of their peacetime predecessors. Yet even they recognised that much of the spending gets wasted.

In 2003, Chancellor Brown commissioned an independent report on government inefficiency and what could be done to tackle it. The report's author was experienced businessman Peter Gershon, who'd already been hired to run government procurement. He concluded that there were huge opportunities to make cost savings without cutting services: within three years there could be annual savings of £20 billion, and 84,000 fewer staff.[289]

Brown accepted all of Gershon's recommendations and set about implementing them with gusto. Indeed, he boasted about how tough he was going to be in cracking down on inefficiency, and subsequently gave taxpayers a running commentary on how well things were going. All over Whitehall, efficiency teams were established and were soon churning out reams of stats and reports supporting Brown's assertions.

However, when the National Audit Office examined progress after three years, they discovered a very different picture. Only one-quarter of the claimed savings were actually provable. The rest comprised a mixture of wishful thinking and deckchair rearrangement.[290] Moreover, several so-called efficiency gains had merely increased costs elsewhere – such as NHS hospitals discharging patients early to save money, only to readmit the same patients as emergencies because they hadn't been well enough to be discharged. As for headcount reductions, while government departments were claiming to have cut 45,000 posts, many of the so-called cuts seem to have been reassignments, and the official National Statistics count showed an overall net decline of only 12,000 – just one-seventh of the original target.

Right up to his final day, Brown continued to insist his efficiency programme was working, but out in the real world

nobody believed it. Gershon had not just been a flop, it had
actually spawned an additional Whitehall bureaucracy dedicated to servicing the efficiency programme itself.

It would be easy to blame Brown and simply add this
failure to his lengthy catalogue of failures. But that would
be unfair, because Gershon was by no means the first such
failed government efficiency drive. Thirty years ago, Prime
Minister Margaret Thatcher brought in Derek Rayner – a
highly regarded Marks and Spencer's director – to advise
her on government efficiency. He set up an Efficiency Unit
inside the Cabinet Office, which in six years conducted 266
'scrutinies' of government departments and claimed to have
identified savings of £600 million annually. However, just as
with Gershon, when the National Audit Office examined the
record, it found that only one-quarter of the claimed savings
had actually materialised.[291]

All recent governments have come to power pledging to
cut waste. They've promised us bonfires of quangos, wars on
red tape and 'better government' efficiency drives. But delivery has never matched up to the promises. For every quango
culled, another springs up in its place. For every regulation
scrapped, two are waiting in the wings – often forced on us
by our EU obligations. And efficiency drives translate all too
easily into more external consultants, doomed IT projects
and a bigger internal bureaucracy.

In 2010, the coalition set up the Efficiency and Reform
Group, basing it – like Rayner's unit – in the Cabinet Office.
In its first two years it reckoned to have saved nearly £10
billion overall, including over £1 billion in consultancy fees
and more than £2 billion in staff cuts. And, at least for those
initial savings, the National Audit Office agreed they were
largely genuine.[292] However, the coalition's target is much

more ambitious, calling for *annual* efficiency savings of £16 billion from central government and a further £20 billion from the wider public sector. Past experience suggests that will prove impossible.

Moreover, savings that are made might well come at the expense of unintended service cuts – because most government departments don't have a clue how their costs relate to service delivery. As the Public Accounts Committee put it: 'Most departments cannot link costs to outputs to identify the consequences of changes in spending. This lack of basic management information is a serious impediment to making sustainable cost reductions that minimise the impact on frontline services.'[293]

On one level, this is an astonishing state of affairs – huge and expensive organisations unable to relate their costs to their delivery. Yet, as we've seen throughout this book, in the public sector it's par for the course.

For decades, successive governments have attempted to tackle waste through imposing better management practices and smarter buying from on high. And for decades the results have been disappointing. Doubtless our politicians must keep the pressure on, but the truth is that a command-and-control public sector is never going to deliver high efficiency.

FOLLOW THE MONEY

Britain has one of the most centralised public sectors in the developed world. From outside, it appears to be composed of many hundreds of separate government departments, quangos, local councils, hospitals, academy schools, universities and other institutions. But behind the scenes all the strings lead back to one place – Whitehall. And that's because Whitehall controls the money.

In Britain, local councils are dependent on Whitehall grants for 85 per cent of their revenue. The comparable percentage across the rest of the OECD is less than half that. And quangos and other entities depend on Whitehall for almost *all* their funding.

Unsurprisingly these organisations must dance to Whitehall's tune. They may not dance particularly well, but it's Whitehall's directives and tick-box lists that always take priority. Unlike Tesco's supermarkets – which must keep their customers satisfied or lose their income – NHS hospitals can keep going whether or not their customers are satisfied. It's their paymasters who really count, and their paymasters are sitting in Whitehall, not lying on trolleys outside A&E.

Of course, Whitehall doesn't want to see the customers poorly treated, just as Soviet planners didn't *want* to see bread queues snaking round the block. It just happens – an inevitable result of trying to deliver services through a sprawling empire under the direction of a distant centralised bureaucracy.

True, our state bureaucracy is supposed to be under democratic control, so, unlike Gosplan, it shouldn't be able to plough on regardless of the consequences. But it's one thing for us to elect fresh waves of politicians who promise more efficiency and accountability, quite another for them to deliver it. Politicians may cut budgets and order departments to be more efficient, but experience shows that doesn't do the trick. The system is organised to look up rather than out, and its heavy unionisation and ingrained conservatism make it very difficult to change at the sharp end.

To make real progress, we're going to have to learn from Tesco. We need to recognise that suppliers have to be directly answerable to customers. We have to reorganise our public services so that satisfying customers is the only way for the suppliers to fund themselves. And more than anything, we must put customers directly in charge of choosing and paying for their services.

THE FUTURE IS ALREADY OUT THERE

Reorganising our public services so they answer to customers is not something we have to invent from scratch. Throughout this book we've found plenty of examples around the world for us to copy.

In healthcare, the European social insurance systems give consumers a choice of health insurers, GP services and hospitals. The combination of choice and competition avoids the inefficiencies of our monolithic nationalised NHS and produces much better clinical results. Yet they still achieve universal coverage, with insurance mandatory for those in employment, and tax-funded support for the poor.

More radically, the Singapore health system requires patients to pay a large part of their own medical costs, funded from mandatory savings accounts into which they contribute throughout their working lives. This is real consumer power, and Singapore has some of the best health outcomes in the world, with infant mortality *half* our own rate. Coverage is universal, yet relative to GDP they spend well under half what we spend.

In education, the trail of choice and competition has already been blazed by others. From Sweden to the US, state-funded schools are being given more independence, and parents more choice. New private providers are bringing fresh ideas into schools, even though their pupils remain publicly funded. And there is clear evidence that school autonomy coupled with accountability to parents drives results. Moreover, organisation can trump money, with some of the very best results in the developed world achieved by the cheaper systems.

On public services generally, the lesson from international studies is that decentralised systems are far more efficient than ours. The most efficient systems tend to be those where the cost of providing local services is born by local taxpayers. Local councils have far more incentive to deliver value if they have to account for costs and delivery directly to their own electors, rather than a distant central finance ministry. And the same goes for the police.

Right across our public services, there are plenty of reforms for us to copy. Reforms that would allow us to save the cash we have to save without destroying the services we need. Reforms that would put power directly in *our* hands, rather than forcing us to depend on Westminster and Whitehall.

Welfare is admittedly more difficult. We are one of many western countries that have allowed welfare commitments to balloon well beyond affordability, but, unlike with our public services, we can't save money by improving efficiency: we can only make savings by cutting someone's benefits. Whether it's middle-class welfare or pensions or housing benefits, it's always going to be painful for the losers, and it's always going to be difficult. There are no easy answers, but one principle we can follow is that benefit cuts should focus on those who are young and fit enough to earn their own way in the world. Just as under the Tudor Poor Laws, the old and infirm should be protected.

So, based on what we've discussed in this book, here's our summary to-do list for cutting waste and making government affordable:

- Break up the NHS and switch to a European social

insurance system. Health insurance to be mandatory – like car insurance – but with a choice of regulated insurers.

- Accelerate current moves to make state-funded schools independent, with as much autonomy as private schools. Encourage new entrants into the sector, including for-profit operators.

- Freeze public sector pay until it comes down into line with the private sector, end national pay bargaining, downgrade the role of unions and charge the full cost of public pensions.

- Abolish universal welfare benefits for those of working age, and cut – or at least freeze – benefit rates to ensure work always pays significantly more than a life on benefits.

- Increase state pension age to seventy by 2030.

- Cut Whitehall grants to local councils and police authorities, decentralise the tax system and make councils responsible for raising the bulk of their own revenue from local taxpayers.[294]

- Cut policing costs by permanently locking up persistent offenders – three strikes and you're out.

A key point about this list is that almost all of the proposals are already in operation elsewhere in the world – this is not experimental blue-sky thinking. And in fairness to the coalition, they're already implementing some of the necessary reforms, such as the new free schools. Indeed, right across the main parties there are politicians who understand that we can't carry on as we are, that we must learn from those who've found more efficient ways to deliver services, and that we have to cut welfare entitlements.

Of course, as reformers, Labour politicians have a serious weakness. Their party's financial dependence on the public sector unions makes it difficult for them to act robustly in the interests of taxpayers as a whole. Annual donations of £10 million argue strongly against confrontation.

But politicians from other parties also hold back. They may believe in hard-edged changes along the lines of our to-do list, but to support them in public risks being branded a brute – nasty, even. Much safer sticking to anodyne statements about efficiency drives.

The critical problem is not lack of ideas, but lack of will.

PUTTING IT OFF

We can all understand why politicians put off decisions like these. Cutting welfare benefits and dismantling familiar public services is never going to be popular in the short term, and, in the long term, even the most successful of today's politicians will be gone. Far easier to defer the tough choices and leave the bill for tomorrow's generation.

Which is why tomorrow's generation faces a future that doesn't add up. As we saw in the previous chapter, on current policies and expectations, government debt is set to spiral out of control. Funding will dry up, and, like Greece, Britain will discover what slash-and-burn fiscal policy really involves.

Yet we can't put all the blame on our politicians. We're the ones who've voted for ever higher government spending, without being prepared to pay the higher tax that goes with it. And we're the ones who shout and scream when politicians do attempt serious public service reform. We may indulge in a bit of ritualised hand-wringing about the debts facing the next generation, but if anyone has robbed them, it's us.

And there's something else we should consider: the next generation might turn on us. Faced with a vicious funding crunch, they could well decide not to honour past promises of state pensions and elderly care. They could say, 'You've spent all our money, you're now totally unproductive, and you're not going to drag us down still further with twenty years of expensive state care.' It might not be *Soylent Green*, but we could easily imagine how the elderly might be a low priority for limited funds.[295]

Putting off difficult decisions is attractive for all of us in the short term. But with government debt still growing unsustainably, we have to face up to them. Much better to take the required action now, while we're still broadly in control, than to wait until we've hit the buffers.

WE *MUST* DO THIS

Four decades ago, Labour Prime Minister Jim Callaghan famously explained to his hostile party conference that the government was unable to manage the economy as previously promised:

> We used to think that you could spend your way out of a recession and increase employment by cutting taxes and boosting government spending. I tell you in all candour that that option no longer exists, and in so far as it ever did exist, it only worked on each occasion since the war by injecting a bigger dose of inflation into the economy, followed by a higher level of unemployment as the next step.[296]

It was a memorable and historic statement of government's limitations, but by the time he made it, Callaghan was no longer in control. He was speaking from desperation, swept along by a raging financial crisis. The markets had lost confidence in his high-spending, high-taxing, high-borrowing government, and were dumping Sterling and British government bonds as fast as they could.

Just a few weeks later, Callaghan was forced to negotiate a humiliating IMF bail-out, conditional on immediate and substantial public spending cuts. His government never really recovered and was ejected at the next election. But our public services endured many more years of management by blunt instrument. Investment was slashed, schools and hospitals were run down, the NHS failed to keep pace with the latest technology and waiting lists grew even longer. State pensions were frozen in real terms for nearly two decades.

The left blamed Thatcher, but the real culprits were her predecessors. It was they who pushed up spending beyond what the country could sustain, and it was they who failed to deal with the problem while there was still time.

Today, even though our fiscal problems are *worse* than they were in the 1970s, thus far we have averted the funding crisis faced by Callaghan. We still have the luxury of time to address our underlying problems.

But the Bank of England can't go on printing money to fund the deficit for ever. And we can't count on global interest rates remaining at historic lows for ever. Sooner or later, the cost of servicing our huge national debt is going to balloon, and if we're going to avoid a worse repeat of 1976 and its aftermath, we have to steel ourselves. We have to take some of those tough decisions now.

If we're serious about maintaining our public services in an era of low growth and high debts, there really is no alternative. We must stop government burning our money.

NOTES

1   Press reports from 8 to 15 July 2012
2   *Fantasy Island*, Larry Elliott and Dan Atkinson, Constable, 2007
3   For an excellent account of the NPfIT debacle, see the speech by Richard Bacon MP to the Westminster Hall debate on NHS IT, 14 June 2011
4   'Farm payment fiasco could cost the taxpayer £620 million says National Audit Office', *Daily Telegraph*, 15 October 2009
5   See Chapter 2
6   See Chapter 2
7   'Crazy town hall non-jobs', *Daily Mail*, 18 February 2011
8   See Chapter 8
9   'Total public sector output, inputs and productivity', UKCeMGA, 2010
10   See Chapter 4
11   See Chapter 6
12   See Chapter 5
13   See Chapter 7
14   'The effects of taxes and benefits on household income 2010/11', ONS, June 2012
15   For a good discussion of the optimal size of government and how excessive government spending erodes GDP, see 'Living with Leviathan', David B. Smith, IEA, 2006
16   *The sources of economic growth in OECD countries*, OECD, 2003; *Government size, volatility, and economic growth*, Afonso and Furceri, ECB, 2008; and for a summary and discussion of all the research see *The Single Income Tax: Final Report of the 2020 Tax Commission*, TPA/IOD, 2012
17   Tony Blair speech to Venture Capital Association, 6 July 1999
18   Efficiency Review by Sir Philip Green, Cabinet Office, 2010

19   'Philip Green's efficiency purge', *Guardian*, 11 October 2010

20   'Defence shake-up aims to cut waste in procurement', BBC News website, 23 December 2011

21   'Unhealthy delays', *Daily Telegraph*, 11 June 2006

22   'Out of control: how government overspends on capital projects', TaxPayers' Alliance, 2009

23   'Underestimating Cost in Public Works Projects: Error or Lie?' by Flyvbjerg, Holm, and Buhl, *Journal of the American Planning Association*, Summer 2002; as reported in 'Government Schemes Cost More Than Promised', Cato Institute, 2003

24   According to the Public Accounts Committee, the original bid included no contingency reserve – contrary to official Treasury rules – and no allowance for security costs. In contrast, it made a highly optimistic assumption about private sector contributions which was not tested in any way. See 'The Budget for the 2012 Games', House of Commons HC85, 2008

25   'Supplementary Green Book Guidance: Optimism Bias', HM Treasury

26   Fulton Report 1965

27   2012

28   See Chapter 4

29   'Progress in improving financial management in government', National Audit Office, 2011

30   'What some CIOs in Whitehall earn', *Computer Weekly*, 6 August 2007

31   '9,000 in public sector get more pay than Prime Minister', BBC News website 20 September 2010; see also *The Public Sector Rich List* and *The Town Hall Rich List*, both published and updated regularly by the TaxPayers' Alliance

32   Survey of personal incomes 2009–10, HMRC

33   'Estimating differences in public and private sector pay – 2012', ONS, March 2012

34   'Total reward: pay and pension contributions in the private and public sectors', ONS, September 2010

35   'Reforming Public Sector Pensions', Public Sector Pensions Commission, July 2010

36   'Does wage regulation harm kids?' Carol Propper and Jack Britton, Centre for Market and Public Sector Organisation, University of Bristol, 2012

37   'Can pay regulation kill?' CEP Discussion Paper 843, Emma Hall, Carol Propper, and John Van Reenen, January 2008

38   'Trade union membership 2011', Department for Business Innovation and Skills, 2012

39   'Trade union density', 2010, OECD StatExtracts

40   See Chapter 4

41   Labour market statistics data tables April 2012, ONS

42   'Taxpayer funding of trade unions 2012', TaxPayers' Alliance Research Note 120. Note that the TPA figures understate the true subsidy because many public sector organisations refused to release the required data.

43   'Tesco's UK Chief Executive quits', BBC News website, 15 March 2012

44   'Incompetent teachers "being recycled" by head teachers', BBC News website, 4 July 2010

45   See the speech by Richard Bacon MP to the Westminster Hall debate on NHS IT, 14 June 2011

46   'Ministers blame officials for farm payment delays', *Guardian*, 24 October 2006

47   'Lockheed appears close to winning big British order', *New York Times*, 20 July 1995

48   'Something old, something new…', *Flight*, 15 May 1996

49   Interviewed by Fox News, 2004

50   See Chapter 10

51   Figures relate to 2007–2011, and are taken from the OECD 'World Economic Outlook 90', 2011

52   The definition of public spending used in this section is spending by the General Government sector, the standard international measure as used by the OECD. General Government comprises central government and local authorities, but excludes public corporations. However, because of various other definitional differences, the OECD's measure of government spending is on average two or three percentage points of GDP *higher* than the measure used by the Treasury.

53   *Public Spending in the 20th Century*, by Vito Tanzi and Ludger Schuknecht, Cambridge University Press, 2000

54   Source: PESA 2011, and 'Economic and fiscal outlook November 2011', OBR. Note that certain smaller categories of spending – such as capital grants – have been omitted from this analysis. Also, spending totals are shown gross of receipts from sales.

55   Pensioner numbers for five largest public sector schemes as of 2010; source: 'Independent Public Service Pensions Commission Interim Report', 2010

56   'Public sector employment – Q3 2011', ONS 2011; 5.8 million excludes the 200,000 employed by the banks nationalised in 2008.

57   Public Expenditure Statistical Analyses (PESA), HM Treasury, 2011

58   For a much more detailed analysis – including the issue of North Sea oil revenue – see 'Unequal Shares: The definitive guide to the Barnett Formula', Mike Denham, TaxPayers' Alliance, 2008

59   The figures are taken from PESA 2011, published by HM Treasury. Technically, our chart shows spending by departmental grouping, which includes, for example, spending funded by local authorities as well as directly from the central government department concerned.

60   The post of Chancellor of the Exchequer dates from the reign of Henry III in the thirteenth century.

61   'Maze of initiatives "like spaghetti"', *Guardian*, 14 January 2003

62   Department of Education and Science, 1964–1992; Department for Education, 1992–1995; Department for Education and Employment (DfEE), 1995–2001; Department for Education and Skills (DfES), 2001–2007; Department for Children, Schools and Families (DCSF), 2007–2010; Department for Education, 2010–

63   'Jibes prompt DTI rebrand U-turn', BBC News website, 13 May 2005

64   'ACA-to-YJB: A Guide to the UK Semi-Autonomous Public Bodies', by Ben Farrugia and John O'Connell, TPA, 2009

65   'Academy funding briefing 2012', Department for Education

66   'Ministers "too involved" in SATS', BBC News website, 22 July 2009

67   'Taxpayer funded lobbying and political campaigning', Matthew Sinclair, TPA, 2009

68   For a more detailed discussion of these studies, and of council finance generally, see Chapter 5 in *How to Cut Spending (and still win an election)*, edited by Matt Sinclair, Biteback, 2010

69   Margaret Thatcher speech to Conservative party conference, October 1979

70   Actually it's a little more complicated than that, but tax collection costs are around 1 per cent of revenue.

71   OECD Health Data, 2011

72   Source: 'NHS Expenditure in England', House of Commons Library, Standard Note SN/SG/724, 2009. Note that the figures shown in the chart relate to the UK, and unavoidably include some minor inconsistencies over time. Updated using PESA July 2011, HM Treasury.

73   OECD Health Data, 2011

74   Figures mainly sourced from the NHS Information Centre, covering the NHS in England.

75   'Hospital Episode Statistics', HESonline, 2011

76   'Commentary Report for the GP Patient Survey 2009/10', Ipsos MORI, 2010

77   'National NHS patient survey programme – Survey of adult inpatients 2009', Care Quality Commission

78   'The Effects of Taxes and Benefits on Household Income', ONS, 2010

79   Source: 'NHS Staff 2000–2010', NHS Information Centre, Department of Health

80 Some add McDonald's to the list, but that's not a fair comparison since many McDonald's restaurants are owned and operated by franchisees and affiliates. Meanwhile, Indian State Railways has slipped down the rankings with a mere 1.3 million employees.

81 Strictly speaking, the NHS does not employ all of its staff directly. In particular, most GPs are independent contractors working for the NHS.

82 MRI scanners use magnetic resonance imaging to build up images of the body's internal structures. They are especially useful in the detection of cancers and other soft tissue problems. But they are notoriously expensive and until recently the NHS has owned a bare handful.

83 See 'Public Service Output, Inputs and Productivity: Healthcare', Maria-Cristina Peñaloza, Michael Hardie, Richard Wild, Katherine Mills, ONS, 2010

84 Joumard, I., C. André and C. Nicq (2010), 'Health Care Systems: Efficiency and Institutions', OECD Economics Department Working Papers, No. 769, OECD Publishing. doi: 10.1787/5kmfp51f5f9t-en

85 'Public Service Output, Inputs and Productivity: Healthcare', Maria-Cristina Peñaloza, Michael Hardie, Richard Wild, Katherine Mills, ONS, 2010

86 'NHS takes two-thirds of government's rich list', *Guardian*, 21 September 2010

87 'BMA team "stunned by GP contract"', BBC News, 31 January 2007

88 'Remuneration of doctors', Health at a Glance 2009, OECD

89 'NHS Pay Modernisation in England: Agenda for Change', NAO, 2009

90 'Trade Union Membership and Influence 1999–2009', Alex Bryson and John Forth, Centre for Economic Performance, 2010

91 'NHS Health and Well-being Review, Interim Report', Department of Health, 2009

92 'The procurement of consumables by NHS acute and Foundation trusts', NAO, 2011

93 'The Pharmaceutical Price Regulation Scheme', Office of Fair Trading, 2007

94 '£207m debt at PFI-saddled hospital trust "should be written off"', *Daily Telegraph*, 29 October 2012

95 'The refinancing of the Norfolk and Norwich PFI hospital', Committee of Public Accounts, Press Notice No. 35 of Session 2005–6

96 'Plans for NHS files are late by two years', *Financial Times*, 30 May 2006

97 'Referral To Treatment Waiting Time Statistics', Department of Health, 2011

98 'Dignity and Nutrition Inspection Programme', Care Quality Commission, 2011

99   There were more than 3,000 such deaths in 2010. Source: 'Deaths involving MRSA' and 'Deaths involving Clostridium difficile', ONS, 2011

100   'NHS targets "may have led to 1,200 deaths" in Mid-Staffordshire', *Daily Telegraph*, 17 March 2009

101   'Issues Highlighted by the 2010 NHS Staff Survey in England', Care Quality Commission

102   'A Century of Change: Trends in UK statistics since 1900', Joe Hicks & Grahame Allen, House of Commons Library 1999

103   Gay, J. G. et al. (2011), 'Mortality Amenable to Health Care in 31 OECD Countries: Estimates and Methodological Issues', OECD Health Working Papers, No. 55, OECD Publishing. http://dx.doi.org/10.1787/5kgj35f9f8s2-en. Note that our chart is based on the Nolte and McKee list of diseases amenable to healthcare.

104   'Wasting Lives 2011', John O'Connell, TaxPayers' Alliance

105   International Road Traffic and Accident Database, OECD, 2011

106   *Memoirs of a Tory Radical*, Nigel Lawson, Biteback, 2010

107   'A healthy improvement: Satisfaction with the NHS under Labour', John Appleby and Ruth Robertson, British Social Attitudes 27th Report

108   'Life expectancy at birth and at age 65 for health areas in the United Kingdom, 2003–05 to 2007–09', ONS, 2011

109   'Securing our Future Health: Taking a Long-Term View', the Wanless Report, 2001, HM Treasury

110   Fiscal Sustainability Report, OBR, 2011

111   'The Clausewitz of the NHS', *British Medical Journal*, 2003

112   From 1948 to 1968, the health job was simply labelled Minister of Health. From 1968 to 1988, it was folded into the Secretary of State for Social Services, an impossibly huge job spanning both health and social services. Since 1988 it has again focused solely on health under the title Secretary of State for Health.

113   Speech by Rt Hon Alan Milburn MP, 11 February 2003: Choices for All, National Archives

114   Tony Blair speech to Venture Capital Association, 6 July 1999

115   'Health at a Glance 2009', OECD

116   OECD Health Data, 2009

117   Joumard, I., C. André and C. Nicq (2010), 'Health Care Systems: Efficiency and Institutions', OECD Economics Department Working Papers, No. 769, OECD Publishing. doi: 10.1787/5kmfp51f5f9t-en

118   'Chocolate stampede as Tesco pays for error', Sky News, 14 October 2011

119   *The Five Giants*, Nicholas Timmins, HarperCollins, 1995

120 All prescriptions are free in Scotland and Wales, and in England the Department of Health says that 90 per cent are issued free.

121 'International Comparisons of Obesity Prevalence', Department of Health, 2009

122 Public Expenditure Statistical Analysis 2011, HM Treasury

123 'Education at a glance 2011', OECD. Ages five to sixteen. For consistency, the OECD shows cost figures measured in US dollars adjusted for purchasing power.

124 'What Students Know and Can Do: Student Performance in Reading, Mathematics and Science', OECD, 2010

125 Joint Council for Qualifications, Results 2011

126 'Students face university entrance test in row over "easy" A-levels', *Daily Telegraph*, 5 June 2009

127 'Is the gold standard looking tarnished?', *Guardian*, 15 August 2006

128 'Tesco boss raps school standards', BBC News website, 14 November 2009

129 'Changes in standards at GCSE and A-Level: Evidence from ALIS and YELLIS', Durham University Curriculum Education and Management Centre, 2007

130 'Talent isn't rationed. Nor should success be', *The Times*, 21 August 2008

131 'Educational reform lessons: an interview with Sir Michael Barber', Education Sector, 2006

132 See 'Medicine in the war zone', Science Museum website

133 'Viewing the United Kingdom school system through the prism of PISA', OECD, 2010

134 'Relative difficulty of examinations in different subjects', Durham University Curriculum Education and Management Centre, 2008

135 Source: Department for Business Innovation and Skills

136 Higher Education Statistics Authority

137 'Dumbing down of university grades revealed', *Sunday Telegraph*, 1 January 2011

138 'Unusual courses: from Beckham to basking sharks', *Independent*, 15 August 2006

139 'Education at a glance', OECD 2011; the private net present value of a degree is estimated at $207,000 for a man.

140 'Graduates in the labour market – 2012', ONS

141 Ex-communist countries excluded; source – OECD StatExtracts and Education at a Glance

142 'Growth effects of education and social capital in the OECD countries', by Jonathan Temple, OECD, 2001

143 'A Family Affair: Intergenerational Social Mobility across OECD Countries', OECD, 2010

144 'Middle classes told to stop using Sure Start', *Daily Telegraph*, 11 August 2010

145 'Changes in children's cognitive development at the start of school in England 2001–2008', Merrell and Tymms, Centre for Evaluation and Monitoring at Durham University, 2010

146 Same fifteen economies used in previous chart; source: OECD PISA and Education at a Glance

147 'Does money buy strong performance in PISA?' OECD, February 2012

148 'Viewing the United Kingdom school system through the prism of PISA', OECD, 2010

149 'Half Our Future', HMSO, 1963

150 It's estimated that average per pupil funding for secondary modern schools was only half that for grammars.

151 The figures in this section are taken from spreadsheets published by the Institute for Fiscal Studies to accompany their paper 'Poverty and Inequality in the UK 2011'. Incomes are shown net of direct taxes and measured at the household level. They are expressed as the equivalent for a childless couple using the Modified OECD equivalence scale. The figures shown here are at 2009/10 prices, and are before taking account of housing costs.

152 To be precise, households at the bottom quartile point of the income distribution in 2009/10 have higher real incomes than those at the top quartile point of the income distribution in 1961.

153 Real net incomes after housing costs: same source as above

154 'Family Spending', ONS, 2011

155 'Poverty and Inequality in the UK 2011', accompanying spreadsheets, IFS

156 Both the poverty line and the income figure are defined as real net incomes before housing costs.

157 'Comparison of UK and EU at risk of poverty rates', ONS, June 2012

158 'Divided we stand: why inequality keeps rising', OECD, 2011

159 Jin Liqun, Chairman of China Investment Corporation, *Daily Telegraph*, 20 October 2011

160 'Ageing Society', DWP website

161 DWP Quarterly Statistical Summary, November 2011

162 The French pension age was cut to sixty under Mitterrand in the 1980s.

163 '21st Century Welfare', DWP, 2010

164 For comparison, the overall population has increased by about 20 per cent.

165 'The Effects of Taxes and Benefits on Household Income', ONS,

2011. Tax credits and council tax benefit have been included in cash benefits.

166 'Briefing Note on Welfare', by Andrew Haldenby and Kimberley Trewhitt, Reform 2010; figure relates to 2007/8

167 'Cost of fiscal churn', Burning Our Money blog, 13 January 2006

168 '21st Century Welfare', DWP, 2010

169 'Welfare Reform in Tough Fiscal Times', by Corin Taylor, Mike Denham, Richard Baron and Andrew Allum, TPA, 2010

170 '21st Century Welfare', DWP, 2010

171 'Fraud and Error in the Benefit System', DWP, 2011

172 'Department for Work and Pensions: 2010–11 accounts', NAO, 2011

173 'Tackling the hidden economy', Public Accounts Committee, 2008

174 'Too fat to work', *The Times*, 19 November 2007

175 'Shannon Matthews trial: The dysfunctional family where children equalled benefits', *Daily Telegraph*, 4 December 2008

176 Source: The Office for National Statistics website Neighbourhood Statistics

177 'Indices of Deprivation 2010', DCLG

178 Dewsbury East Ward profile, Kirklees Council, 2011

179 'Parties clash over Shannon case', BBC News website, 7 December 2008

180 'Underclass +10', Charles Murray, Civitas, 2001

181 'The Foundation Years: preventing poor children becoming poor adults', Frank Field, HMG, 2010

182 British Social Attitudes Survey 2009. See also 'There is an appetite for welfare reform', Penny Young, *Guardian*, 27 January 2012

183 'Report from His Majesty's Commissioners for Inquiring into the Administration and Practical Operation of the Poor Laws', 1834 (p. 228)

184 1871 Census of England and Wales, 'General Report'

185 'Welfare Reform in Tough Fiscal Times', by Corin Taylor, Mike Denham, Richard Baron and Andrew Allum, TPA, 2010

186 'Labour productivity Q2 2011', ONS

187 'Government evidence to the Low Pay Commission', 2011

188 The best recent exposition of this proposal is *In Our Hands: A Plan To Replace The Welfare State*, by Charles Murray, AEI Press, 2006

189 Figures relate to 2010 to be consistent with household income figures.

190 The calculations are set out in 'Welfare Reform in Tough Fiscal Times', by Corin Taylor, Mike Denham, Richard Baron and Andrew Allum, TPA, 2010. The proposed arrangements are implemented through a negative income tax.

191 'Universal Credit: Welfare that works', DWP, November 2010

192 'Social Insurance and Allied Services', report by Sir William Beveridge, Cmnd 6404, 1942; see also Alan Deacon in *The Boundaries of the State in Modern Britain*, by S. Green and R. Whiting, Cambridge University Press, 1996

193 'Does getting tough on the unemployed work?', *Guardian*, 16 June 2010

194 It's estimated that the CPI lags behind the RPI by an average 0.5 per cent per annum.

195 'Housing was Labour's great failure. Now it gets worse', *Guardian*, 13 July 2010

196 'Universal Credit: Welfare that works', DWP

197 'Universal Credit: much to welcome, but impact on incentives mixed', IFS, 2011

198 'Welfare Reform in Tough Fiscal Times', by Corin Taylor, Mike Denham, Richard Baron and Andrew Allum, TPA, 2010

199 'The Introduction of the Work Programme', National Audit Office, 2012

200 'Work for free and "be of benefit" to a multinational like Tesco', John Harris, *Guardian*, 16 February 2012

201 'Employment and Support Allowance', DWP website

202 'Grandad declared capable of work by testing firm died one month later', *Daily Mirror*, 17 February 2012

203 'Residents living in fear', *Rutherglen Reformer*, 9 May 2012

204 'Government at a glance 2009', OECD. Note that Public Order and Safety also includes fire services, accounting for about 10 per cent of the total.

205 2009/10 figures sourced from 'PESA 2011', HM Treasury

206 'European Sourcebook of Crime and Criminal Justice Statistics', WODC Ministerie van Justitie, 2010

207 'Crime in England and Wales 2010–11', Home Office

208 'International Statistics on Crime and Justice', UNODOC, 2010

209 'European Sourcebook of Crime and Criminal Justice Statistics', WODC Ministerie van Justitie, 2010

210 'Crime in England and Wales 2010–11', Home Office

211 'Don't let the truth get in the way of a bad crime story', *Guardian*, 23 October 2007

212 'Supplementary Volume 1 to Crime in England and Wales 2010/11', Home Office

213 'Crime in England and Wales 2010–11', Home Office

214 See *Wasting Police Time* by PC David Copperfield, Monday Books, 2006; also the excellent Inspector Gadget blog

215 'The economic and social costs of crime', Home Office Research Study 217, 2000

216 'The economic and social costs of crime against individuals and households 2003/04', Home Office, 2005

217 'Police service strength', Home Office, various years

218 '"Numties in Yellow Jackets": The Nature of Hostility Towards the Police Community Support Officer in Neighbourhood Policing Teams', Bryn Caless, *Policing*, 2007

219 'Police get four hours overtime for just answering a phone call after their shift has ended', *Daily Mail*, 3 February 2009

220 'Police Service Strength: 30 September 2011', Home Office

221 'Police Funding', House of Commons Home Affairs Select Committee, 2007

222 'Demanding Times', HMIC, 2011

223 'Crimes detected in England and Wales 2010/11', Home Office, 2011

224 The last Labour government decided it was in the national interest for this to be made a criminal offence, punishable by up to six months in prison.

225 'Sentencing Statistics England and Wales 2009', Ministry of Justice, 2010

226 'Clarke calls for Monckton inquiry', BBC News website, 19 December 2005; also 'Big increase in murders by criminals on parole', *Daily Telegraph*, 6 December 2006

227 'The history of life', BBC News Magazine, 16 June 2006

228 Speech to the Conservative party conference, October 1993

229 *Newsnight*, 13 May 1997

230 'Arizona criminals find jail too intents', CNN, 27 July 1999

231 'Criminal Justice: The Way Ahead', Home Department, 2001

232 The think tank Civitas has done a lot of excellent work on this subject. See, for example, 'Prison is a Bargain', David Green, *The Times*, 12 May 2004

233 'Compendium of reoffending statistics and analysis', Ministry of Justice, 2010

234 'Supervision of community orders in England and Wales', HC (2007/08) 203

235 'Adult reconvictions: results from the 2009 cohort', Ministry of Justice, 2011

236 'Compendium of reoffending statistics and analysis', Ministry of Justice, 2010

237 'Adult reconvictions: results from the 2009 cohort', Ministry of Justice, 2011

238 OECD World Economic Outlook, May 2012

239 'Public Sector Efficiency: An International Comparison', by Afonso, Schuknecht, and Tanzi, European Central Bank Working Paper No 242

240 Efficiency relates to the year 2000 and spending relates to the average over the previous decade. We've included a simple regression line to highlight the overall pattern, but the important distinction is between big and small, as the ECB report makes clear.

241 2002–2012; source: OECD

242 For an excellent historic overview, see *The Welfare State We're In*, James Bartholomew, Politico's, 2004

243 See Chapter 6

244 'The meaning of Poverty', by Peter Townsend, *British Journal of Sociology*, 1962

245 Note that official measures of poverty are always expressed in terms of an 'equivalised' household, adjusting for the fact that bigger households need a higher income to enjoy the same standard of living as smaller ones.

246 'Polly Toynbee: How can she attack free schools when she educated her own children privately?', Toby Young, *Telegraph* blogs, May 2010

247 *The Spirit Level: Why More Equal Societies Almost Always Do Better*, Richard Wilkinson and Kate Pickett, Allen Lane, 2009

248 For an excellent discussion and critique of Happiness Economics, see *...and the Pursuit of Happiness*, edited by Philip Booth, IEA, 2011

249 'Does absolute income matter?', R. H. Frank in *Economics and Happiness: Framing the Analysis*, Oxford University Press, 2005

250 'Is inequality iniquitous?', BBC News website, 27 January 2010

251 See, for example, 'The Spirit Illusion', Nima Sanandaji, Arvid Malm and Tino Sanandaji, TaxPayers' Alliance, 2010

252 *Financial Times*, 23 March 2009

253 'An overview of growing income inequalities in OECD countries', OECD, 2011

254 *Public Spending in the 20th Century*, Vito Tanzi and Ludger Schuknecht, Cambridge University Press, 2000

255 'Distribution of incomes before and after tax 2009–10', HMRC

256 'The effects of taxes and benefits on household income 2008/09', Office for National Statistics, 2010

257 *Beatles Anthology*, Weidenfeld & Nicolson, 2000

258 Luke 2:1, King James Bible

259 'America', Sydney Smith, *Edinburgh Review*, 1820

260 The population increased by about 30 per cent over this period.

261 'Tony Blair's *Newsnight* interview', *Guardian*, 21 April 2005

262 For an extended discussion of how such a tax system would operate, see 'The Single Income Tax: Final Report of the 2020 Tax Commission', TPA/IOD, 2012

263 'The effects of taxes and benefits on household income 2010/11', Office for National Statistics, 2012. Note that our figures relate to the average for non-retired households, and incorporate all the taxes identified by the ONS, including certain allocated business taxes.

264 Budget 2012, HM Treasury

265 2011/12

266 The data for 1821 is taken from 'Taxation in England during the Industrial Revolution', RM Hartwell, *Cato Journal*, 1981

267 For an excellent analysis of green stealth taxation, see *Let Them Eat Carbon*, Matthew Sinclair, Biteback, 2011

268 Projection for 2012/13, 'Budget 2012', HM Treasury

269 All debt figures from 'Financial Statistics', ONS

270 Budget 2012, HM Treasury

271 Early data is sourced from the excellent website ukpublicspending.co.uk; from 1858 onwards, all data is sourced from the Public Sector Finances Database, published by HM Treasury; from 1974/5 onwards, we switch to the PSND in place of the old national debt.

272 'The World Economy: A Millennial Perspective', Angus Maddison, OECD, 2001

273 *Public Spending in the 20th Century*, Vito Tanzi and Ludger Schuknecht, Cambridge University Press, 2000

274 *Wall Street Journal*, February 1993

275 For a detailed discussion, see 'The Real National Debt: A Decade of Reckless Growth', by Mike Denham, TaxPayers' Alliance, 2010

276 'Independent Public Service Pensions Commission: Interim Report', October 2010

277 See 'Wider measures of public sector net debt – Dec 2011', Dave Hobbs, ONS; 'A broader picture of the public sector balance sheet: State pension and other pension obligations – An update at April 2012', David Hobbs, ONS; and 'Pensions in the National Accounts – A Fuller Picture of the UK's funded and unfunded pension liabilities', by Sarah Levy, ONS, 2012

278 Figure relates to non-financial assets; 'Fiscal Sustainability Report', Office for Budget Responsibility, 2011

279 'Fiscal Sustainability Report', Office for Budget Responsibility, 2012

280 See Chapter 5

281 Debt Management Office website

282 *The Cash Nexus: Money and Power in the Modern World, 1700–2000*, Niall Ferguson, Allen Lane, 2001

283 'Fiscal Sustainability Report', OBR, 2011

284 'It doesn't exist', *Newsweek*, 5 December 2008

285 'Fiscal Sustainability Report', OBR, 2011

286 See 'The History of State Pensions: 1948 to 2010', by Bozio,

Crawford and Tetlow, Institute for Fiscal Studies, 2010; also 'The Pensions Primer', Pensions Policy Institute

287 'Plans to raise state pension age not radical enough says Lord Turner', *Daily Telegraph*, 3 July 2009

288 'A Sustainable State Pension – Impact Assessment', DWP, 2011; figures are at 2011/12 prices, and savings shown net of additional benefits payments to those remaining jobless for an additional year.

289 'Releasing Resources to the Front Line', Peter Gershon, 2004

290 'The Efficiency Programme: A Second Review of Progress', Report by the Comptroller and Auditor General, 2007

291 'The Rayner Scrutiny Programmes', Report by the Comptroller and Auditor General, HMSO, 1986

292 'Cost reduction in central government: summary of progress', NAO, 2012

293 'Cost reduction in central government', Public Accounts Committee, 2012

294 This would be a switch from national to local taxation – overall taxes would not automatically increase. For more detail on this, see 'The Single Income Tax: Final report of the 2020 Tax Commission', IOD/TPA, 2012

295 *Soylent Green* is a science fiction film in which the elderly are euthanised and recycled into a protein supplement.

296 Speech to Labour Conference, 1976

ABOUT THE AUTHOR

Mike Denham is an economist who has worked in both the public and private sectors. He was at HM Treasury during the Callaghan and Thatcher governments, and subsequently spent twenty years in the City. In recent years he has written extensively on government waste, public sector reform, and the need for lower taxes in Britain. He authored the government waste blog Burning Our Money, and he's currently a Research Fellow at the TaxPayers' Alliance. Mike graduated from Oxford University and has a Master's degree from the London School of Economics.

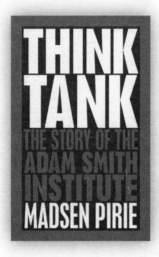

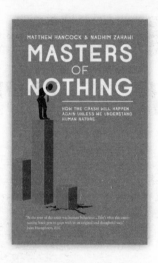